OFFICE MANAGEMENT PROBLEM SOLVER

Office Management Problem Solver

Joseph L. Kish, Jr.

with contributions from
Keith Costello, Joel Culmone, Margo Corson

A Norback Book

CHILTON BOOK COMPANY   RADNOR, PENNSYLVANIA

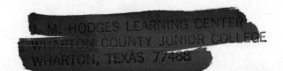

Copyright © 1983 by Norback & Company, Inc.
All Rights Reserved
Published in Radnor, Pennsylvania 19089, by Chilton Book Company
Designed by Jean Callan King, Metier Industrial, Inc.
Manufactured in the United States of America

Library of Congress Cataloging in Publication Data
Kish, Joseph L.
  Office management problem solver.

  Includes index.
  1. Office management. I. Title.
HF5547.K535 1983   651.3   80-70349
ISBN 0-8019-7011-3
ISBN 0-8019-7370-8 (pbk.)

1 2 3 4 5 6 7 8 9 0   2 1 0 9 8 7 6 5 4 3

*To Yolanda and Robert Lucadamo
on their Golden Wedding Anniversary*

Preface

The elements of office management are so varied, and the skill requirements of the office manager position so numerous and diverse, that the availability of practical, up-to-date resource literature is essential. Yet, there is a distressing lack of such materials available today. Unlike computer programming, marketing or accounting, resource literature has not kept pace with the professional development requirements of today's office manager. Consequently, an office manager would be hard-pressed to find current books and magazine articles that were sufficiently comprehensive to meet his or her needs and that approached the subject from a practical as well as a theoretical point-of-view. In the absence of a single-source reference, the office manager invariably experiences needless delays, frustration and expense.

Given this background, you will readily understand my excitement and enthusiasm when given the opportunity to draw upon my 25 years as an office management practitioner, teacher and consultant and write a reference resource that would:

Develop the background, concept and rationale of each element of office management

Present, in reference format a sequential "nuts-and-bolts" approach, using the various steps involved in the implementation and/or application of each aspect

Contain supplemental chapters by three highly respected, successful office managers, discussing the office management function in light of their own experiences

Answer 77 questions of general concern to office managers

Office Management Problem Solver is a single-source reference that will prove as valuable to the newly appointed office manager as to his or her more experienced counterpart. The former will find this volume valuable as a means of quickly and economically gaining the background and knowledge required to successfully function in that new position. The latter will find it to be an excellent source of new, innovative ideas and techniques and a valuable tool in upgrading knowledge through self-instruction.

Numerous people have contributed to the development and production of *Office Management Problem Solver*. My personal thank you: to Craig T. Norback, who recognized the need for such a resource, conceived its format and invited me to author it; to Tom Ford of Norback & Co., and Lydia Driscoll of Chilton Book Company for their fine editing and production efforts; to my friend and mentor Stan Fenvessy whose expert advise was most helpful; to fellow consultants Marshall Graham, J. Porter Henry, Charley Elitch, and Belden Menkos for sharing their specialized knowledge and critiquing certain ideas; to John Gregory and Kathy Mayer of the American Management Association for their help in conducting many of the informal surveys reported in this book; to Phyllis Kalmback and Dee Brannen who typed the manuscripts; and most importantly to my wife Elissa, daughters Grace and Frances and son Joe, for their patience and encouragement.

JOSEPH L. KISH, JR.
July, 1983
Westfield, New Jersey

Contents

Contents

Contents

CHAPTER 1

The Position of Office Manager in Theory

Nearly a century has passed since Frederick Taylor, Frank Gilbreth, Ivy Lee, J. M. Jurand, and others first introduced the concepts of *scientific management* and *industrial engineering* to manufacturing and warehousing functions. Through these concepts techniques such as work-saving methods and equipment, coordinating floor plans with workflow, and monitoring performance levels have produced significant, continuing cost savings and operational efficiencies. Rare indeed is the manufacturing or warehousing function that has not been planned, operated, and monitored in accordance with these concepts.

However, the same organizations that have strived so diligently for efficiency and cost reduction in their manufacturing and warehousing operations have paid only minimal attention to their office operations. They have designed their offices without regard either to workflow or to communication and supervision requirements. The same care used in selecting material handling equipment, tools, and safety equipment has not been exercised in selecting office typewriters, filing equipment, or furniture. Further, clerical personnel have been added to the office staff without the same scrutiny and justification that would have been necessary to hire an additional factory worker or warehouseman. Perhaps the reason for this is that *individual* office costs are generally lower than manufacturing and warehousing costs and are therefore less visible. Or many executives may feel that given a limited amount of time and funds for improving the cost-effectiveness and overall efficiency of their organization they would be wiser to concentrate on more visible profit-generating activities rather than overhead and support activities. Consequently, as manufacturing and warehousing operations have become more efficient, economical, and productive, office costs have skyrocketed. Office productivity has, on the whole, not kept pace with increases in work load, and high rates of turnover among office staff have become the norm.

This situation can best be illustrated by comparing recent figures (1979-1980) from the Small Business Administration that contrast manufacturing productivity costs per unit of output in different industries. In the household appliance industry, manufacturing productivity costs decreased by 17%, while indirect labor costs rose by 15%. Similar trends were noted in the construction industry, the industrial equipment manufacturing industry, and the warehousing and storage industry. This suggests that decreasing factory and distribution costs and rising indirect labor costs represent the norm among American businesses regardless of their industry, size, or geographic location. As a result American businesses are producing more per manhour in their factories and less per manhour in their administrative offices.

The effect of this inattention to the administrative office is dramatically illustrated when one realizes that few if any office activities generate accountable income for the organization so that any expenses incurred by such activities come directly off the bottom line of the organization's profit and loss statement. However, any increase in office efficiency will also increase the ultimate profitability of the company.

To illustrate, let us assume that an organization's sales are $1 million annually and that it is netting 10% on sales, or $100,000. Let us further assume that the costs involved in operating the administrative office are

$500,000 a year. If these costs could be reduced by 10%, the $50,000 savings would increase profits from $100,000 to $150,000, an increase of 50%. If the costs of operating the administrative office were reduced by 20%, profits would double, from $100,000 to $200,000.

Cost-conscious organizations interested in growth during periods of rising costs and increased domestic and foreign competition would be well advised to take a long, hard look at their administrative office's systems, staffing, and operations. American businesses can no longer afford to ignore the ever-increasing costs of office space, equipment, and personnel.

It is imperative that every organization establish a group whose sole purpose is to manage the administrative office and its various functions. Headed by an *office manager,* the administrative office would be responsible for developing cost-reducing, efficient ways to provide services, ranging from the selection and layout of office space to the development of programs for efficient utilization of personnel and equipment and of the actual procedures involved in the functions of the administrative office.

THE ORGANIZATIONAL ROLE
OF THE ADMINISTRATIVE OFFICE

The administrative office of any organization may correctly be viewed as a service group that provides various administrative support services such as mail pickup and delivery, and duplicating and office copying services. By assuming responsibility for such services the administrative office allows manufacturing, marketing, financial, and other personnel to devote more time and attention to financing, manufacturing, and marketing the organization's products and services.

The value of a smooth-running administrative office becomes readily apparent when one realizes that the administrative office enables executives and managers to free themselves from the many administrative details inherent in any office operation. For example, a qualified office manager makes it unnecessary for a production planning manager to be concerned with the printing and stocking of departmental forms or for the regional sales manager to schedule routine maintenance and replacement of the company vehicles assigned to the sales staff.

AN OVERHEAD FUNCTION

As we noted earlier, the administrative office in most organizations serves the company's personnel, not its customers. Therefore, its activities rarely generate income for the organization directly.

Of course, there are exceptions to this principle. For-profit companies such as management consulting firms, CPAs, and lawyers who provide professional services to clients usually bill for services such as typing, mailing, reproduction, and drafting. These are the most common exceptions. As a general rule, however, the costs of the various personnel, materials, equipment, and facilities allocated to the administrative office are nonrecuperable and must be borne by the organization itself directly out of sales income. Sound management practice calls for the company to treat the administrative office function in exactly the same light as it does any other non–revenue–generating aspect of its business (from the sponsorship of a bowling team to a tuition reimbursement program)—as an expense that is unavoidable and that will result in tangible or intangible benefits commensurate with the costs involved.

In order to gain an accurate picture of the cost of office operations, an organization should "charge back" the cost of the administrative support service provided to the various user departments. The costs charged back should be *true costs*—that is, they should be the actual costs incurred in providing the service. True costs include such expenses as

> A proportion of the salaries paid the people providing the service (including a pro rata share of the office manager's and unit supervisor's time) based upon the portion of their working day devoted to planning and supervising the function
> The dollar value of the fringe benefits paid such employees
> The amortized value of the equipment involved
> Annual maintenance and service costs of such equipment
> The annual value of consumable supplies
> Occupancy costs (space, utilities, cleaning services) for the space assigned to the administrative support service

The sum total of the above will indicate the *annual operating costs*. To develop a realistic chargeback cost, one of the two following methods may be used.

Actual-use method. Records of the actual use made of the office's services by each department can be kept, and at the end of each month the total-use figures (such as number of copies or pages prepared or miles driven) are divided into one-twelfth of the annual operating cost, providing a cost per unit for that month. This unit cost is then multiplied by the actual number of copies, pages, or miles produced by or for each department. The resulting figure is charged back to the user department for that month.

Sampling method. With this method, once every year each department's actual use of support services is sampled (over a four- to six-week period). On the basis of this sampling each department's use of a particular support service is calculated as a percentage. For example, the Personnel Records Department made 1,500 copies out of a total of 45,000 copies made; therefore, their use is 3.3% of the total. The annual operating cost of providing the copying service is then multiplied by each department's percentage of use. The answer is the dollar cost charged back to each department for the entire year for that support service. The copying service costs $150,000; Personnel Records' use is 3.3% of total; therefore, their annual chargeback is $4,950.

By using one of these approaches an organization in effect duplicates the situation in which CPAs charge their clients for typing and reproduction services in connection with their annual audits.

This approach—charging for actual use rather than allocating part of the costs to all departments without regard for their use—has three primary advantages over the allocation approach. It discourages unnecessary use of the services; it provides management with an accurate set of costs against which it can judge the quality of services provided; and it places greater accountability on the office manager, thereby reducing the likelihood of empire building.

The term *empire building* refers to a practice common among managers in virtually every organization of every size and activity of indiscriminately adding to their department's staff, equipment, and services without first ensuring that the additional costs incurred will be offset by tangible and intangible benefits. Unfortunately some job classification systems, upon which salary grades are largely based, encourage empire building, since they assign more weight and therefore more importance to managers who oversee larger staffs and larger budgets. Identifying and eliminating empire building in any organization is a sure way to reduce operating and overhead costs and to improve overall profitability.

In point of fact organizations do not require in-house capability in all aspects of office operations. Many companies enter into contractual relationships with commercial service organizations to provide services such as payroll preparation and record keeping; microfilming, copying, and duplication services; and word-processing transcription services. Usually these companies either lack sufficient sales volume to justify the costs of an in-house operation or have found that they can reduce overall costs by purchasing the various services as required.

The various functions of an administrative office can therefore be provided in one of two ways: (1) by establishing an in-house capability overseen by the office manager or (2) by contracting with an outside commercial service and relying upon the office manager to monitor the performance. Viewing the administrative office function as an overhead factor and establishing a chargeback system, so that the in-house capability is viewed as merely another source of supply, are cost-effective, realistic approaches.

HISTORICAL DEVELOPMENT
OF THE OFFICE MANAGER'S POSITION

The title *office manager* has been in popular use only since the 1920s; however, the concept of office manager dates back to the Industrial Revolution. In commercial offices of that period it was common practice for owners to delegate responsibility for clerical operations and the supervision of office personnel to their chief clerks, allowing themselves to devote more of their time to the managerial and profitmaking aspects of their businesses.

As businesses grew in complexity and size, so did their offices. Quill pens and ledgers gave way to typewriters and a variety of office equipment designed to facilitate the performance of routine office activities. Coupled with the need to provide such support services as filing, communications, and mail, and to develop new and improved work methods and procedures, these changes led to the creation of a new position in many organizations—that of the office manager.

Initially the office manager was a middle-level executive who reported to the treasurer or the comptroller in large organizations or to the president in small ones. His or her responsibilities included such matters as selecting, purchasing, and maintaining office appliances, furniture, and equipment; purchasing, stocking, and issuing stationery, forms, and other office supplies; and supervising such centralized support services as the typing pool, the mailroom, the central files, and the switchboard.

As organizations continued to grow and as the number of persons assigned to each aspect of the administrative office function increased, it became necessary to define the office manager's duties more precisely. Intermediate levels of supervision were added between the office managers and the various persons who actually provided the services. The supervisors at the intermediate level were working supervisors rather than managers; they not only supervised the day-to-day operations of their function but also performed the various tasks involved in providing the service. For example, the central files supervisor actually classified records and coded them for filing; the mailroom supervisor sorted incoming and outgoing mail and probably even had an internal mail pickup and delivery route. The office manager, on the other hand, evolved into a true manager rather than a working supervisor. His or her duties became confined strictly to planning, organizing, controlling, and communicating—the basic responsibilities of all managers. The office manager's position became that of a generalist who could apply creativity and managerial know-how to provide administrative services to the entire organization. By and large this development has continued to the present.

The change in business organizations that followed World War II had a marked effect upon the office manager's job. Formerly a centralized unit, the administrative office now became decentralized, and the office manager's role was not only to continue to provide for the remaining centralized activities but to provide guidance to the decentralized groups as well. Today the responsibilities of the office manager include establishing work methods and procedures, setting equipment standards, and supervising training, as well as the traditional responsibilities of earlier generations of office managers.

In large organizations today the office manager is on a directorial or even a vice-presidential level, reporting to an executive vice-president.

In many organizations the office manager has also been assigned responsibility for overseeing computer operations and all aspects of information processing.

SCOPE OF RESPONSIBILITIES

There is a decided commonality of responsibilities among office managers, even though the actual activities for which they are responsible differ from one organization to the next, depending upon the size and complexity of the organization served, management's philosophy concerning centralization of common services, and, of course, the skills and "clout" of the individual office manager. Still, it is possible to define the scope of the office manager's job in two categories: (1) organizational and managerial responsibilities and (2) administrative systems and services.

Organizational and managerial responsibilities. Included in this category are those business activities that involve organizing, staffing, and equipping the organization so that it can operate cost-efficiently—activities such as the selection of office facilities, the planning and designing of office space, the managing of personnel, and the purchasing, stocking, and issuing of office supplies.

Administrative systems and services. This category includes all tasks involved in assisting the profitmaking departments to do their job more effectively as well as at lower cost. Included are such activities as developing new and improved work methods and providing support services such as facilities for transcribing dictated and handwritten drafts or for copying small quantities and duplicating large volumes of written materials; mail pickup and delivery; records storage and retrieval; and telephone and other communications services.

Since each of the various business activities and support services will be examined in detail in subsequent chapters of this book, they will be mentioned only briefly at this point in order to provide the reader with an understanding of the unusual diversity of the office manager's responsibilities.

ATTRIBUTES OF
THE SUCCESSFUL OFFICE MANAGER

Within the areas of responsibility just mentioned, the office manager must continually apply managerial expertise to ensure that maximum productivity and cost savings are achieved without adversely affecting the speed or quality of the services provided. Specifically, the office manager must be able to perform certain basic functions if he or she is to succeed at office management.

Functions

Planning. Making plans for the development and implementation of cost-effective, operationally efficient, and (if applicable) user-responsive business activities, and services falls within the office manager's area of responsibility. Such planning involves:

Assessing the organization's current, short-term, and medium-term requirements for facilities, personnel, equipment, supplies, systems, and administrative services

Translating these requirements into a series of clearly defined objectives

Formulating a strategy for achieving these objectives

Selling that strategy to top management in both written and verbal presentations. (After getting management's approval), conducting or overseeing studies designed to

Identify alternate investments and courses of action

Select the best of the preceding alternatives, effecting the necessary tradeoffs between operational requirements and budgetary constraints

Organizing. This function involves organizing the various available or allocated resources (personnel, equipment, and budgeted funds) to achieve the goals identified by planning. In doing so the office manager must recruit or select personnel, structure them into logical working groups, provide the equipment and supplies they require in order to function properly, establish lines of authority and reporting arrangements, and ensure that adequate communications facilities are provided.

Controlling. This essential function involves controlling the various operations overseen by the office manager through the use of operating budgets, performance reporting, the establishment of individual and group productivity standards, and similar measures.

Motivating and training. To ensure their efficient, enthusiastic participation in the activities of the office, employees must be highly motivated and well trained. The ability to communicate concisely and clearly, taking into account the different educational and intellectual levels of various employees, is essential to this function.

Personality Traits

Given these primary requirements, what personality traits and intellectual abilities should the successful office manager possess? To resolve this question, the author queried participants at an American Management Association course (Chicago, November 1981). The following traits were determined to be desirable in any office manager.

Service orientation and sensitivity. First, and possibly most important, the office manager must be service-oriented and sensitive to people, since all of the office manager's areas of responsibility are service functions. In addition, these are labor-intensive areas in which constant inter-action between user departments, on the one hand, and the office manager's function on the other is the norm. The office manager must have a genuine desire to help these departments by doing all within his or her power to provide the needed services in the time dictated. Too often office managers forget that theirs is a true service function that must be responsive to the users' changing needs. They sometimes tend to view the departments they serve as antagonists and adopt a "them versus us" attitude; as a result the overall organization suffers.

In hiring office management personnel (and especially in selecting the office manager), the interview should be conducted so that the applicant's service orientation and sensitivity toward people are clearly determined. This can be done effectively by asking whether the applicant has ever worked in a service function and, if so, how he or she viewed the requirements and demands of the departments served.

Proven managerial ability. This important trait is the demonstrated ability to perform the managerial functions of planning, organizing, controlling, motivating, and training. A number of other traits must be possessed in order to accomplish this.

Knowledge of business. The office manager must have a keen understanding of a wide range of business subjects—from problem solving to coping with union representatives. He or she must be a generalist, or must be able within a short time to become one. The duties of the office manager are simply too broad for a technician or specialist to function efficiently.

Ability to innovate. The office manager must be an innovator with a questioning mind, unwilling to accept the status quo because "that's how we've always done it" or to assume that what worked best for another company is therefore best for this one. The office manager will commit large sums of money in the form of equipment, people, supplies, and facilities to performing certain administrative office functions. Unless he or she is innovative, it is doubtful whether these investments will return anywhere near their potential cost savings and productivity.

Communications skills. The office manager needs above-average written and verbal communication skills, coupled with an ability to adjust communications to meet the intellectual level of the audience. The manager must understand what motivates people and adjust communications accordingly. To illustrate, top management would be motivated by the hope of achieving increased productivity and lower operating costs; thus, in communicating with these managers one should stress those benefits. Lower-level employees, however, would probably take a more parochial view, considering "How will this affect me and my job security?" In communicating with these employees one would emphasize individual benefits rather than those that the owners or stockholders would receive.

Teaching skills. The office manager should possess teaching skills—a requisite for the successful development of his or her subordinates.

Ability to say no. The office manager should be able to say no tactfully to superiors, peers, and subordinates alike. This is an essential quality in anyone responsible for a service function in which multiple demands require the setting of priorities and the regulation of work.

Decisiveness. The ability to reach decisions without having the complete facts is another attribute that the office manager should possess. Often in assessing a potential situation, not all the information needed will be available. For example, suppose one must answer the question, "What would be the effect upon our ability to provide twenty-four hour word processing service if we were to remove certain restrictions on the work that will be accepted for processing?". In such instances the ability to reach a decision on the basis of an intuition, an educated guess, or a "gut" feeling tempered with experience is of primary importance.

Ability to admit mistakes. The ability to make effective decisions should be tempered with the flexibility and confidence in oneself to admit that a decision may not have been right and that a change may be required. Such a character trait is very valuable in an office manager.

It is apparent that many of these attributes are innate: an individual either possesses them or not. Many can be refined and improved, however, through a planned management development program consisting of:

> Participation in the activities of professional groups such as the Administrative Management Society, the Association of Records Managers and Administrators, and the Association for Systems Management
>
> Continued reading of trade publications such as *The Office, Administrative Management,* and *Information and Records Management*

Attendance at the annual conference and trade shows of the Business Equipment Manufacturers Association and the Administrative Management Society

Participation in training seminars and extension courses conducted by the American Management Association, Executive Enterprises, Inc., and AMR International

CHAPTER 2

Organizational Responsibilities of the Office Manager

Once the decision has been made to establish an office management function within an organization and to appoint an office manager to perform this function, two critical decisions must immediately be reached: (1) How will the office management function be organized? (2) What authority and responsibilities will be assigned to the office manager?

Unfortunately there are neither standard nor simple solutions to these questions. Each organization must evaluate and identify its own operational and administrative needs and must then develop an approach to office management that will meet these needs and be consistent with the organization's managerial philosophy. Failure to organize the office management function or to structure the office manager position in accordance with the company's needs will markedly impair the potential contribution of an office manager to the company's productivity and cost-effectiveness. Conversely, if both the office management function and the office manager position are well structured, with a proper arrangement of personnel and a logical allocation of functions and responsibilities, organizational objectives will be accomplished that cannot be achieved by persons acting individually.

ORGANIZING THE
OFFICE MANAGEMENT FUNCTION

Determining the Scope

The initial task in organizing the office management function is to decide which administrative and support services will be included. To a great extent this decision depends upon the size and complexity of the organization involved. As a rule the smaller the organization, the more functions the office manager will have to perform. Indeed, in a small, single-location organization, it is not uncommon for the office management function to include almost all overhead activities (data processing, supplies management, administrative services, human resources, industrial relations, facilities management, payroll, and systems and procedures).

Conversely, in a large organization the office management function is typically much narrower in scope. In such companies the office manager is generally responsible only for supplies management, administrative services, and facilities management. Data processing, human resources, industrial relations, and systems and procedures are assigned to other administrative executives, who, along with the office manager, report to a single top-level executive such as the vice-president for administration.

This latter arrangement reinforces rather than undermines the concept of office management, since it implies the recognition that the modern-day office is so complex in its scope that few single individuals will have the skills, time, or ability to manage all its component activities. In effect, therefore, in organizations of this type, responsibility for all nonmanufacturing and nonsales activities no longer rests with the office manager but with a new administrative executive—the vice president for administration. Usually this official is a generalist rather than a specialist. The office manager and the director of data processing now usually report to the vice president for administration. In addition, in larger organizations where such activities are not under the organizational umbrella of the office manager, the director of human resources and the director of industrial relations also report to the vice president for administration: In effect, all the traditional office management activities are still performed, but they are the responsibilities of several specialists who report to a single generalist.

The Dartnell Institute of Business Research recently surveyed over three hundred employees who were responsible for the administration of their companies' business offices and asked them to describe the activities for which they were directly responsible. Over 60% of the respondents indicated they were responsible for activities that could be classified as aspects of *supplies management, industrial relations,* and *administrative services,* while more than half indicated that they were responsible for *facilities management* and *human resources.*

To determine which of these activities should fall within the office management function in a particular company, the person responsible for establishing the office management function must

  Identify each administrative support and clerical activity that is performed within the organization
  Determine the degree of skill required to supervise and administer each such activity properly, as well as the time that would be required for a motivated person to acquire such skills
  Ascertain the time that would probably be involved in the proper supervision of each such activity
  On the basis of the above, determine which administrative support and clerical activities will be assigned to the office management function and which will be assigned to other organizational elements

Establishing an Organizational Structure

Once the decision has been made as to which activities will comprise the office management function, an organizational structure for the function can be designed. Three structures have been successfully employed for the office management function:

Centralized: in this structure the office manager is responsible for establishing, administering, and supervising the specific activities under her or his control and the employees assigned to each.

Decentralized: in this structure the separate organizational elements are responsible for identifying their own needs for administrative support and clerical services and for providing for these needs as they choose by establishing, administering, and supervising the specific activities and employees.

Decentralized under centralized control: in this structure the office manager is responsible for establishing and overseeing the various administrative support and clerical activities, but the day-to-day operation of each activity and the supervision of the employees involved remains the responsibility of the various department, division, staff office, or other organizational element for which the administrative support and clerical activities are performed.

Figures 2-1, 2-2, and 2-3 illustrate each structure.

Frequently a single organization utilizes a combination of these structures rather than just one. For example, mailroom functions may be centralized, the word processing function may be decentralized under the office manager's control, and the reception services may be performed on a totally decentralized basis.

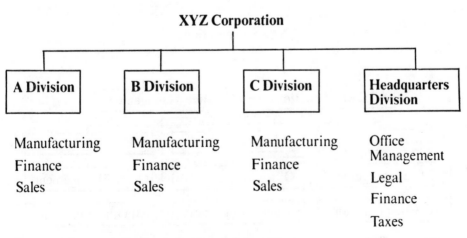

Figure 2-1. Centralized Organizational Structure

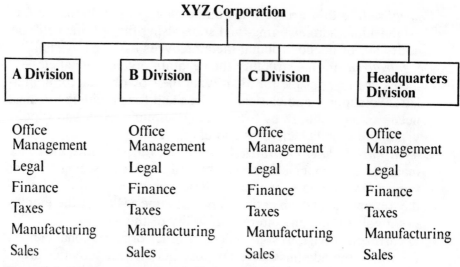

Figure 2-2. Decentralized Organizational Structure

Advantages and Limitations of Each Structure

There are several distinct advantages and limitations to each of the three structures. The persons establishing the office management function must weigh these advantages and limitations carefully in order to

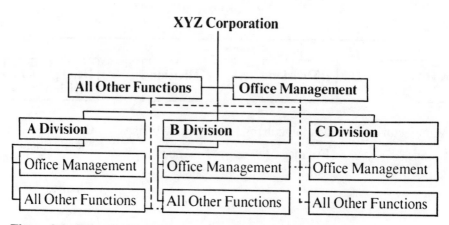

Figure 2-3. Decentralized Structure Under Centralized Control

ensure that the structure selected will be both cost-effective and compatible with the organization's management philosophy.

CENTRALIZED STRUCTURE

Advantages

Under this structure the various office management functions are overseen by qualified, knowledgeable specialists who work at their specialties full-time. Under the decentralized structure, managers who are often neither skilled nor experienced in the various techniques must take time away from other, primary duties to oversee an office management function.

It ensures a career path to which all office management personnel can aspire, decreasing turnover.

It permits a cost-efficient use of facilities and manpower and eliminates duplication.

It facilitates the identification and control of overhead costs, since standard procedures, performance standards, quality controls, and the reporting of performance are more easily developed within a centralized office.

Disadvantages

The major disadvantage is the lack of a close working relationship between the various office management personnel and the departments or units they serve. The complaint is often heard in a centralized structure that office management personnel neglect the departments' needs and concentrate instead upon their own goals.

Conflicting priorities and deadlines must be resolved by a disinterested party such as the function's supervisor or the office manager, who, being human, may base their judgments upon what is politically expedient rather than what is just.

User departments may have to modify their needs to satisfy the limitations of the centralized function. This often leads to lower efficiency and effectiveness than if a dedicated decentralized system were developed to meet each user's unique needs.

Decentralized Structure

Advantages

Communication and supervision are greatly simplified.

A closer working relationship is generally established between office management personnel and the user departments.

A higher degree of personal attention is generally noted.

Workers obtain greater psychological satisfaction.

Decentralization fosters the idea of profit accountability.

The system provides maximum flexibility to meet changing and unique operating needs.

Disadvantages

Decentralization is generally the most costly approach to providing for office management needs. Usually each decentralized group staffs and equips to satisfy peak requirements, resulting in unnecessarily high costs.

"Empire building" is more common in a decentralized environment than in any other.

Decentralization makes it difficult to establish and administer uniform operating procedures, quality controls, and performance standards.

The quality of supervision afforded the various office management functions is usually lower within a decentralized system.

Decentralized Structure Under Centralized Control

This structure is designed to combine the strengths and advantages of both the centralized and decentralized structures while avoiding their disadvantages.

Advantages

The decentralized structure provides professional, full-time advice and guidance to user departments while allowing them to remain responsible for the day-to-day operations of their office management functions.

It ensures that the decentralized functions will be organized and operated in accordance with established techniques and controls.

It provides for an overseer to reduce the likelihood of empire building, overstaffing, improper equipment selection, and the like.

It provides for organization-wide coordination and control, since all functions are monitored by the office manager.

Disadvantages

Coordination is more difficult than under a centralized approach.

The "squeaky wheel" principle tends to be followed; since time is usually limited, the office manager tends to concentrate his or her efforts on users who request those efforts, rather than on those that need it or would benefit from it the most.

Evaluative Criteria

Four factors must be taken into account when selecting one of these structures for the office management function: (1) span of control; (2) ability to cross organizational lines; (3) delegation of authority from the office manager to other executive and supervisory personnel; (4) logical division of work.

Span of control. This refers to the number of subordinates that the office manager can directly supervise. The basic principle applicable to the span of control may be stated as follows: No supervisor should have more persons reporting to him or her than he or she can effectively supervise. The number of persons an office manager can effectively supervise depends in large part upon the type of activities that fall within his or her area of responsibility. Where the activities are relatively simple and are routine and repetitive, an office manager can reasonably be expected to supervise as many as a dozen persons who report directly to him or her as well as perhaps several score more who report to those various supervisors or lead persons. Conversely, when the activities are diversified or are complex, the number of subordinates that the office manager can effectively supervise is significantly reduced.

Determining a span of control generally involves trial and error. If too large a span is established, it will usually be necessary to reduce the number of persons that report directly to the office manager by adding an intermediate reporting level.

Ability to cross organizational lines. This ability is essential if the office manager is to supervise, either directly or indirectly, the various activities included in the office management function. The office management function must be assigned to the highest organizational element among those serviced. This means, for example, that the office manager should be assigned to either the corporate staff or to the "landlord" division in a multidivisional organization, or to the president's or general manager's offices in a single-divisional setup.

Delegation of authority. This is essential to a smooth-running, efficient office management function. When the organizational structure impedes the office manager's ability to delegate authority, the overall office management function becomes cumbersome; decisions are made slowly, and both upward and downward communication is impeded.

Logical division of work. To divide work in an effective, coordinated manner is a major goal of any organization. Such division of work is necessary to ensure the maximum utilization of each individual's time and energies. In the office management function, logical division of work involves each individual employee's learning only a small segment of the overall task rather than all of its aspects. This simplifies training, makes work measurement and coordination possible, and facilitates the use of time- and labor-saving equipment and work methods.

Three principles must be kept in mind when planning for the logical division of work

A work load should never be subdivided if it will require less than one person's time. The only exception to this rule is if there are space limitations. In such instances additional work must be found to round out the employee's time until it equals a full-time job.

The subdivision of any task should be accompanied by the development of uniform methods and procedures as well as of a method for measuring, monitoring, and reporting each employee's productivity and performance.

If additional duties are assigned to any employee to round out his or her work day, such duties should be learned by other employees as well, so that sufficient backup will be available if the primary employee is absent.

ESTABLISHING THE AUTHORITY AND RESPONSIBILITIES OF THE OFFICE MANAGER

Once a decision has been made about how to organize the office management function, defining the authority and responsibilities of the office manager becomes a relatively simple, straightforward task. The following steps must be taken:

Organization charts are prepared indicating the functions over which the office manager exercises direct and indirect authority, the persons to whom the office manager reports, and the persons who report to him or her. The organization charts also indicate the relative position of the office manager and the office management function vis-à-vis the other executives and organizational elements and their functions.

Position descriptions are developed defining the principal responsibilities of the office manager, the nature of his or her authority, and his or her accountability for meeting these responsibilities.

Performance criteria are defined to provide a series of cost, service, and other criteria against which the office manager's performance can be realistically measured and appraised.

Policy statements and guidelines are issued detailing the interrelationship between the office management function and the remainder of the organization.

Implementing procedures are established detailing the methods, forms, and controls that will regulate requests for and provision of services to other parts of the organization.

THE OFFICE MANAGER'S POSITION:
FOUR CASE HISTORIES

In order to gain an understanding of how the office management function and the office manager's position may differ from one organization to the next, let us examine how they have been structured in four different companies. In each case the name of the company has been disguised; however, details concerning the office management function and the office manager position are accurate and unmodified.

Breathe-Easy Respiratory Service, Inc.

Breathe-Easy Respiratory Service, Inc., based in Westchester County, New York, is involved in the sale and servicing of respiratory devices to hospitals located in the northeastern and middle Atlantic states. Founded five years ago with a staff of three, the firm has experienced rapid growth. Its gross sales have increased by over 85% and five new employees have been added during the past year alone. Currently Breathe-Easy has twenty-one employees, ten of whom are employed in the business office.

The business office is run by an office manager who has been employed by the firm since its founding. Originally a combination secretary-to-the-president/girl Friday, the office manager was promoted to her present position three years ago when the office staff grew to four clerks.

She has gained the knowledge and skills required for her present job largely through independent efforts. She has studied at various local colleges that offer courses in office administration during evening hours, attended American Management Association seminars on office management, and has become actively involved in the local chapter of the Administrative Management Society. Continued reading of such trade publications as *Information and Records Management* and of the various books that have been written in the field of office management has enabled her to upgrade her skills and knowledge so that she is able to function effectively as her organization's in-house expert on administrative support and clerical activities.

Breathe-Easy has totally centralized all activities other than those directly relating to the sales and servicing of respiratory devices as part of the office management function. The activities include

Personnel management, which covers the recruitment, testing, and hiring of new and replacement personnel; the recommending of standard and incentive wage scales; the administering of employee benefits; and the evaluation and training of employees.

Facilities management, which includes the control of office space as well as its layout, the selection and assignment of office furniture, and the maintenance of office facilities, grounds, and parking lots.

Administrative services, which includes mail service, telephone service, records management, word processing, office copying and reproduction services, and the maintenance and replacement of company-leased vehicles.

Accounting services, which includes payroll and petty cash, cash management, accounts receivable and payable, billing and collections, and the preparation of monthly trial balances and aging of accounts receivable.

Supplies management, which includes the standardization, purchasing, and inventory of the operating supplies required by the company.

Systems and procedures development. Currently, all systems are manual, although plans are under way to conduct a study to determine the feasibility of computerizing various operating systems or procedures, using either a commercial service bureau or a company-owned or leased minicomputer system.

Since Breathe-Easy is not unionized, the business office performs no industrial relations duties. Surprisingly, there is no formal grievance procedure: "The need to establish one has yet to occur," the office manager explained.

The office manager has wide decision making authority. Reporting directly to the president, she has been delegated authority to approve or reject all requests for expenditures in her areas of responsibility up to $5,000. Beyond that, the president's approval is also required.

The office management function is expected to continue to operate in its present form in this company in the foreseeable future. The president explained that because the company is a sales and service orgainzation he wishes to keep the office management function as lean as possible. Therefore the size of this function, in terms of both number of employees and activities performed, is not expected to change significantly. The president estimated, "In all probability, we'll add an assistant office manager in two or three years to help our office manager stay abreast of her work load, but it's unlikely that we'll add any other supervisory or management personnel to this function in the foreseeable future."

Breathe-Easy has structured its office management function along traditional lines, with a totally centralized function headed by a single executive who reports to the chief operating executive of the company. This structure has proved to be quite satisfactory for most small organizations and for those that have highly routine, simple office operations.

Ashby & Collins, P.A.

Ashby & Collins, P.A. (Professional Association), is a Nashville-based law firm that offers legal services to a broad range of clients—individuals, corporations, and municipalities. The firm is organized by types of clientele; a senior partner heads each practice area and has full operating and profitmaking responsibility.

In keeping with this management philosophy each senior partner has full responsibility for staffing and equipping his or her practice area and for providing the office management functions needed. The firm's philosophy is that any senior partner should have freedom to manage his or her own practice area as he or she wishes, so long as he or she maximizes the services provided the firm's clients, the profits made, and the productivity of the employees assigned.

The firm has centralized the office management function by establishing a General Services Department headed by an office manager. This department is responsible for maintaining the firm's office facilities and for providing the various administrative support and clerical services that are required by the various practice areas. It is in the utilization of these centralized activities that Ashby & Collins' approach is unique. Each administrative support and clerical activity provided by the General Services Department is charged back at cost to users, making the cost of the office management function self-liquidating. However, each of the various practice areas is free either to use the centralized services or to obtain them in any other way they choose (by, for example, contracting with a commercial service bureau, purchasing equipment themselves, or establishing their own capability), if they decide that the costs charged by General Services are higher than would be available from an alternate source or that the speed or quality of service provided is unsatisfactory. In effect, therefore, Ashby & Collins' General Services Department becomes simply another vendor that must compete on both a cost and a service basis with all other potential vendors. In the words of an Ashby & Collins senior partner,

This approach keeps General Services on their toes, and just about eliminates any possibility of featherbedding or empire building. If either of these occurred, the costs would increase to the point where the practice areas would use other sources, and General Services would be unable to charge back its operating costs as they are required to do by our policy. The same is true of their service: if it's too slow or too many errors occur, we'll look for other alternatives, and General Service's costs will again fail to be totally charged back. If that should happen for too many months, first the rank-and-file workers will be cut back, and eventually the firm will look for a new department head.

The advantage of this approach is aptly summarized in this partner's statement. The approach provides an effective challenge to the centralized office management department: services must be provided in an efficient and economical manner or the services will be obtained elsewhere. Truly cost-conscious organizations would do well to consider such an approach.

United Chemicals Corporation

United Chemicals Corporation is a large, multidivisional manufacturer of agricultural, industrial, and specialty chemicals. Headquartered in Atlanta, United has more than twenty-five manufacturing locations throughout the United States. United Chemicals is organized into three divisions: Agricultural Chemicals, Industrial Chemicals, and Specialty Chemicals. Each division is headed by a vice president general manager who, in keeping with the corporation's management philosophy, is virtually autonomous and has full responsibility for the profitability of his or her division. The Atlanta headquarters office of United Chemicals houses a small corporate staff, as well as the vice president general manager of each of the three divisions and their divisional headquarters.

In accordance with United's management philosophy, the office management function is totally decentralized. In the headquarters, each of the divisions, as well as the corporate staff, has its own office manager and provides for its own administrative support and clerical services. Each, for example, sets up and operates its own mailroom; purchases, inventories, and controls its own office supplies; recruits, hires, and administrates its own personnel; and develops its own manual and automated systems and procedures. Little if any interaction occurs between the office managers of the corporate staff and those of the various divisions. It is, in effect, the situation one would anticipate if four independent companies were located in the same building.

There is no similarity in the backgrounds of the four office managers, since there have been no corporate-wide position description or selection criteria relating to that job. Consequently one office manager is a former head of the word processing pool who has had little experience in other administrative support and clerical activities; two were formerly personnel professionals, and the other had had extensive experience in office services but little in personnel work. Each reports to different persons in the organizational hierarchy: the corporate office's office manager reports to the vice president for human resources; two of the divisional office managers report to the divisional controller; and the fourth reports to the divisional vice president for administration.

Both the corporate and divisional managements are aware that this decentralized structure has definite built-in inefficiencies and is, in the long run, more expensive than a centralized structure would be. They realize, for example, that in the areas of supplies management and personnel management there could be substantial cost savings if the whole organization were served by a central supply room or employment office. However, in light of their desire to give each division maximal control over its own operations and operating expenses, they feel that more would be lost by centralizing the various administrative support and clerical activities than would, in the aggregate, be saved. So each time the question of consolidation is broached, a decision is made to continue the decentralized pattern. It should be noted, however, that within the past year two of United's divisions have begun to work toward forming a purchasing pool, by planning to enter into joint purchasing agreements with office supplies and equipment vendors so that they can save by buying in bulk.

The decentralized office management structure is generally impractical in large and medium-sized organizations. The duplication, overlapping, and increased numbers of personnel that are typical of such structures generally more than offset any benefits that may be realized.

Fixed-Wing Aircraft Corporation

Fixed-Wing Aircraft Corporation is a Texas-based manufacturer of commercial and military aircraft that maintains eight large production facilities in states located west of the Mississippi. As a matter of corporate policy adopted nearly twenty-five years ago, Fixed-Wing established a corporate staff comprised of the highly skilled specialists needed for each area of the company's business. For example, there is a corporate director of organization planning, a corporate director of long-range planning, and a corporate director of purchases. The function of each of these officers is to establish guidelines under which the business activities for which he or she is responsible are to be carried on within each division. The corporate-level specialist has staff rather than line authority and operates in an advisory capacity. The persons in the various divisions under the jurisdiction of the corporate-level specialists are divisional rather than corporate employees and are hired, promoted, supervised, and terminated by the divisional managers to whom they report; however, they are subject to periodic audit and appraisal by the corporate-level specialist, whose job it is to see that the business activity for which he or she is responsible is being efficiently and accurately carried out throughout the company.

The office management function within the corporation is organized in terms of the decentralized operation, centralized control concept. At the corporate level there is a general office manager, a person with more than twenty years experience in office management, whose job is to establish the guidelines under which the divisions organize and operate their own local office management activities. In addition, the general office manager is responsible for periodically auditing each division's office management operation and making recommendations for improvement. The general office manager also serves as an in-house consultant, providing assistance, on demand, to the operating divisions in matters dealing with office management.

Each of the eight factories has its own office management operation headed by an office manager who generally reports to the controller. Functionally, however, the divisional office managers look to the general office manager for advice and direction in matters dealing with office management functions.

Each local office manager is responsible for the cost-effectiveness of his or her own office management operation, and while the general office manager's approval is not required for major equipment, staffing, and organizational acquisitions, the general practice among local office managers is to "walk such matters by the general office manager before proceeding for the final approval."

Fixed-Wing's approach has proved to be successful in organizations in which there are highly procedurized operations and multiple locations. Since a specialist in office management is on the corporate staff to serve as "guru," the local operating divisions can run high-quality, user-oriented office management operations without incurring the expense of hiring an office management consultant. Consequently, overall costs, even after the general office manager's prorated salary has been taken into account, are much lower than if the decentralized operation, centralized control structure were not employed.

The wide diversity of the office manager's organizational and operating responsibility is readily evident from these four examples. The potential office manager must, it is obvious, be informed about a variety of administrative functions if he or she is to succeed in his or her chosen profession. The chapters that follow focus on some of these specific office management functions.

CHAPTER 3

Setting Up an Office

Establishing an office for even the smallest of organizations is no simple task for even the most seasoned office manager (see Chap. 15). Besides the obvious operational decisions (such as choosing the location and size of the facility), there are a variety of other financial, legal, and public relations considerations that must be addressed early on if the new office is to provide for the organization's immediate, intermediate, and long-term requirements in a cost-effective manner.

For this reason it is recommended that a company that is considering establishing a new office form a task force headed by the office manager to

Ascertain the feasibility of establishing the new office
Define the various requirements for the office
Evaluate various locations and means of acquiring the facility
Recommend the location and means of acquisition that best meet
the organization's current and projected requirements
Oversee the actual establishment and operation of the new office,
as well as the move (in total or in part) to the new facility

The office manager will head the task force, and the other members include representatives of the following functional areas:

Tax department (or, in the absence of such a person, the organization's CPA)
Legal department (or, in the absence of such a person, its outside legal counsel)
Personnel department
Architect or space planner
Insurance adviser or broker
Real estate consultant or broker
Construction consultant

The composition of the task force will ensure that all the aspects of business operations that might be affected by the location and layout of the new office are represented, reducing the possibility that an important aspect will be overlooked. It should be noted that many of these individuals will serve as on-call advisers or resources rather than as working members of the task force. This will help to keep the task force from getting bogged down as a result of having too much input or of difficulty in arranging meeting times that suit all members.

FEASIBILITY AND REQUIREMENTS STUDY

Why is the New Office Needed or Desired?

The initial job of the task force is to determine the goals that management hopes to achieve by establishing the new office. A typical motivation is the desire to acquire new space—more space for present or projected employees, equipment, or work areas; a more space-efficient layout that will be better suited to workflow; or simply a space that "looks better." Sometimes the primary motivation is the wish to relocate in a new area—one that is closer to public transportation or more easily reached by car; one that is closer to clients, suppliers, and other companies with which the organization must frequently interact; one that has a superior labor market or less active labor unions; one that offers tax reductions or rebates; or one that is in a more prestigious neighborhood.

The motivation can be readily and accurately determined by interviewing top management. Naturally, for a variety of reasons (such as not wanting to alarm the present workforce until something definite has been decided) the feasibility study must be conducted discreetly. For that reason many organizations choose to retain a single real estate consultant or broker to work on their behalf, who generally does not reveal the identity of the client until the decision is nearly made.

Once the objectives have been determined, the task force can begin to define the space, equipment, and security requirements for the new office.

Space and Equipment Requirements

Space requirements for the new office include

The space required for housing individual executive, professional, technical, and clerical personnel

The floor space required for equipment such as word processors, filing cabinets, data processing equipment, and office copiers

The space required for support areas such as conference rooms, reception areas, supply rooms, restrooms, and cafeterias, as well as for corridors, aisles, and other access areas

Since specific instructions for determining the space requirements for each of these three categories is given in Chapter 7 ("Office Layout and Design"), only the main steps will be described here. First, the task force determines what departments and functions will be housed in the new office. It then seeks to establish the staffing needs of the new facility. This is done by determining, through discussions with the managers of each department, current and projected staffing levels. The title of each currently authorized position in a department, the number of persons currently holding the position, and the types of duties each performs are established. On the basis of projections of future work loads, the task force also estimates how each department will be staffed in each of the next five years.

Once staffing needs have been determined, the task force establishes what equipment will be needed in each department and how much space the equipment will require. First a physical inventory is made of the equipment currently assigned to each department, including type and model, dimensions, and usable and available equipment capacity. Then, on the basis of its estimates of future work load and staffing needs, the task force arrives at an estimate of the equipment that will be needed in each department during each of the following five years.

The next step is to determine *workplace standards* for each position—that is, the exact quantity and type of space that must be provided for each employee and for the equipment to which he or she is entitled. Then the applicable workplace standards are multiplied by the number of staff members for each position to determine the space that will be required to house all the personnel currently employed, as well as the space needs projected for the next five years.

To the floor space required for personnel must be added the space required for the various support areas and corridors. Finally, the space required for any office equipment not included in the workplace standards is computed by adding 21.5% of the square footage of floor space occupied by each item to provide for access and circulation space. These figures, like the others, are computed not only for the current year but also for each of the next five years.

By adding up space required for personnel, equipment, and support and access areas, the task force will finally arrive at a figure for the total floor space required in the new facility.

Access and Security Requirements

It is important to determine whether there are any unique access or security requirements that must be provided for. If, for example, there is a second-shift data entry operation, one must make sure that the building will be open, elevators will be operating, and heating, ventilation, and air conditioning systems will be functioning during that time. Likewise, if a need for physical security necessitates taking special precautions such as restricting access to the office area, barring windows, or instituting a guard patrol of the premises during nonworking hours, these must also be identified at this time.

Unique Operational and Workflow Requirements

Finally, the ideal configuration of the total office space is determined by taking into account the type of work that will be performed, the workflow from one department to another, and inter- and intradepartmental communication requirements. Should it be, for example, a one-floor rectangular facility or would a square, multifloor office be more suitable?

Profiling the Optimum Facility

It should now be possible, on the basis of the data that has been gathered, to develop a profile of the type of facility that will suit the organization best. In addition to specifying floorspace, configuration, and special access and security needs, the profile would specify the access to transportation facilities required and the desired traits of the new office location in terms of zoning requirements, prestige, proximity to specific clients or suppliers, available labor market, tax rates and rebates, jurisdiction of specific union local and district lodges, neighborhood stability, and availability of additional space.

Identifying and Costing Alternatives

Calling upon the task force's real estate consultant or broker and its construction consultant, the possible geographic locations that fit the optimum facility profile are now identified. On the basis of prevailing construction, space, and occupancy costs in each such area, estimates are made of the costs involved in each of these alternative ways of acquiring a facility:

Erecting a new building
Renting an existing building or a portion of one
Purchasing a new or existing building and arranging its subsequent
   sale to and lease back from an investor

For purposes of comparison, a study will also be made of the options of:

Occupying the entire premises
Occupying only part of the premises and leasing the rest to other
   companies for periods designed to expire as the leasor organization requires more space

Upon completion of such analyses the task force will be able to
present management with its recommendation in a report that details

The possible locations for the new office
The costs of constructing or leasing such an office
The various characteristics, advantages, and limitations of each
   possible location vis-à-vis the optimum facility requirements

Management Review

Ideally, management will react promptly to the report by authorizing
the task force to proceed to examine in detail the feasibility of establishing the new office in one or more of the suggested locations. Management may also instruct the task force to consider other possible locations. Regardless of the number of locations involved, the evaluative
process now proceeds along the following lines.

SELECTING THE NEW SITE

The office manager and the real estate consultant or broker contact the
leading commercial real estate broker in each of the geographic areas
under consideration to determine the availability of existing buildings
that satisfy or could be remodeled to satisfy the organization's current
and projected requirements. Each building suggested is evaluated and
ranked in terms of the following characteristics.

ACCESSIBILITY

This is an important consideration if visitors will routinely come to the
office or if the company operates what may be classified as a "walk-in

business" (such as a stock brokerage or insurance agency). To facilitate accessibility,

The office should face the main thoroughfare.

There should be adequate traffic flow (both pedestrian and vehicular) to ensure maximum exposure to potential clients.

Parking facilities (on and/or off the street) should be available at no, or minimal, cost.

The building in which the office is located and its street entrance should be prominent

Unless the office is on the ground floor, elevator service should be available.

CONVENIENCE FOR EMPLOYEES

All potential locations will be evaluated in terms of their convenience for employees. Specifically:

If 25% or more of the employees will rely upon public transportation for getting to and from work, such transportation should be easily available.

Unless the company intends to provide eating facilities either on a full scale or through vending machines, inexpensive restaurants and coffee shops should be located nearby.

The building should provide modern, clean restrooms that are adequately supplied with soap, towels, and toilet tissue.

The heating, ventilation, and air conditioning system should be adequate to ensure the comfort of both employees and visitors and be operative during scheduled working hours (for additional discussion, see Chap. 7, "Office Layout and Design").

Ideally, the office should have a northern exposure, ensuring a maximum amount of comfortable light. If a northern exposure is not available, the next preferable alternatives are eastern, southern, and western.

The building's exterior and interior should be clean and well maintained. Any noncompany building personnel with whom employees or visitors are likely to come into contact (such as elevator operators or maintenance personnel) should be courteous and present a professional appearance.

Turnover among the building's tenants should be minimal. An unstable tenant base should be taken as an indication that others have found the building's management, services, or maintenance unsatisfactory.

RENOVATION

Aside from redecorating and minor renovations, little or no remodeling should be required to prepare the offices for occupancy. In particular,

Electrical wiring should be adequate to accommodate the various word processing, data processing, communications, and other equipment that the organization currently uses and that it is likely to use in the future.

If mechanized filing equipment or other heavy equipment will be used, is the floor load adequate, or will reinforcement be necessary? Naturally, the former is desired.

The installation of material handling systems such as dumbwaiters, horizontal conveyors, and pneumatic tube systems should be possible with minimal disturbance of existing walls, ceilings, floors, and ductwork.

TERMS

The landlord should be willing to share in the cost of renovating the premises to meet the organization's needs. Ideally, the lease should provide for subleasing or early cancellation subject to a nominal penalty. Rent escalation should be permitted only to reflect rises in property taxes, utility costs, and labor costs.

It is recommended that the task force assign a relative weight to each of the above factors and evaluate them on a scale of 1 to 5—1 being the highest and 5 the lowest rating. By multiplying each rating by the assigned weights and summing the results, a comparative overall rating will be arrived at for each facility. Additional factors that may be evaluated in the same way are

Annual rental costs
Availability of expansion space
Date upon which the facility will be ready for occupancy

Exploring Methods of Acquisition

Three possible methods of acquiring (and financing) the new office that the task force will investigate are lease, purchase, and sales-leaseback.

LEASING

Advantages
Leasing minimizes the amount of capital that must be tied up.
It enables the company to maintain maximum flexibility for future relocation.
It facilitates budgeting, since the cost of occupancy is predetermined to a great extent by the annual rental costs.

Disadvantages
There is no buildup of equity.
If the organization outgrows its leased quarters, additional space may be unavailable.

PURCHASING

Advantages
All other factors being equal, ownership of an office building is a good investment.
The organization builds an equity in the building.
There is certain prestige in a company's owning its own building.
Since there is a greater likelihood of remaining longer in owned than in leased premises, the cost of remodeling the facility to meet the company's needs will generally be justified.

Disadvantages

As owner, the organization must maintain and repair the building and maintain the grounds.

Large amounts of capital will be tied up.

Ownership is a less flexible arrangement than leasing. If the neighborhood declines or the location becomes less desirable in the future, ownership will make the decision to relocate more difficult to justify.

SALES-LEASEBACK

This is the option in which an organization buys a new or existing building for its own use, sells it to an investor, and then leases the building back from that investor.

Advantages

It enables an organization to obtain a building that meets or can be modified to meet its unique requirements without tying up large amounts of capital.

It frees the organization from the need to provide its own maintenance and repair services.

Disadvantages. In addition to the disadvantages cited for the lease option (which apply to this option as well), the sales-leaseback option has one additional disadvantage: There is a possibility that the building may be sold to another investor whose repair and maintenance services may not be as satisfactory as those of the original investor.

Roles of the Task Force Members

The various members of the task force should have clearly defined responsibilities in selecting the facility. The following functions can be performed by each specialist:

In a *lease* situation:

Real estate consultant or broker: helps locate and evaluate each possible facility and assists in negotiating lease.

Tax accountant or CPA: performs cost analyses to determine relative financial benefits of lease, purchase, and sales-leaseback options and recommends most financially beneficial option.

Legal counsel: negotiates the lease.

Architect/space planner: develops space requirements. Helps determine how well facility meets current and projected space, workflow, and communications needs, helps lay out the office.

Construction consultant: helps plan for remodeling of the facility. Represents the organization in dealings with the general contractor and the various subcontractors.

In a *purchase* or in a *sales-leaseback* situation:

Real estate consultant or broker: helps locate and evaluate each possible facility. Helps negotiate the purchase or sales-leaseback arrangement.

Tax accountant or CPA: performs cost analyses, structures and helps arrange financing.

Insurance adviser or broker: determines and arranges for necessary insurance coverage.

Architect or space planner: develops space requirements. Helps determine what remodeling or renovation is necessary to adapt the building to the owner's requirements. Assists in laying out the offices.

Construction consultant: as in the case of leased premises, helps plan for remodeling and renovation of the facility. Represents the organization in dealings with the general contractor and the various subcontractors.

RELOCATING TO THE NEW FACILITY

If any section of the organization is to move to the new facility, an integral part of the task force's responsibility is to coordinate the move and make sure that all goes well. Ideally, a moving company with experience in office relocation should be engaged, since such a mover can provide valuable advice on how to schedule and conduct the move.

Relocations are usually scheduled over one or more consecutive weekends, beginning after the close of business on Friday and continuing until Sunday evening. The moving schedule will provide for the simultaneous relocation of only as many departments as the mover can transfer from the old to the new location in a single weekend, since a prime requirement of the move is that any department be set up in its new quarters and ready to resume operations on the first day of the business week following the move (typically the opening of business on Monday morning).

Several measures can make the move more efficient:

Records retention schedules can be applied before the actual move so that all eligible records are destroyed or sent to inactive storage rather than being transported to the new facility, placed in file cabinets, and shortly afterwards being removed for destruction or transfer.

All surplus equipment can be sold, reassigned to other departments that need it, donated to a charitable organization for tax deduction purposes, or placed in a surplus property pool.

New filing systems, equipment, and supplies can be installed at the time of or immediately after the move.

As a final step all suppliers, customers, and other organizations are notified of the relocation and of the new address and telephone numbers. In addition, a news release is prepared and sent to the newspapers that serve the area in which the company was formerly located and the area in which it is relocating, as well as to all trade publications and periodicals that serve the organization's industry.

CHAPTER 4

Establishing Office Systems and Procedures

Office systems and procedures, in the broadest sense, may be defined as *predetermined plans for accomplishing specific office operations, functions, or tasks;* they are the methods whereby every professional, managerial, and clerical employee performs his or her job. Office activities go hand in hand with systems and procedures; for every task that is performed in the office, a system and procedure must be formulated to ensure its successful completion.

Systems and procedures are of two types—formal and informal. When they are formal, all employees performing a particular task are required to follow the same prescribed, standard method. When they are informal, no single method has been prescribed, and in the absence of a standard system and procedure each employee (or group of employees) is free to establish his or her own method of performing the assigned duties.

Just as there are alternate routes by which a traveler may reach a desired destination, so are there different approaches that may be used to accomplish a given office operation. Some approaches may be completely automated; some may involve only manual operations; still others may be partially automated and partially manual. For any given problem each of these approaches may prove satisfactory.

However, the fact that a particular approach accomplishes a given office operation successfully (in the sense that it provides results) does not mean that the approach is necessarily the best or most desirable. Alternatives may make it possible for that job to be performed more quickly, with less effort, or at lower cost—and therein lies the difference between a good systems approach and a mediocre one.

SYSTEMS ANALYSIS

An office system, whether it is totally automated, totally manual, or a combination of the two, is composed of three basic elements: people, equipment, and procedures. The degree to which these elements are matched to the specific work that must be done will to a great extent determine the cost-effectiveness and operational efficiency of the system.

The standard approach to developing new and revising old systems and procedures is known as *systems analysis*. This approach works equally well for computerized and manual applications, as well as for jobs that are performed by both single individuals and groups.

Systems analysis is a management tool that helps the office manager to examine any office operation, function, or task of any size or complexity, recognize the alternate approaches that might be more efficient and economical, and select the one alternative that is superior to all others. The rewards of such an effort are reduction of personnel, supplies, or equipment; less duplication of effort and unnecessary work; increased productivity; and coordinated and controlled administrative and support activities.

Pareto's Principle

An important limitation of systems analysis is expressed in Pareto's Principle. Pareto's Principle (paraphrased) states that 80% of the total operational and cost benefits attributable to any systems analysis may be achieved with 20% of the effort. To increase the attainable benefits beyond the 80% level will require a disproportionate expenditure of time, effort, and money. Consequently, striving for systems perfection is both uneconomical and inefficient *unless* the threat of failure or error is too great to justify Pareto's "80% results from 20% efforts" approach.

It should be realized, therefore, that the method of performing any job or task may be improved *provided* that one is willing to devote the necessary time, effort, and funds to such improvement. With this fact in mind, let us now discuss how a systems analysis of office procedures is made.

The Six-Step Approach

The six steps of making a systems analysis are simple and logical:

Select and define the functions or procedures that are too costly or operationally deficient.
Gather all background information and facts concerning that function or procedure.
Analyze all the facts completely.
Develop several alternate improved methods.
Select and implement the best alternative.
Periodically reevaluate the new methods to ensure that they are performing as projected.

SELECTING AND DEFINING THE PROCEDURE

Simple though this step may sound, it is critical to the success of the overall improvement of the office system and involves several steps. The objectives are fourfold:

To select the function or procedure to be systematized or improved
To define the problem clearly, accurately, and completely
To ascertain the objectives or goals to be accomplished in improving the function or procedure
To specify the scope of the study

Selection Criteria

Care should be taken in the selection of a function or procedure to be improved to ensure that the three following conditions exist:

The function or procedure is one that the office manager has the authority and ability to revise.

The function or procedure is worth improving—it is both productive and necessary.

The costs of making the study will be recoverable within two years.

In selecting a function or procedure for study, the office manager will be alert for telltale signs that indicate that change is necessary. These are some warning signs:

The function or procedure has been the target of complaints from customers or from other personnel within the organization.

Outside auditors have recommended that this phase of company operations be studied.

There is a constant backlog of work in this area.

Errors occur frequently.

Bottlenecks and unaccountable processing delays occur routinely.

The turnover rate among the personnel involved in this function is higher than elsewhere in the organization.

Other *indicators of inefficiency* are present:

Excessive make-ready or preparation time

Overly elaborate controls

Improper matching of job requirements to personnel skills

Absence of written procedures

Operating costs are too high.

Repetitive computations or transcriptions are common.

Data are posted or summarized from one report or form to another.

Project Definition

Project definition involves (1) defining the problem; (2) ascertaining the objectives of the study; (3) delineating the scope of the study—that is, the points in the overall system or the procedure at which the project will begin and end, the record-keeping media to be used, and so forth.

Defining the Problem

"A problem well-defined is half solved" (Charles Kettering). The first step in any systems analysis is to accurately define the problem. This frequently turns out to be far more difficult than one might expect. When a problem exists in the way a task is being done in the office, the employees involved are usually aware that there is a problem, but they are rarely able to describe the real root of the trouble. For this reason it is important that the office manager defer any action revising a function or procedure until all aspects of the problem have been evaluated. Correcting one aspect of a problem, such as a poorly designed form, may provide some relief, but it will not achieve the results possible when an entire function or procedure is analyzed as a whole and revised in order to fulfill clearly defined objectives.

As a rule, the deficiencies that point to the need for improving a particular function or procedure will generally point the way to the basic problem. For example, a constant backlog and high error rate in the processing of customer inquiries about the status of orders suggest that the problem is an inability of the customer service department to rapidly and accurately supply customers with information about the fulfillment of their orders. Likewise, continual overtime in the word-processing division, coupled with a frequent use of temporary assistance and complaints of missed deadlines, suggest that the word-processing department is unable to stay abreast of current work loads with its present procedures. The office manager should not hesitate to re-examine and, if necessary, revise the original problem definition as new data are gathered.

Writing a two-part "problem definition" can be very useful. The first part describes the operational objectives of the function or procedure under study; the second estimates the underlying problems that impede accomplishing the objectives. For example:

The Records Archives Department is designed to provide a secure, low-cost alternative to office files for those records that are referenced fewer than three times per file drawer per month. However, as a result of this department's inability to process requests for return of inactive records in under three days, many departments refuse to store any but their oldest records in this facility.

ASCERTAINING THE DESIRED GOALS

Having defined the basic problem, the office manager can now set the goals that he or she intends to accomplish as a result of the systems analysis. For example, the goals might be

Increased productivity
Elimination of overtime
Lower operating costs
Faster processing times
Fewer errors
Fewer customer complaints

Again, goals need to constantly be re-evaluated, and revised as new information becomes available.

DELINEATING THE SCOPE OF THE STUDY

By delineating the scope of the study the office manager establishes the ground rules as to what operational, recordkeeping, and personnel functions are to be evaluated. For example, the scope of a study designed to improve the cost-effectiveness and accuracy of the crime statistics compilation and reporting system of a large midwestern police department was described as follows:

This study is concerned with the processing of reports of criminal actions, commencing with its original capture and recording, and ending with its storage in magnetic media format and its subsequent retrieval. Included are all manual and computerized processing activities involved in the capture, maintenance, and dissemination of crime statistics by the police department.

Delineating the scope of the systems analysis completes the project definition phase. The office manager has now (1) identified the purpose of the selected procedure, (2) ascertained the factors that impede the achievement of that purpose, (3) established specific objectives and goals to be accomplished as a result of the systems analysis, and (4) clearly outlined the operations, personnel, equipment, and other factors to be evaluated during the course of the study. The gathering of background information can now begin.

FACT GATHERING

Before beginning the fact gathering effort, the office manager needs to become as familiar as possible with the organization and operations of the departments involved in the function or procedure under examination. He or she will need to examine organization charts and personnel assignment rosters, review any production standards that have been established for the department, and scrutinize any pertinent reports or surveys previously made.

Having done so the office manager will then hold a meeting to announce the study *and its purpose* to all personnel concerned. He or she openly and truthfully addresses the possible effect of the study upon the employees and their jobs. Naturally the office manager stresses any benefits that are likely to occur. For example, if one of the goals of the systems analysis is to increase productivity by eliminating some data entries in an order-taking procedure, the employees involved are likely to be more cooperative if they are told that as a result their tasks will be made less tiring or repetitive. A frank but diplomatic approach will help to overcome any hostility that the employees may feel toward the study.

Purposes

The fact gathering phase has three purposes:

To obtain all available information and data relating to the function
or procedure under study, including
Organization and staffing
Operating policies and procedures
Record-keeping and reporting practices

Workflow, forms, and controls
Productivity standards
Equipment and supplies
To verify or validate the accuracy of such information
To develop systems requirements for the new or revised function or procedure on the basis of the information that is gathered during either the problem selection and definition phase or during the fact gathering phase

At the outset, two words of caution are in order. First, one must avoid reaching any conclusions or forming any opinions during the fact gathering phase. During this phase one is merely obtaining the material for future analysis. To attempt to analyze any of the data at this time would be both counterproductive and premature. Second, care must be taken to separate facts from opinion. The former are essential for a competent analysis of the problem; the latter, while often indicative of underlying problems, should not be a part of any such analysis.

Methods

Methods of gathering the necessary information include interviewing the personnel involved; examining pertinent records (that is, written policies, procedures, correspondence forms, and records); and work sampling.

INTERVIEWING

Interviewing personnel is usually the most useful fact gathering device. The office manager starts at the beginning of the procedure—the point at which the initial transaction occurs that sets the procedure in motion. This could be the creation or receipt of a form, a report, an item of correspondence, or even a verbal message. For instance, a purchasing procedure might be started when the signal that stocks of a particular office supply have been reduced to the reorder point is received.

The office manager in effect assumes the role of the individual transaction, tracing each step in the overall process in the same way that a form or other record would and noting at each step what is done, who does it, what equipment is involved, and what skills are required. To do so, the interview method is ideal.

As one traces through the processing cycle, one speaks to the people involved to find out what they do and why. One asks them to explain their particular tasks and, as they do so, makes notes of what they say. Brief notes on 3-by-5–inch index cards are usually sufficient for recording information during fact gathering interviews. The use of elaborate forms and detailed note taking are likely to inhibit the informal atmosphere that is essential to a relaxed, informal interview. Suspicion by the interviewee that his or her comments will reach the boss's ears is also an inhibiting factor, so any verbatim recording of comments is avoided, as is the open taking of names. Above all, one avoids commenting upon or criticizing anything the interviewee does or says; the task at this point is to gather facts, not to pass judgment.

It is wise to allow the interviewee to do most of the talking. One can guide the person being interviewed towards the essential topics by asking the right questions. One must be careful not to dominate the conversation, since in that way much valuable information could be lost. After the interview has been concluded, the office manager can inconspicuously note the name of the person interviewed and the data of the interview.

EXAMINING RECORDS

Next the records that are used in the function or procedure under study are examined. The office manager wants to find out what is done with every copy of each form or item of correspondence that is generated. He or she will also determine what manual and mechanized equipment is used to prepare or process the various records and information and learn who gets what copy of each record and what each recipient does with the record after it has been received.

Any available written descriptions of relevant policies and procedures are carefully scrutinized to learn how management expects the function or procedure to operate. Once this has been done one notes any deviations from the prescribed policy or procedure that have been observed.

This information, too, is recorded on index cards. As with the interview notes, source and date are recorded.

WORK SAMPLING

If work volumes are not known, reliable estimates must be obtained of the volume of forms or other documents that are received for processing and actually processed through the function or procedure in a given period. Rather than conduct a time-consuming, costly work load analysis for a two- to three-month period, one can use a sampling technique whereby work load for a limited period is projected across longer periods to estimate average volumes. The length of time selected for the sampling varies depending upon such factors as existing backlogs, seasonal peaks and valleys of activity, and labor unrest. A long enough period must be studied to eliminate the distortion that would occur if a period were selected in which the work load was not truly representative (i.e., either too light or too heavy as compared with the annual average). In most situations, sampling over a period of a few weeks will be sufficient.

During the fact gathering phase the office manager also notes any observations he or she has made of things that appear to have some bearing upon the efficiency of the function or procedure. This means noting such factors as absenteeism, chronic lateness, excessive use of the telephone, and unusually long rest or personal breaks. Such behavior suggests the need for closer supervision.

Recording and Organizing the Gathered Facts

The information gained from interviews, examination of records, and work sampling and recorded on index cards must now be put into a format that will facilitate subsequent analysis. In most instances a simple flow chart will provide the best format.

Lengthy narratives that record and explain all the details gathered can be difficult to read and clumsy to refer to. On the other hand, the graphic flow chart, which combines illustrations and abbreviated narrative, can be comprehended and referred to quickly and is an excellent device for organizing information on how a process is performed.

A number of flow-charting symbols are currently used. They range from the simple symbols, dubbed "therbligs," developed by Frank and Lillian Gilbreth at the turn of the century to the more complex mechanized data processing flow chart symbols. A set of charting symbols based upon the four basic therbligs is shown in Table 4-1.

A well-designed flow chart contains all the facts that one must know in order to properly evaluate a given function or procedure. It describes what is being done at each step in the process as well as who is doing it, where they are doing it, and how they are doing it. Figure 4-1 shows a simple flow chart. It is obviously easy to read and analyze, but of far greater value to the office manager is the fact that the flow chart allows one to visualize an office function or procedure with all of its aspects in proper perspective. Many defective or questionable aspects of a given function or procedure may become apparant when such a flow chart is examined critically.

Table 4-1. Flow Chart Symbols

Symbol	Meaning
◎	A record is created.
⊘	A positive action is taking place (calculations are being made, transcription is occurring, etc.).
○	Nonproductive make-ready or cleanup actions are occurring (e.g., papers are being typed, carbons are being collated).
→	The records or data are being transported from one location or person to another.
▭	Data are being inspected or verified.
D	No processing is occurring; a delay has occurred (e.g., an item is being held until additional information is received or until funds are released).
▽	Records are filed and stored pending subsequent reference.

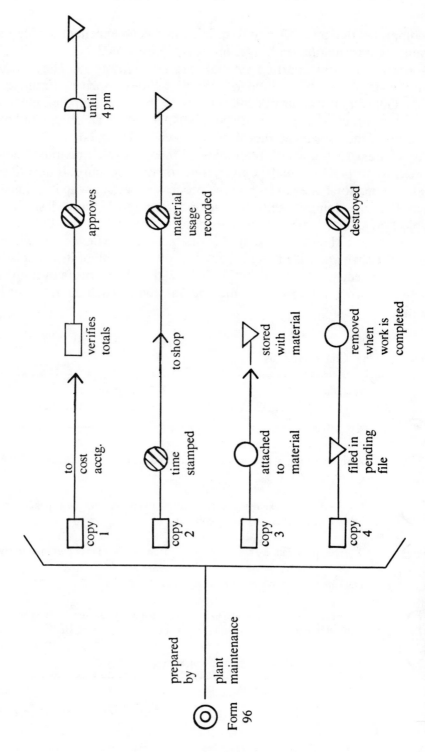

Figure 4-1. Typical Flow Chart

Validation and Verification

Before proceeding to analyze the available facts, the accuracy of the information must be checked. This can be done easily by once again walking through the processing cycle and comparing the flow chart and notes to what is actually being done. The accuracy of work load data can be checked either by follow-up sampling or by review with the persons involved in the processing cycle. Regardless of the method used, validating the information before entering the next phases of the systems analysis effort is an essential step.

Establishing Systems Requirements

Systems requirements are the constraints and conditions that must be met by any new or revised system that the office manager chooses to implement. Systems requirements are imposed by factors outside the control of the office manager. For example, one company might decide that any word processing equipment must be made in America; this system requirement would limit the equipment that could be recommended for use. Still another company may decide that any data processing system must utilize "user friendly" language, a systems requirement that would restrict hardware to only a handful of computer systems.

Systems requirements exist in virtually every organization. Delineating them is an essential part of the fact gathering phase.

ANALYSIS

Flow-charting the process under study will probably reveal some improvements that could be made relatively easily. The temptation may be great to get caught up in the process of making these improvements immediately. Such possibilities should by all means be exploited as quickly as possible but one must avoid becoming so engrossed in the selective improvement of individual steps that one fails to vigorously attack the problems in the given function or procedure as a whole. To reduce the likelihood of forgetting the major goals, it is important to review the original problem definition regularly.

Having become reacquainted with the basic objective of the procedure under study, the office manager is now in a position to evaluate every step in the function or procedure to see whether it is aimed at achieving the objective. Specifically, every aspect of the function or procedure will be evaluated in terms of the factors of need, people, placement, time and method.

Need. Each form, report, duplicate document, or item of correspondence should serve a necessary, demonstrable purpose. Anything found to be superfluous should be eliminated. It is not enough simply to establish that a record is put to some use. The cost of preparing the record must be weighed against the usefulness of the record. If the information is found not to be worth the cost or if it costs more than any mishap it is meant to prevent, then the record is uneconomical and should be eliminated.

People. This factor involves the question of how well the people involved in the given function or procedure are performing their jobs. From the notes taken during the fact gathering phase, and after comparing the actual procedures and policies being followed with the official written versions, one can determine whether any employee is malingering or deviating from expected work methods. Just how long it should take the average employee to perform most of the tasks involved in the procedure should also be determined at this point. One can then consider whether certain tasks might be performed better somewhere else, or by lower-priced employees, or possibly by computer or other mechanized equipment.

Placement. Sometimes the reordering or elimination of procedural steps will make the overall function or procedure more economical and efficient. For each processing step, consider the possibility of relocating or eliminating that step to reduce the total time and cost. For example, rather than key-enter data from a source document when the document is received, it might be sound to encode the source document and input into a "porta-punch" card at the source, avoiding the need to enter the data manually later.

Timing. Timing of activities can obviously affect efficiency. If the peaks and valleys of activity in a given procedure can be leveled by deferring or rescheduling work, or if the frequency with which a function or procedure is performed can be reduced, the need for additional personnel or overtime work and the frequency of errors may decrease sharply.

Methods. The speed, accuracy, and cost of the various methods available to process and handle the data that are used in the function or procedure must be determined, and all available types of manual and mechanized preparation and handling methods must be considered. It is usually desirable to automate any process if cost savings will result.

DEVELOPING ALTERNATIVES

After each aspect of the function or procedure has been evaluated, various alternate ways of achieving the desired objectives will suggest themselves. Each of these alternatives must be illustrated with a flow chart, and an estimate is developed of both the initial implementation cost and the cost of maintaining and operating the new function or procedure once it is fully operational.

Each alternative is evaluated in terms of how well it fulfills the desired objectives, its compliance with systems requirements, and its initial and continuing costs. A numerical weight is assigned to each of these three factors; the comparative weights are determined by the relative importance that the office manager and his or her associates attach to each of these criteria. It is then a simple matter to rank each alternative in order of its total weighted score; the top-rated alternative is the one that under normal circumstances will be the "best" for the office manager's organization. However, rarely will one alternative be best in terms of all criteria, and a tradeoff among the three will usually have to be made.

SELECTING AND
IMPLEMENTING THE "BEST" ALTERNATIVE

Once the office manager has evaluated, flow-charted, and ranked the various alternatives, the next step is to "sell" management on adopting the new or revised procedure of function. In addition to making flow charts, whatever directives are required to implement the procedure are also be written out at this time. These directives in draft from will help the office manager communicate to management exactly what is involved in the change.

However, before the actual proposal is forwarded for consideration, it is wise to make one last review of the changes with the employees who will actually be involved. The office manager should listen carefully to their reaction to the method selected, bearing in mind that they will probably have some tendency to resist change. The object is to note any potential trouble spots or deficiencies. One should evaluate these with an open mind and stand ready to make changes if they appear justified. If substantial opposition is encountered during the review, one might be wise to consider running the old and the new systems in parallel for a brief tryout period to see whether the objections are valid.

The recommended new or revised function or procedure is now ready for examination by top management. Hopefully it will be approved, and implementation can be scheduled. However, if the proposal is rejected, one must find out why management disapproved. If it was a question of poor timing or an inadequate budget, the proposal can probably be resurrected at a later date for further study. But if the idea was considered too outlandish or against company policy, its future adoption is very unlikely.

Let us assume, however, that the proposal has been approved and that the office manager has been given the green light to implement the new system. There are usually a host of chores that must be performed before the change can be fully implemented. For instance, equipment may have to be ordered, computer programs written, tested, and debugged, forms ordered, and training sessions held. Time must be allowed for accomplishing these tasks. Depending upon its nature, the new function or procedure will probably have to be pretested to uncover operating "bugs" before it actually goes into use. Possibly the old and the new systems can be operated in tandem for a short time, with the office manager and the persons who are using the new method working together to smooth out any difficulties that occur. Once the new system is found to be operating reliably, the office manager can direct the persons involved to switch to it, completing the implementation phase.

PERIODIC FOLLOW-UP AND MODIFICATION

It is sound practice to re-evaluate a newly implemented function or procedure three to six months after it has been installed. The office manager talks freely to the persons who are using the new system to find out how well it is working and to try to correct any persistent problems that remain. Even after the new methods are working well, the office manager must be continually on the alert for needed modifications, bearing in mind that systems improvements are always possible.

CHAPTER 5

Personnel Management

Personnel management, as defined in the Association of Consulting Management Engineers' (ACME) publication *Body of Knowledge Required by Management Consultants,* relates to "developing and administering policies and programs for providing . . . qualified employees, equitable treatment, advancement opportunities, job satisfaction, and adequate security."

THE RATIONALE
FOR PERSONNEL MANAGEMENT

Unlike manufacturing and warehousing functions, in which automation has led to a reduction in personnel, the introduction of computers, word processors, and other mechanized equipment to the office has been accompanied by an increase in the workforce. The following data released by the U.S. Department of Labor are illustrative:

In 1929, one out of every twelve employed Americans worked in
an office.

By 1954, the figure had risen to one in every eight.

By 1981, the ratio had increased to one employed American of
every three.

The conditions that have contributed to this growth in personnel (that
is, the need to comply with increased governmental regulatory and
reporting requirements; more complex and diversified organizational
structures; the expansion of product lines and markets; and the growth
and acceptance of the *administrative-specialist* concept) still exist today,
and it is reasonable to assume that they will continue to exist in the
foreseeable future. Consequently, the office workforce will continue to
increase both in actual numbers of persons employed and as a cost of
doing business. A program for assuring the most effective utilization of
people—probably the most critical and valuable asset of any organization—is a necessity for any organization.

ELEMENTS OF PERSONNEL MANAGEMENT

Personnel management has four basic elements: (1) the recruitment and
selection of new or replacement personnel; (2) the training and development of employees to ensure that the future needs of the organization
are met; (3) the establishment and updating of direct compensation
progams; (4) the development and updating of fringe benefit programs.

PERSONNEL RECRUITMENT AND SELECTION

Objectives

Personnel recruitment and selection has two primary objectives. The
first is to place the most qualified person available in the position being
filled, reducing the likelihood that the job will be given to the wrong
person. Naturally a primary goal is to avoid hiring completely incompetent workers, but one also wants to avoid hiring someone who is not so
incompetent as to warrant firing but who does not perform really well.

The second objective is to reduce operating costs by minimizing employee turnover. The costs of employee recruitment and selection have risen significantly during the past five years (1976-1981). According to the American Management Association, the median cost of hiring an employee (including newspaper advertising, agency fees, investigation expenses, interviewing time, and administrative costs) is approximately $1,750 per employee hired (Erwin S. Stanton, *Successful Personnel Recruiting and Selection.* New York: AMACON 1977). Hasty, haphazard or inadequate recruitment and selection procedures add significantly to this cost, since unsatisfactory employees must be terminated and replaced, a process that also involves costs not related directly to recruitment and selection. Hiring a person who is overqualified for a position also leads to undesirable turnover, since boredom and lack of challenge are major causes of resignations.

Many office managers whom the author has consulted cite poor recruitment and selection procedures as one of their major concerns. They point out that employee attendance, morale, and productivity are directly related to matching a person's skills and interests to his or her position. As one office manager explained, "We pay the penalty for any incompetent and overqualified employees we select. Their poor attendance, lack of interest and enthusiasm, and lower levels of productivity come home to roost by placing the burden to maintain high levels of output upon those of us who allowed such individuals to be selected for our departments." Thus it is essential that the office manager establish an efficient, effective system for recruiting and selecting personnel.

Procedure

The following nine-step procedure is recommended for recruiting and selecting new and replacement personnel:

A department head requests that a new or replacement employee be recruited.

The office manager ascertains that there is a valid need for the employee.

Together with the department head, the office manager defines the education, skills, work experience, and other attributes that the applicant for the position should possess.

The office manager and the department head identify the possible sources of qualified applicants.

The office manager contacts these sources to notify them of the job opportunity.

As applications and résumés are received from interested persons, the office manager and department head review them, rejecting those applicants who are obviously unqualified and inviting those who appear qualified to come in for an interview.

The office manager conducts a preliminary interview with each applicant. If on the basis of this interview the applicant still appears to be qualified, he or she is then tested (if appropriate) and interviewed by the department head or by any others that the latter feels should be consulted.

A "short list" of no more than five applicants whom the department head would be willing to hire is prepared. The office manager conducts reference checks on each of these applicants.

The office manager and the department head review all available information concerning each applicant on the short list and select one for the position. The factors leading to the decision to hire or reject each of the five candidates are then documented.

Office managers who institute such a procedure in their own organizations may feel confident that they are minimizing the possibility of overlooking a key selection criterion and are reducing the risk of inadvertently violating the numerous federal, state, and local laws and regulations that pertain to the recruitment and selection of personnel. Let us now examine each step in greater detail.

INITIATING THE REQUEST

The department head who wishes to hire a new employee or to replace an employee who is leaving prepares a job requisition form and forwards it to the office manager.

DETERMINATION OF NEED

The office manager, upon receiving the job requisition form, visits the department concerned and by such methods as work measurement analysis, examination of existing work methods, and analysis of equipment, decides whether the employee is needed. The office manager keeps in mind the following circumstances that may make the hiring of the employee unnecessary.

> The work measurement analysis indicates that employees are not meeting prescribed standards of performance. Retraining them and providing closer supervision to raise productivity levels may make the additional employee unnecessary.
>
> Examination of work methods indicates that time can be saved by simplifying procedures, forms, or controls. The time saved in this way may eliminate the need for the additional person, since the remaining workers may be able to attain higher productivity levels.
>
> The analysis of the equipment in use indicates that more efficient equipment is available. Replacement may increase productivity to the point where the requested employee is not required.

If after completing this review the office manager is convinced that the employee is needed, he or she countersigns the job requisition form.

DEFINITION OF QUALIFICATIONS

Working with the department head, the office manager then develops two written guidelines that are critical to the selection of a suitable person.

Position description. This carefully worded statement clearly and specifically describes the following aspects of the position:

> Title and grade
> Salary range
> Title of supervisor to whom position reports
> Specific duties and functions

Position incumbent specification. This less formal statement specifies the qualifications that candidates for the position should have, including

Desired education (both level of education attained and subject areas studied)

Desired work experience (including number of years, businesses in which employed, and positions held or functions performed)

Specialized knowledge or abilities (such as ability to take shorthand, familiarity with specified office equipment or programming languages, or minimum typing speed)

Physical requirements (such as ability to lift boxes of a specific weight)

Other desirable or required characteristics (such as possession of a valid driver's license or willingness to relocate, travel, or work alternating shifts)

In developing such specifications care must be taken to avoid violating federal, state, and local laws and regulations dealing with discriminatory employment practices. While it is permissible to specify minimum qualifications, it is illegal to develop those specifications so that any individual is systematically excluded solely on the basis of sex, race, age, marital status, or national origin. It has been my experience that many companies inadvertently and quite unintentionally exclude certain classes of applicants, and thereby violate one or more of the several equal employment opportunity statutes, by setting position incumbent specifications that far exceed the requirements of the job (after all, is a high school diploma really necessary for a supply clerk's job?), as well as by not adequately briefing the department heads on what constitutes discriminatory hiring practices. Too often, department heads are free to impose their own particular preferences and prejudices upon the position incumbent specification and in doing so violate the equal employment opportunity laws, opening their organizations to charges of discrimination and the possibility of significant punitive damages.

In a recent decision, *Griggs* v. *Duke Power Company* (401 U.S. 424-1971), the Supreme Court ruled that any job requirement resulting in the exclusion or rejection of a greater proportion of minority members (such as women or blacks) than of white males was discriminatory unless it could be proved beyond a doubt that the requirement was essential to the successful performance of the job.

All office managers should be aware of the implications of the *Griggs*

v. *Duke Power Company* decision and make certain that in establishing a position incumbent specification they are able to fully justify and document the need for any of the following requirements:

Minimum educational levels

Possession of a high school diploma, a baccalaureate degree, or a specified graduate degree

Age

Sex

Minimum work experience

Physical attributes such as a specified height, weight, overall appearance, or lack of physical handicap

Ability to achieve minimal scores on standardized tests

If there are any questions concerning the legality of a particular requirement, the organization's legal counsel should be consulted. Caution is well advised.

IDENTIFYING SOURCES OF APPLICANTS

The next step is to decide where applicants for the position will be recruited. The most successful strategy is to seek applicants from as many sources as possible, to increase the likelihood of finding the best-qualified applicant.

The following methods of locating applicants are useful.

Internal search. Most organizations choose to give their existing employees the opportunity to apply for any job openings, feeling that such opportunity for promotion from within helps to minimize employee discontent and turnover. The usual method of notifying employees of job opportunities is the "job posting," a bulletin board notice that gives key details about the job (title, grade, pay rates, person to whom position reports, etc.) and spells out the qualifications the successful applicant should have. The job posting also describes how to apply for the job and specifies a deadline for doing so.

A variation of this technique is to ask employees to suggest acquaintances from outside the organization who might fill the job. Many organizations even pay a nominal "finder's fee" to an employee whose referral leads to the hiring of a new employee. While employee referrals are an excellent source of applicants, many personnel professionals caution against the overuse of this source, claiming that it leads to a workforce that is too inbred and homogeneous and an atmosphere that frequently lacks the stimulation that persons of differing backgrounds and experiences bring.

Newspaper advertising. Help wanted ads have traditionally proven to be an excellent source of job applicants. The major problems with this approach are wording the ad in such a way that the job is accurately and fairly presented, and ensuring that equal employment opportunity laws are complied with.

There appears to be a tendency for employers to oversell office jobs in newspaper ads by making them sound more challenging and responsible than they actually are. This should be avoided, since it will lead to overqualified persons applying for the job. If they are hired, they will probably become dissatisfied and disillusioned, which contributes greatly to low productivity, frequent errors, and high turnover.

In wording newspaper ads, the following guidelines should be strictly adhered to, to reduce the possibility of noncompliance with equal employment opportunity laws:

Do not indicate any sexual preference. Place the ad in the "Help Wanted—Male/Female" section.

Do not specify any age requirement or use such adjectives as "young," "mature," "recent graduate," or the like.

At the bottom of every ad include one of the following descriptions of the company:

"Equal Opportunity Employer—Males/Females"

"Equal Opportunity Employer—Males/Females May Apply"

"Equal Opportunity Employer—Males/Females/Handicapped Persons"

Employment agencies. Both private and state employment agencies are established sources of applicants and, since they prescreen applicants, can do much to ensure that the persons referred at least meet the minimum standards for the job. Private agencies charge a fee to the persons they successfully place in jobs, and in many instances this fee is picked up by the employer. State agencies charge no fees.

Executive search firms. This source is used to assist in the recruitment of candidates for upper-middle and senior management jobs, as well as for those technical positions where applicants are in short supply. Of all the sources this is perhaps the most expensive: the employer contracts to pay the executive search firm a fixed fee (typically 33⅓% of the first year's salary) plus all expenses for telephone calls, interview travel, and so forth incurred by the executive search firm if the person presented is subsequently hired. If not, then the search firm is still reimbursed for all out-of-pocket expenses.

College and school placement offices. These are excellent sources for applicants for entry level positions. Some secretarial schools and business colleges charge a nominal fee if the applicant is hired, but most schools provide the placement service at no charge to either the employer or the applicant.

Professional and trade associations. Virtually every professional and trade association has an employment committee that works to bring job opportunities to its members. There is rarely any charge for this service. Listing a job vacancy with such an organization provides access to persons who are at least experienced in the relevant field and who often can step right in and begin functioning in the position.

Local business organizations. Many companies that are moving to another area or reducing their staff attempt to place their terminated personnel with other organizations in the vicinity. I have used this source of both professional and clerical personnel with good results.

The decision about which source of applicants to use for a particular job will be based upon a variety of factors, such as the anticipated availability of applicants, the recruiting budget, the desire to attract certain types of applicants, and past experience with each source. Once the sources have been selected, it becomes a simple matter to contract the source and make specific arrangements.

INITIAL SCREENING OF APPLICANTS

The applications and résumés received by the office manager are forwarded to the department head for initial screening. In reviewing them, the department head will write on any from obviously unqualified applicants the reasons why the applicant appears to be unqualified and return them to the office manager. The office manager, in turn, promptly writes to the unsuccessful applicants, informing them that they are no longer being considered for the position and thanking them for applying. Such applications must be retained for at least twelve months to satisfy the recordkeeping regulations set by the U.S. Department of Labor.

Applications and résumés received from persons who do appear to be qualified are ranked by the department head on a scale of 1 to 3, as follows, with a brief annotation of the reasons for the ratings:

1: appears to be highly qualified
2: appears to have average qualifications
3: appears to be marginally qualified

No attempt is made to contact any applicant or to further refine the ratings until the deadline for receipt of applications has been reached. The office manager then contacts each applicant who received a 1 rating and invites him or her to appear for an interview at a time that is mutually convenient for the applicant, the office manager, and the department head.

PERSONAL INTERVIEW

Each applicant is initially interviewed by the office manager, whose responsibility it is to

Describe the organization and its products or services
Answer any questions the applicant may have about working
    hours, company benefits, performance reviews, or compensation
    policies
Obtain any information about the applicant that was omitted or not
    readily determinable from the application or résumé
Form a *preliminary* judgment about the applicant's suitability
Administer and grade any required pre-employment test

The office manager carefully documents his or her reactions to and opinions about the applicant and attaches this documentation to the application or résumé. He or she then escorts the applicant to the department head for the second portion of the interview. Naturally, all relevant information (test results, the office manager's reactions and comments, etc.) are delivered to the department head at this time.

In structuring the interview the department head should be careful *not* to ask for the following information, since to do so would violate federal equal opportunity laws:

The applicant's age or date of birth (nor should one request a birth or baptismal certificate)

The birthplace of the applicant or his or her parents

Whether the applicant is a native-born or naturalized citizen, as well as whether his or her parents or spouse are native-born or naturalized

The applicant's lineage, ancestry, national origin, descent, parentage, or nationality

The nationality of the applicant's parents or spouse

The applicant's marital status

The applicant's religious preference, house of worship, or religious holidays observed

Information relating to applicant's spouse (e.g., employer, occupation, etc.)

Number of children and their ages

Organizations to which the applicant belongs (fraternal, social, political, etc.) when such information is not relevant to his or her ability to perform successfully in the job applied for

Whether the applicant has ever been arrested (however, it is legal to request details of any crimes of which the applicant has been *convicted*)

Whether the applicant has any physical or mental disability, or whether he or she has ever suffered from a specific illness, disease, or condition

The applicant's mother tongue, the language generally spoken at home, or, if applicable, how the applicant learned to read, write, or converse in a foreign language

In addition, if the applicant is a woman it is against the law to ask

Whether she is married or plans to marry

Whether she has any children and, if so, what their ages are

Whether she plans to have children

What child care arrangements have been made

What birth control methods she uses

It is strongly advised that the department head prepare for such interviews by having a list of questions to ask all applicants as well as questions to ask specific individuals. Examples of the type of penetrating, productive *general* questions that can be asked include

What were your major accomplishments at your previous or current position?

How have you improved your skills and knowledge in the past year?

How will you contribute to our organization should you join us?

What do you consider to be your strengths? Weaknesses?

What type of pressures did you encounter in your previous or current position? How did you cope with such pressures?

What can I tell you about our organization or the job for which you are applying that will help you to decide whether you are both interested in and well suited for this position?

What did you enjoy most about your previous or current job? What did you dislike most about it?

In addition, a review of individual applications and résumés will suggest specific areas that the department head may wish to pursue. For example, frequent job changes may lead to questions about the applicant's long-term employment goals or long tenure without advancement may lead to questions designed to elicit the applicant's motivation and desire for additional responsibility.

After the interview the department head briefly documents his or her opinion of the applicant's qualifications and assigns a new rating to the applicant, using the rating scale described previously.

PREPARING THE SHORT LIST AND CHECKING REFERENCES

At the conclusion of the interviews the office manager and the department manager select the five top-ranked applicants. The office manager then conducts a telephone reference check with previous employers, asking such questions as

What duties did the applicant perform for you?

How would you rank the applicant's performance compared to his or her peers?

What would you consider to be the applicant's strengths? His or her weaknesses?

Why did the applicant leave your employ?

Would you reemploy the applicant if you had an opening? If not, why not?

The office manager also verifies the applicant's job title, dates of employment, and approximate annual earnings.

Selecting the Successful Applicant

Once all reference checks have been completed, the office manager and the department head review all of the available information and decide which of the applicants will be offered the job. If the decision is not to offer the job to any of the persons named on the short list, another group of five is selected, and the reference check and selection procedure are repeated until an applicant is selected.

The office manager then contacts the selected applicant to make the offer of employment. If the applicant declines the offer, the office manager and the department head select another person from either the same or another short list until an applicant accepts the job. When this occurs, all unsuccessful candidates are notified that another person has been chosen and are thanked for applying. As mentioned previously, applications and résumés received from unsuccessful job applicants must be kept for at least twelve months to comply with federal law.

As was recommended previously, the factors that led to the hiring of the successful candidates and the rejection of the unsuccessful applicants should be briefly documented and kept on file as an integral part of the application and résumé.

PERSONNEL DEVELOPMENT

The second objective of a personnel management program is to ensure that short-, medium-, and long-term personnel requirements are met.

This involves (1) evaluating current manpower resources and projecting future requirements; (2) determining what will be required to upgrade current manpower resources to meet the projected needs; (3) devising and implementing training and development programs to achieve such upgrading.

Evaluating Manpower Resources and Requirements

The objective of this phase is to determine whether current personnel possess the knowledge and ability to perform their assigned duties in an efficient, accurate, and timely manner both at the present time and in the future. Each department is studied separately, and the following questions must be answered:

How will this department's operations differ in each of the next five years, in terms of
>
> *Work load:* Will the volume of work increase, decrease, or remain constant? What will be the estimated percentage of annual increase or decrease?
>
> *Work processing methods:* Will automated techniques such as word processing, robotics, or data processing replace manual procedures? Are any additional controls or inspections being considered for inclusion in the present work processing methods?
>
> *Processing times* (*turnaround times*): Will these tend to stay at their current levels? If not, by what percentage are they likely to be increased or decreased?

Is the department adequately staffed to meet projected work load and turnaround requirements?
>
> Estimating on the basis of current rates of productivity adjusted to reflect new or revised work processing methods, how many employees will be required in each of the next five years to ensure that the estimated work load will be efficiently processed within scheduled turnaround times?
>
> Does the department's current personnel possess the skills needed to function successfully in their jobs, taking into account projected changes in work load, work processing methods, and processing time requirements? If not, what

additional knowledge, skills, or abilities are required for them to do so?

A good way to get the answers to some of these questions is to hold a brainstorming session involving the office manager, the director of systems and data processing, and knowledgeable department personnel. During this session each participant will present his or her ideas and reactions in response to each of the preceding questions until a general consensus is reached. A profile may then be developed describing personnel requirements for each of the following five years. Such a profile will also estimate when any additional skills or capabilities must be available.

In addition, knowledgeable professional associations such as the American Management Association, the American Institute of Certified Public Accountants, and trade associations such as the Business Equipment Manufacturers Association or the National Micrographics Association can be contacted to obtain educated projections of future industry growth rates, equipment improvements, and the like. These should enable the brainstormers to further refine their projections.

Upgrading Employee Skills

THE INDIVIDUAL IMPROVEMENT PLAN

During this phase the office manager and department head review together each employee's personnel file, performance evaluations, and productivity reports to assess whether his or her current knowledge and experience matched what has been projected to be the minimum requirements for the employee in that position to function successfully in the future. Once this assessment has been made, in cases where some improvement in knowledge and skills appears necessary an individual improvement plan can be developed for each employee affording him or her the opportunity to upgrade his or her skills to the required level.

The office manager and department head go over the individual improvement plan in detail with each employee, explaining why it is in his or her best interest to cooperate with the plan and upgrade his or her skills. There may of course be some mitigating circumstances that prevent the employee from starting to effect the plan immediately (such as the need to complete after-hours study already under way, a difficult family situation, or anticipated work load increases or overtime requirements that would limit the employee's time). However, these are exceptions; as a rule, implementation should begin immediately.

SOURCES OF ASSISTANCE

The improvements recommended for each individual ordinarily involve upgrading existing skills and acquiring new ones—goals that can readily be achieved through a combination of formal education and informal readings, as well as by on-the-job training.

There are numerous resources for obtaining such knowledge. In the area of formal education, the following organizations may offer programs that will meet the employees' needs:

The American Management Association.
The professional association that serves the particular function in which the employees are involved (e.g., for records management, the Association of Records Managers and Administrators; for credit work, the National Association of Credit Management). Such associations not only conduct formal seminars but also offer correspondence courses aimed at bringing members up to date on current practices.
Local colleges, adult education centers, and business schools, for evening and weekend courses.

For informal education and reading, and attendance at professional meetings and trade shows, the American Management Association can help first by recommending an appropriate bibliography and then by referring the inquirer to various experts in the field who can suggest professional groups, meetings, and trade shows that would be useful. Most experts, when asked for such advice, are very cooperative, and the American Management Association's personnel are both eager and able to provide assistance in almost every area of business.

The final method of upgrading personnel skills is on-the-job training—the most effective method, provided an experienced employee serves as the trainer and takes the time to explain the intricacies of the job. The department head should periodically monitor the training to see that in-depth explanation is being given.

EVALUATING PROGRESS

The upgrading represents an investment on the part of both the employees and the organization. Care should be taken, therefore, to ensure that the desired results are obtained. This necessitates monitoring each employee's progress through a series of individual conferences during the life of the plan. Should it be determined that the rate of upgrading is too slow, additional or replacement sources of assistance should be considered. Upgrading employee skills holds the promise of a return in productivity and efficiency that will far outweigh the costs involved. For that reason, individual improvement should form a part of every organization's personnel management function.

COMPENSATION AND BENEFITS

There are two types of employee compensation:

Direct compensation: the weekly wages and periodic salaries that are paid to employees

Indirect compensation: the various cash bonuses and incentive payments, insurance coverage, and other benefits and perks that an organization provides to its employees at no cost or at a lesser cost than would normally be charged. Indirect compensation is always paid in addition to direct compensation.

A primary objective of any personnel management program is to develop a total compensation program that will enable an organization to attract and retain qualified employees.

Development of Direct Compensation Programs

The establishment of a continuing program to ensure that salaries and wages for specific positions are competitive with those paid by other employers in the locale for the same positions is called *wage and salary administration*.

Value of Direct Compensation Programs

Wage and salary administration programs have one primary objective—to ascertain the "going rate" that organizations in a specified geographic area are *currently* paying incumbents of a particular job. Such determination should be a key responsibility of every office manager's job and should be a part of every organization's personnel management program. The consequences of not having a wage and salary program, or of having an inadequate one, are serious. For example, if, as the result of not knowing what constitutes the going rate, an organization sets the pay scale for a given position at too low a figure, the company will experience difficulty in recruiting qualified personnel to fill the job, and will also experience high rates of turnover as incumbents resign to accept positions with other area employers whose pay scales are more in line with the going rate. Conversely, if the pay scale established for a given position exceeds the going rate, the organization will incur needless operating expenses, find that its profitability is adversely affected, and, all other things being equal, be at a competitive disadvantage with those organizations whose pay scales are more attuned to the going rate.

Determining the Going Rate

Determining what other organizations in the area are currently paying is a relatively simple task: a variety of sources are at the disposal of every office manager.

The first task is to accurately and clearly define the duties that incumbents of the position are expected to perform, as well as any other requirements (such as minimum years of related experience or the necessity of working second, third, or weekend shifts). Once such information has been gathered, one can begin to investigate the going rate in the area for that position.

The first step is to review the classified help wanted ads in the local newspapers to see whether any other organizations are also recruiting for the position. If so, one compares the duties and requirements of the advertised positions with those of the organization, noting whether the advertised positions require a person of greater, lesser, or approximately the same qualifications. Finally one can note the salary or salary range specified in the ad.

A second source is to call other office managers in the vicinity and offer to exchange salary information with them. This approach will usually prove successful and will often lead to other opportunities for the exchange of information that will be beneficial to all participants. The advantages of becoming acquainted with and able to call upon other office managers for advice and exchange of information is a powerful argument in favor of every office manager's becoming involved with his or her local chapters of such professional associations as the Administrative Management Society and the Association for Systems Management.

State employment services and local employment agencies are other sources of reliable salary information. If the office manager informs such agencies that he or she is reviewing pay scales for the company, the desired information will generally be provided.

There are also a number of excellent, reasonably priced, and readily available publications that can be helpful:

> *Area wage surveys:* these are statistical analyses of wages and salaries paid to the incumbents of scores of common professional, technical, clerical, and maintenance positions in specific geographic areas of the United States. Published by the U.S. Department of Labor's Bureau of Labor Statistics, these surveys may be ordered from the:
>> Superintendent of Documents
>> U.S. Government Printing Office
>> Washington, D.C. 20402
>
> A very valuable feature of these surveys is the fact that they subclassify each position according to the level of skills and experience required.
>
> *Salary surveys:* these are periodically conducted and published by various professional associations and many of the periodicals serving a given profession or industry.

National Survey of Administrative, Technical, and Clerical Pay:
  this is another publication of the Bureau of Labor Statistics that
  may be ordered from the superintendent of documents. It reports
  average salaries paid in the United States to the incumbents of
  twenty-one common office occupations and is also subdivided to
  further analyze those salaries according to skill and experience
  levels.

After collecting and analyzing data from these sources, the office manager will be able to reliably determine going rate of pay for the position.

Evaluating Salary Scales .

The organization then has to decide how to react to this knowledge.
There are three possible courses of action:

  To set direct compensation at a level that equals or approximates
    the going rate
  To set direct compensation below the going rate and rely upon indi-
    rect compensation to bring the total compensation for the posi-
    tion up to a level that will enable the company to successfully
    recruit and retain qualified persons
  To set direct compensation at or just below the going rate and give
    employees the opportunity to participate in an incentive compen-
    sation program (described in Chap. 10) that will enable them to
    increase their earnings well above the going rate.

Once a course of action is chosen, the office manager will need to
closely monitor the recruitment of new and replacement personnel for
the position and the resignations of employees from the position. The
results of the monitoring may indicate that an adjustment of direct compensation levels is necessary.

Periodic Pay Adjustments

It is common practice for organizations to periodically review and adjust the salary ranges of various positions in response to increases and
decreases in the cost of living index for the geographic area in which the

company is located, or an inability to attract and retain personnel for positions for which qualified applicants are in great demand and short supply.

As a rule, companies periodically adjust their salary ranges to reflect changes in the cost of living index. While the amount of such adjustments rarely equal the percentage of change of the index, they do enable the organization to help to stabilize their employees' purchasing power.

When a position is in great demand but qualified personnel are in short supply, many organizations recruit for that position at a higher salary than the entry level salary. If the salary ranges are competitive with those of other area employers, this will usually result in more applicants and less turnover.

Employee Benefits Management

Employee benefits, or, as they are also known, *fringe benefits,* refer to any indirect compensation that an organization furnishes its employees in addition to their basic salaries. Included among the more common employee benefits are life insurance, hospitalization, disability, and dental insurance; tuition assistance programs; college scholarships for employees' children; matching education and charity contributions; paid sick leave, vacations and holidays; free legal assistance; and the privilege of obtaining the organization's products or services at a cost below that charged to the general public.

As one might expect the cost of providing such benefits is high. Indeed, in many companies the cost of providing fringe benefits averages between 30 and 35% of the total annual payroll. Obviously no organization, regardless of how paternalistic or benevolent its attitudes towards its employees, can continue to expend such money on a continuing basis unless it realizes intangible benefits in return—and it does.

Cost-conscious organizations employ specific types of benefits to help them accomplish specific objectives, such as

Inducing qualified people to apply for and accept employment
Upgrading the quality of the workforce by removing many of the financial deterrents to after-work study, memberships in professional associations, and attendance at seminars and conferences

Reducing employee turnover by providing benefits attuned to employees' predictable needs—the so-called "golden handcuffs" approach. For example, the organization may provide college scholarships for the employees' children, offer free medical checkups, or tie amounts of paid vacations to years employed.

Countering union organizing efforts by providing the same benefits that the union promises to work for (for example, family medical and dental coverage or a liberal sick leave policy)

Through the foregoing measures, improving employee morale and achieving a more harmonious, stable workforce—factors that invariably result in productivity gains and improved quality of output as well as reduced costs of operation

DETERMINING WHICH BENEFITS TO OFFER

The sophisticated approach to deciding which benefits to offer involves

Determining exactly what objectives are to be accomplished by providing the benefits

Determining which benefits will help achieve those objectives

Estimating the annual cost of providing each benefit

Establishing an annual budget for overall employee benefits

Determining, on the basis of a cost/benefits analysis, which benefits will be offered

This approach recognizes a basic truth—not all employees respond to the same benefits. A recent college graduate with no dependents would not necessarily be enthused about paid family dental care or a liberal pension plan. Conversely, the older employee with family responsibilities who might be interested in such a benefit would not be as excited by tuition assistance or paid time off to fulfill military reserve obligations as might a younger coworker. Each organization must assess its own objectives and then develop a combination of benefits that will increase the likelihood that the objectives will be realized.

Table 5-1 briefly describes some of the more common fringe benefits (other than legally mandated ones such as Social Security and Workmen's Compensation). The table lists the basic features of each benefit and the group to whom that benefit will probably appeal the most.

Table 5-1. Basic Features of Fringe Benefits

Type of Benefit	Basic Features	Likely to Appeal Most to
Group life insurance	Provides benefits in event of death or total disability. Typically the policy's amount is tied to a multiple of each employee's annual salary and is provided at either no cost or at very low cost to the employee.	All employees, but especially those who have dependents or who are unable to qualify for or to afford individual life insurance coverage.
Hospital and surgical benefits	Covers specific hospital, doctor, drug, and other medical expenses for employees and their dependents. Typically the employer pays the entire cost of the employee's benefits, while the employee contributes all or part of the expenses involved in covering his dependents.	All employees
Major medical insurance	Provides coverage for medical, hospital, and surgical bills over and above the basic hospital and surgical benefits. As a rule, major medical plans provide for payment of 80% of medical, hospital, surgical, and drug bills after a specific deductible has been met.	All employees

Long-term disability compensation	Provides for payment of benefits up to a specified amount to employees who must remain out of work for prolonged periods of time due to illness or accident. Such coverage is meant to provide salary continuation once the employee's paid sick leave has run out.	All employees
Paid sick leave	Provides for payment of salary or wages during periods of absence due to sickness. As a rule the number of days of paid sick leave for which each employee is eligible depends upon his term of employment, with the individual receiving a specified amount of paid sick leave every pay period, month, etc.	All employees
Maternity/paternity leave	Provides for time off with pay prior to or immediately after the birth of the employee's child.	Persons of child-bearing age
Tuition assistance	Provides for reimbursement of tuition, fees, and books for college-level courses taken and passed by the employee. Many organizations limit such assistance to business-related courses; others have no restrictions.	Younger employees who wish to earn a baccalaureate or advanced degree
College scholarships for employees' children	Provides scholarships for college-level study for children of employees.	Middle-aged employees

Table 5-1. Basic Features of Fringe Benefits (*continued*)

Type of Benefit	Basic Features	Likely to Appeal Most to
Pension plan	Organization contributes a sum calculated as a fixed percentage of employee's earnings to a pension plan payable upon retirement or (to designated beneficiaries) upon death. Employee may either be afforded option of making voluntary payments to plan or be required to make such contributions.	Middle-aged and older employees
Profit sharing	Organization contributes a percentage of its annual earnings to be distributed to its employees in the form of profit sharing. Typically each employee's distribution is based upon annual salary.	Employees with adequate service to participate in the plan
Time off for jury duty and military service	Organization pays employee full wages less any additional payment received while latter is absent from work for jury duty, National Guard training, etc.	All employees
Employee discounts	Employee is permitted to purchase the company's products or services at prices below those charged the general public.	All employees

In an effort to improve their cash flow during this era of tight money and high interest rates, many companies have chosen to insure some of the insurance coverages included in their employee benefits package themselves. By "self-insuring," or assuming the risk of loss themselves, an organization retains money it would otherwise pay out in the form of insurance premiums and agent or broker commissions.

The decision to self-insure should be based upon a detailed economic analysis. The savings resulting from the nonpayment of premiums and commissions must be compared to the expense involved in establishing and administering the self-insured program.

Knowledgeable insurance risk analysts with whom the author has consulted recommend that anytime that an organization is able to predict its losses with any degree of accuracy (as in the case of Workmen's Compensation), it should consider self-insurance. This is an area in which the office manager should obtain qualified assistance, for while a correct decision to self-insure will lead to significant cost savings, the converse is also true.

SUPPLEMENTING THE WORKFORCE

Efficient use of manpower necessitates that an organization staff for average work load and acquire any additional personnel required to cope with periodic peaks by encouraging employees to work overtime, employing temporary personnel, or (if the work to be performed makes such action feasible) contracting the overflow work out to a commercial service bureau. It is wise to anticipate the need for such temporary assistance by finding sources of additional manpower *before* the need arises. Some ways of doing this are to

Recruit people who are willing to accept short-term, temporary
full- or part-time assignments

Find temporary assistance agencies (Olsten, Kelly Girls, etc.) that
can supply persons with the necessary skills, and negotiate a
contract for temporary assistance on a demand basis

Find out which of the commercial service bureaus can process the additional work load, and develop a service timetable and cost schedule for this

Cross-train some permanent employees so that they can step in if necessary to provide the necessary help

Developing a multifaceted strategy for coping with a varying work load should be the goal of every office manager. This is one area in which advance planning will prove to be of great value.

CHAPTER 6

Administrative Services

Services

Administrative services, or, as they are also called, *office services*, include the various support services that every executive, department, or staff office requires in order to perform its assigned functions economically and efficiently. Administrative services include reception services; mail and messenger services; records management services; copying services; telephone services; and word processing services.

RECEPTION SERVICES

Purposes

Reception services are needed

To foster goodwill by ensuring that suppliers, customers, prospective employees, and other visitors are greeted promptly and courteously upon their arrival, made to feel welcome, and are made comfortable while they wait to see someone in the company

To improve internal security by discretely controlling access to the offices

To increase productivity by making it more difficult for suppliers and other people to just "pop in" unannounced on employees, and to provide a reception area that is removed from the general office areas and from the normal flow of traffic where employees and their visitors may converse in private without disturbing other employees.

Types of Reception Services

There are two types of reception services, depending upon whether an attended or an unattended reception area is used.

In attended reception areas receptionists greet visitors at the various entrances to the offices (for example, at the main entrance of a multi-level building served by elevators or at the entrance to a floor of a multilevel building).

In unattended reception areas there are no receptionists at the entrances. Visitors use other means, such as

Telephoning the employee from a phone in the reception area and, if required, being admitted by that person.

Speaking to a central control point (a guard station or switchboard operator) through a closed-circuit television system and being admitted only after the person to be visited gives permission.

Using a special plastic entry card to activate doors and gates.

Selecting one of these two types of reception services involves making a tradeoff between costs and the level of service provided. The attended reception area is more personal and definitely leaves the visitor with a more favorable impression of the organization, but it is more expensive. The unattended reception area is less costly because there are no continuing staffing costs, but there is a decided note of impersonality in talking to a central control station through a television system or telephone. The use of card-activated doors and gates involves issuing such cards to nonemployees who may thereafter gain access to the facility at any time.

More and more, as costs take on increasing importance, companies are reducing their reliance upon attended reception areas and are turning instead to unattended areas utilizing telephones or closed-circuit television. Those companies that have managed to justify the cost of continuing to use attended areas have often found it necessary to assign additional duties, such as typing or answering all calls placed to the organization's main number, to the receptionist.

MAIL AND MESSENGER SERVICES

In virtually every one of the more than two hundred organizations for whom I have served as a consultant, I have observed that little work was done before the morning's mail was distributed and read. This one act seems to be the signal that the workday has begun. Yet in most of these companies the first mail delivery rarely occurs until after the office force has reported to work. Most companies have expended considerable time and money on installing faster and faster information-processing equipment such as computers and word processors to improve the speed and accuracy of their internal and external communications, but have paid little attention to their systems for distributing the letters and other materials that are the output of such systems. As a member of a recent American Management Association seminar on office operations explained "We spend thousands of dollars on word-processing and copying equipment in order to be able to produce correspondence and reports in hours, and then we distribute them using an internal delivery system and a U.S. Postal Service that require days under the best of circumstances." These two situations typify the problem with most mail and messenger services: they are too slow; they use antiquated systems and equipment; and they are not geared toward the users' needs.

Since postage rates increase almost annually and since the salaries paid mailroom and messenger personnel escalate at the same rate as those of most other nonprofessional office workers, cost-conscious office managers can no longer afford to ignore their mail and messenger services. They must take a fresh, hard look at these services and make regular inspections to ensure that they are operating in the most cost-efficient, user-responsive manner possible, given the constraints of budgets, space, and unions. In making such an evaluation, the following factors will be given careful consideration; (1) controlling postage costs; (2) mail handling and delivery equipment and procedures; (3) scheduling of pickups and delivery, and layout of routes; (4) use of alternatives to the U.S. Postal Service such as courier and messenger services, private delivery services, and electronic mail.

Controlling Postage Costs

Constantly increasing postage rates necessitate that the office manager periodically review the mailroom's operations and check with the post office for current regulations in an attempt to reduce or at least minimize the impact of the increases. These expenses can be controlled by

Selecting the most economical postage classification or class of service consistent with delivery requirements

Packaging to achieve reduced mailing rates

Using bulk mailing to specific addresses to receive special reduced rates

Presorting first-class mail by zip code to receive reduced rates

Establishing controls to reduce the incidence of employees mailing personal correspondence at company expense

Ensuring that postal scales are properly calibrated and in proper operating order

Establishing efficient procedures for receiving, opening, sorting, and distributing incoming mail and for picking up, weighing, stamping, and mailing outgoing items

SELECTING RATE CLASSIFICATIONS

In response to demand, the U.S. Postal Service has developed a wide variety of mail delivery services (or rate classifications) that differ in terms of speed of delivery; cost; and size, weight; and type of material accepted. By acquiring a working knowledge of each of these rate classifications and establishing definitive guidelines for their use, one can significantly reduce an organization's overall postal expenses.

The important details to be learned about each rate classification include

The type of materials that can be mailed under the classification
Any limitations on dimensions or weight
Locations served
The time required to reach each location served as expressed in the Postal Service's current service standards

Table 6-1 summarizes this information for each rate classification. The reader is cautioned that this information is subject to change as revisions in mail handling, changes in weather and transportation conditions, and the like occur. However, the information in the table should permit the reader to form an idea of how the various rate classifications work.

Once the rate classifications are understood, one can establish guidelines within the company for using them. While these rules will vary from one organization to another, according to delivery requirements and management's operating philosophy, the following guidelines are applicable to most organizations.

Use first class rather than airmail for (1) all letters being sent up to 600 miles away; (2) all letters, regardless of destination, that are mailed on either Thursday or Friday.

Take care to separate first-class materials from second-, third-, or fourth-class materials being sent to the same address. If a single mailing contains both a first-class letter and materials such as manuscripts, films, brochures, or catalogs that can be mailed at cheaper rates, the letter should not be put into the same envelope with the other materials; otherwise everything will go at the higher first-class rate. Instead, second-, third-, or fourth-class materials are inserted in a large envelope, and the appropriate postage for that class is placed on the envelope. The letter is put into a smaller, sealed envelope, the proper first-class postage is affixed, and the smaller envelope is glued to the larger one. In this way, the higher rate is paid only for the first-class material.

Coordinate mailing schedules with those of the post office. To ensure that using less expensive services does not cause excessive delays in

Table 6-1. Rate Classifications for Postal Delivery

Classification	Type of Materials Acceptable	Limitations Weight	Dimensions	Service Standard Delivery Times
First class	Letters, postcards	To 12 ozs.	3½×5 in.-minimum to 6½×11½ in.-maximum; surcharge if larger	*Next-day service*: to zip codes in immediate area if mailed before 5 P.M. *Second-day service*: to zip codes within 600 miles *Third-day service*: nationwide
Priority mail	All first-class over 12 ozs., and parcels	12 ozs. to 70 lbs. in United States 12 ozs. to 60 lbs. in Canada	To 100-in., girth plus length	Handled as first-class mail with same delivery time as that classification
Express mail, next day	Letters, parcels, to 800 designated post offices	To 70 lbs.	To 100-in., girth plus length	Delivered 365 days a year to addressee; mailed by 5 P.M.—delivered by 3 P.M. next day; *or* mailed by 5 P.M.—may be picked up at 10 A.M. next day if so specified at mailing

Express mail, air-port	Letters, parcels, to 51 U.S. airport mail facilities	To 100-in., girth plus length	Bring mail to airport. Same day service to receiving airport. Addressee may pick up.
Fourth class—surface preferential	Books, printed matter	To 70 lbs.	Available to all points within United States, Canada, and Mexico: Next-day service: up to 150 miles Second-day service: 151–300 miles Third-day service: 301–600 miles Fourth-day service: 601–1,000 miles Fifth-day service: 1,001–1,400 miles Sixth-day service: 1,401–1,800 miles Seventh-day service: 1,801 or more miles
Mailgrams	Letters		Available to all United States and Canadian destinations. *Next-day delivery* to all destinations delivered to by regular mail.

Table 6-1. Rate Classifications for Postal Delivery (*continued*)

Classification	Type of Materials Acceptable	Limitations Weight	Dimensions	Service Standard Delivery Times
Second class	Newspapers and periodicals			Available to all points within United States, Canada, and Mexico: Fourth-day service: up to 150 miles Fifth-day service: 151–300 miles Sixth-day service: 301–600 miles Seventh-day service: 601–1,000 miles Eighth-day service: 1,001–1,400 miles Ninth-day service: 1,401–1,800 miles Tenth-day service: 1,801 miles or more
Third class	Advertisements,	To 16 ozs.	3½×5-in. minimum	Available only to U.S. destinations:

94

Class	Item	Size/Weight limits	Delivery
	parcels, printed matter	to 6⅛×11½-in. maximum; surcharge if larger	Fourth-day service: up to 150 miles Fifth-day service: 151–300 miles Sixth-day service: 301–600 miles Seventh-day service: 601–1,000 miles Eighth-day service: 1,001–1,400 miles Ninth-day service: 1,401–1,800 miles Tenth-day service: 1,801 miles or more
Fourth class— parcel post	Parcels	To 84-in., girth plus length To 40 lbs. (between large post offices) To 70 lbs. (between small post offices) To 100-in., girth plus length	Available only to U.S. destinations: Second-day service: up to 150 miles Third-day service: 151–300 miles Fourth-day service: 301–600 miles Fifth-day service: 601–1,000 miles Sixth-day service: 1,001–1,400 miles Seventh-day service: 1,401–1,800 miles Eighth-day service: 1,801 miles or more

delivery, the delivery of outgoing mail to the post office should be timed to coordinate with the post office's schedule for processing and dispatching outgoing mail. By finding out from the local postmaster what is the latest time that outgoing mail must arrive at the post office to ensure its dispatch the same day, one can schedule the organization's internal mail processing to meet that deadline.

Two guidelines that cannot be derived from Table 6-1 concern the use of certified and registered mail, and of special delivery and express mail.

When proof of receipt is needed, distinguish between registered and certified mail. Do not use registered mail unless the item has an insurable value. If it is necessary to establish proof of delivery of uninsurable materials such as correspondence, the less expensive certified mail provides such proof. But certified mail is never used for an item having an insurable value. *When speed and reliability are of the essence, use express mail rather than special delivery.* Never address special delivery mail to a post office box, but only to a street address.

PACKAGING

There are a number of things that one can do to help reduce mailing costs:

Ensure that all mail meets the Postal Service's requirements with respect to packaging. Again, this will require a periodic review of the postal regulations as well as consultation with the local postmaster.

Encourage the use of lightweight mailing envelopes and enclosures, where this is feasible.

Work with the various departments in an effort to reduce mailing costs (for example, have the department specify lightweight enclosures; print on two sides of the page rather than one; eliminate or consolidate enclosures where this is feasible and would reduce weight).

BULK MAILINGS

Companies that routinely dispatch two or more letters to the same addressee each day (for example, to field offices, suppliers, customers, or advertising agencies) will find bulk mailing economical. Everything going to one such address is held until the end of the day and then inserted into a single preaddressed envelope and mailed under regular first-class rates. The savings from bulk mailings can be sizeable. To illustrate, if four purchase orders were mailed separately to the same supplier, 80 cents postage would be required. If the four purchase orders were mailed in a single envelope, the total postage would be only 20 cents.

Presorting by Zip Code

Discounts of 2 cents per first-class letter and 1 cent per postcard are available to companies that presort their first-class mail in zip code order. To qualify for these discounts, however,

A minimum of 500 or more pieces must be involved in the mailing.
The individual envelopes and postcards must be presorted in zip code order and bundled with
10 or more pieces to the same five-digit zip code
50 or more pieces sorted to be sent to the same sectional center (as indicated by the first three digits of the zip code).
Mail that cannot be sorted by five- or three-digit zip codes due to insufficient volume is known as *residual mail*. Residual mail does not qualify for the presort discount rate, but it can be counted towards the daily minimum of 500 items.

Implementation of the new nine-digit zip codes will bring additional opportunities for postage discounts, according to knowledgeable Postal Service sources. When nine-digit zip codes are implemented the Postal Service will probably offer a higher discount than the existing 2 cents per first-class letter and 1 cent per postcard as an inducement to companies to presort and bundle their outgoing mail in nine-digit zip code order.

Reducing Unauthorized Use of Postage

In virtually every organization some employees send their personal mail to the company mailroom for stamping and mailing. Most office managers are aware of this practice, but many seem to feel that the situation is either uncontrollable or involves so few dollars that any attempt to curb it would cost more than could possibly be saved. This is not true. The misuse of company mail can be minimized, and the dollar losses from such misuse are substantial. Consider, for example, that if each employee mailed just one personal letter each week at the company's expense (obviously a very conservative figure), over $10 per employee per year would be wasted. If the organization had fifty employees and averaged profits of 6% of sales, this unauthorized use of postage funds would offset the net profit on over $4,000 of sales.

Some solutions are to

Eliminate the use of postage stamps by using a postage meter. While this will not totally eliminate the use of the organization's postage for personal use, it will eliminate pilferage of stamps and will somewhat reduce unauthorized mailings.

If the company uses a postage meter that both seals the envelope and applies the metered stamp, require that all but confidential mail be forwarded unsealed to the mailroom. This has been found to effectively reduce the mailing of personal mail at company expense.

Finally, institute a chargeback system so that each department or staff office is billed for the cost of their postage. Given the department heads' interest in reducing their budgets, such billing will motivate them to control postage costs and to clamp down on the personal use of the company mail.

ENSURING THE ACCURACY OF POSTAL SCALES

All postal scales should be checked each day to ensure that they are accurately calibrated. Merely place nine pennies on the scale—they should weigh exactly 1 ounce. If they do not, the postal scale should be adjusted.

According to postal expert Stanley J. Fenvessy, inaccurate postal scales "could increase postage costs by as much as 10%." Equally undesirable is the postal scale that underweighs. Such a scale could well cause customer and supplier complaints about mail received with postage due.

Handling the Mail

The truly significant way to reduce the costs of mail and messenger operation is to develop efficient procedures for processing incoming and outgoing mail. In many organizations the mailroom has been virtually ignored; its systems, like Topsy, have been allowed to just grow. Consequently there is considerable room for operational and cost improvement through better work methods, the use of labor-saving equipment, and more efficient scheduling and assigning of personnel.

For ease of discussion four aspects of mail handling will be considered: (1) The physical layout of the mailroom; (2) staffing; (3) processing of incoming mail; (4) processing of outgoing mail.

PHYSICAL LAYOUT

Using the techniques described in Chapter 7, "Office Layout and Design," the office manager can follow the flow of both incoming and outgoing mail as it passes into and out of the mailroom. Unless a conscious effort at efficient design was made at the time the mailroom was first set up, one will undoubtedly find numerous ways in which the layout can be changed to improve workflow—changes such as reducing travel distance and time, moving supplies closer to where they are used, and matching space allocations to the functions performed.

STAFFING

The assignment of personnel to the mailroom is often done on a hit-or-miss, arbitrary basis. A series of work load counts should be conducted for at least two months to ascertain a day-by-day, hour-by-hour count of the volume of incoming and outgoing mail that must be processed. Standard time quotas can then be developed so that staff can be matched to work load.

Opportunities for improvement will generally be found in all phases of the processing of incoming mail, from initial receipt to delivery to individual employees.

Initial receipt

The first thing to decide is who will pick up and deliver the mail to the organization. The alternatives are the Postal Service, company employees, or a commercial delivery service. In deciding which method to use, the schedule of Postal Service's deliveries and the volume of mail involved must be considered. If the volume is small and if the Postal Service can deliver before or shortly after the start of the business day, it is probably best to rely upon the Postal Service. If the volume of mail is large and if more deliveries are desired during the day than the Postal Service provides, or if the delivery time is well after the start of the workday, it is best to either have employees or a commercial delivery service pick up the mail.

Many companies use a combination arrangement: they have their bulk mail (third-class mail, magazines, etc.) delivered to a post office box and pick up this mail themselves, and they have their first-class mail (payment checks, purchase orders, etc.) addressed to their offices and delivered by the Postal Service. This arrangement, they point out, provides an automatic presort.

If Postal Service delivery is chosen and if volume is adequate, the company can request that all first-class (or *"white"*) mail be delivered in trays. As a rule this will ensure that such mail arrives in better condition than if it were merely banded and delivered in mail sacks.

Dumping

When the mail arrives at the mailroom it is "dumped" on a work table (called a *dumping table*) and then sorted according to size (large envelopes, small envelopes, periodicals, packages, etc.). To simplify the process and reduce travel distance and time, the dumping table should be located just inside the entrance to the mailroom, should be waist high, and should have a raised partition around the sides and back so that the mail does not slide off while being dumped or sorted.

Mail opening and removal

Several pieces of equipment are available to perform this task, ranging from manual letter openers to high-speed machines that slit envelopes open and extract the contents in a single, combined motion. It is strongly recommended that every company that receives at least 100 pieces of mail per week purchase an electric letter opener. For low volumes of mail a small electric slitter capable of opening 50 envelopes a minute will cost approximately $100. The savings in personnel time alone will soon recoup such expenses.

Organizations that process more than 500 incoming envelopes a day may find it advantageous to purchase a more expensive, faster, and more sophisticated device that both opens the envelope and removes its contents. The price of such devices range from $1,000 to $7,500, but given the volume of mail the equipment generally pays for itself very rapidly.

Sorting and distribution

After opening the mail is taken to the sorting station—a work station consisting of a sorting rack mounted upon a waist-high work table. The sorting rack contains numerous bins, each of which is assigned to a specific employee or department. The mail is placed on the table, and a clerk examines each address and places the envelope in the bin assigned to the addressee. Only when no individual or department is noted on the envelope does the clerk read the enclosure to determine to whom the letter should be forwarded. For speedy processing, mail with addressees who cannot be readily identified is held until after all sorting has been done before any attempt is made to determine the recipient.

After sorting, the mail is ready for delivery to the various addressees. There are a number of ways to distribute the mail within the company:

Foot messenger: a mail clerk goes from one location to another delivering incoming mail and picking up any outgoing mail for delivery to the mailroom or to other employees or departments. Such clerks are usually equipped with mail carts that are sectioned off so that each employee's or department's mail can be readily located. It is sound practice to require that the clerk immediately sort all mail that he or she picks up in each department so that letters addressed to employees and departments that the clerk will visit later on the route are delivered on that same mail run rather than a subsequent one.

Conveyors: according to postal expert Stanley J. Fenvessy, organizations that employ more than two messengers for delivering and picking up mail should consider using mechanical conveyor systems instead. Conveyor systems may range from simple, low-cost dumb waiters, running between the mailroom and each floor, to more complex pneumatic tubes, to sophisticated belt-conveyor systems that transport mail and packages in electrically controlled tote boxes.

Mail-delivery robots: these devices, which cost approximately $15,000 each, are self-propelled vehicles that travel a fixed route at a speed of approximately three miles per hour by following an invisible guide path that has been sprayed on the floor. The mail-delivery robot continues along this guide path until it reaches a preprogrammed stop signal. When the signal is reached, the robot stops, and employees in that area can remove their incoming mail and load on their outgoing mail. Mail-delivery robots have usually proved to be an excellent investment; depending upon personnel costs, a twenty- to thirty-month payback period is not unusual.

PROCESSING OF OUTGOING MAIL

The processing of outgoing mail also involves several subsystems that are often fruitful areas for cost and operational improvements.

Pick up

The same delivery system used to deliver incoming mail is used to pick up outgoing mail and bring it to the mailroom. Two words of caution are in order: as already mentioned, mail picked up from the various departments should be sorted en route, so that any mail intended for persons not yet reached will be delivered during the same run. Mail runs should also be coordinated with deliveries to the post office to ensure that all outgoing mail is processed and dispatched by the Postal Service on the day it is mailed. This usually means mailing often and early during the day.

Dumping and sorting

When it arrives at the mailroom, outgoing mail is unloaded onto a dumping table and separated into internal mail and external mail. Internal mail is treated as though it were incoming mail. It is sorted by addressee into the appropriate mail-sorting bins and delivered by the foot messenger or mechanical delivery devices. External mail is delivered to the weighing and metering work station.

Weighing and metering

This process involves placing the individual envelope or package on a properly calibrated postal scale, ascertaining its weight, referring to a postage rate schedule or chart to determine the correct postage, and affixing the postage to the item.

A wide variety of scales are available. The volume of mail to be weighed and the average weight of the items are the primary determinants in selecting a scale. Small-volume users whose mail consists largely of business correspondence will probably find a low-cost balance scale adequate. Such scales, which are similar to those used by many dieters to weigh their food portions, cost under $10 but have a very small weighing platform and a capacity of only 16 ounces. They cannot be used for bulky or heavy packages, catalogs, or books.

Organizations that mail large volumes of mail of varying weights and classes will require more expensive, more versatile scales. The most sophisticated of these are electronic scales that use microcomputer technology to weigh the item and display its weight in digital readout form. A mail clerk then keys in the class of mail involved, and the scale instantaneously computes and displays the correct postage.

Postage meters are also available to meet every mail user's requirements. Such equipment ranges from low-cost, manually operated meters that rent for about $10 a month to electronic postage meters that not only affix correct postage and seal envelopes automatically but also perform various cost-accounting functions, such as charging back the costs of postage.

Dispatching

Once postage has been affixed the mail is ready to be dispatched to the post office. Like other mail experts, Mort Raymond, president of Datamation Systems, urges that all outgoing first-class mail be arranged in mail trays with the addresses and postage facing in the same direction to expedite postal processing and routing. Raymond also urges that third- and fourth-class mail be dispatched to the post office in mail sacks, again to simplify handling and speed up processing. Both mail trays and mail sacks are available from the post office upon request.

Private Delivery Services and Electronic Mail

Organizations of every size and business activity, including such diverse ones as the Rochester, N.Y., School District, BASE, Inc., and Andre Staffelbach Designs, use the private delivery services offered by companies like American Airlines, Federal Express, and United Parcel Service (UPS) for delivery of packages. These companies guarantee speedy delivery. The decision about when to use them must be made intelligently, since they are more expensive than the Postal Service; however, when a contract, payroll, or vital component of an expensive piece of machinery must arrive within hours, the private delivery services are well worth the additional costs.

Electronic mail—facsimile transmission of textual and graphic materials by a technique that reduces the material to digital format for transmission over telephone wires—is also growing in popularity as a way to ensure the timely receipt of essential mail. Again, this technique is more expensive than traditional first-class or even express mail, but when there is a great need for speed such additional costs are of minor significance.

Mail experts foresee increased utilization of such alternatives to the Postal Service. However, due to the costs and (in the case of electronic mail) the specialized equipment involved, it is unlikely that either will ever supplant the Postal Service as the prime mover of business mail in the United States. Office managers, therefore, must learn as much as possible about the Postal Service and mailroom operations so they can continually reappraise and improve the mail processing procedures, personnel, and equipment.

RECORDS MANAGEMENT

Records represent an organization's memory. They record its past, detail its present, and project its future. Certain records must be retained not only to help in decision making but also to fulfill a company's obligations to its employees and stockholders, as well as to comply with the legal and regulatory requirements of various federal, state, and local governments. It is not necessary for a company to retain every record that it creates and receives in the normal course of business. In fact it would be downright inefficient and uneconomical to do so. Instead progressive, cost-conscious office managers are instituting records management programs to ensure that a record is promptly destroyed once it is no longer of administrative, operational, research, or legal value.

Such a program involves establishing low-cost storage areas for inactive records, where, through the use of low-cost equipment and efficient archival procedures a file drawer of records can be stored for one-fourth to one-fifth the cost of keeping it in active office files. Records that must be retained for some specified period of time for legal, regulatory, or internal reference purposes but those not referred to frequently enough to justify their retention in expensive office areas and filing equipment can be sent to this inactive records storage facility. This program of systematic transfer of records from office files to inactive storage or destruction is known as *records management*. Such a program reduces overhead costs by freeing filing equipment and supplies for more relevant use, by reducing the time required to file and retrieve records, and by reducing the floor space required for in-office records storage. Records management involves the development of policies concerning *records retention* and the establishment of *retention schedules* that specify the length of time (or *retention period*) that each type of record will be kept in office files or in the inactive-records storage area.

Goals

A records retention system has three primary goals: to reduce costs, ensure compliance with the law, and improve operating efficiency.

REDUCING COSTS

Costs can be reduced through

The timely destruction of records no longer required for legal, administrative, or operating purposes

The recovery and reuse of filing equipment, supplies, and floor space occupied by such destroyed records

The use of low-cost inactive records storage systems for maintenance of records whose frequency of reference does not warrant high-cost in-office storage and immediate accessibility

ENSURING COMPLIANCE WITH THE LAW

Compliance with the law can be ensured by

Making sure that all records required by any federal, state, or local governmental agency or regulatory body are available during the period when such organizations have investigatory or regulatory jurisdiction

Making sure that all records required to protect the organization against legal action brought by a third party are maintained for the period during which such actions may be brought

IMPROVING OPERATING EFFICIENCY

Operating efficiency can be improved by

Reducing the volume of records that must be searched to answer a reference request

Providing an index of the records maintained throughout each department of the organization

Eliminating unnecessary duplication in recordkeeping

Establishing a Records Retention Program

Four steps are involved in the development of records retention policies and the establishment of records retention schedules:

Inventory: the determination of what records are maintained throughout the organization, as well as the obtaining of key data concerning the information each record contains, the record's use, and its reference frequency

Appraisal: an analysis of the legal, regulatory, audit, statistical, and reference value of each record and the development of preliminary record retention periods for each copy of each record

Negotiation: the review, appraisal, and approval of each recommended retention period by the relevant manager, legal counsel, tax counsel, and various other executives whose records are to be covered by the schedules

Issuance: the preparation of each record retention period in a form that will simplify their issuance and will facilitate compliance by all relevant departments

Inventory

PURPOSE

The inventory phase, which involves determining what types of records are maintained, the information each type contains, and how each type is used is crucial to the development of an efficient, workable records retention schedule. During the inventory phase, data is gathered upon which to base decisions as to

The relevance of information in the records to legal, regulatory, and auditing requirements

The length of time the records must be retained in office files to ensure easy access to them

Whether the information in the records should be maintained on microfilm rather than on paper

The degree of duplication of records among and within various departments, and the justification (or lack of it) for the duplication

PROCEDURE

The equipment needed includes a stamp that numbers consecutively (costing approximately $20) and several thousand white, pressure-sensitive file folder labels. The file-folder labels are numbered consecutively with the stamp, beginning with the number *00001*. These labels will be used to identify every file drawer or storage container examined during the inventory.

Inventory may now begin. The inventory of *office files* can start with any department. To prepare the way, the office manager calls the department manager to arrange for a convenient time and briefly explains what will happen—that all files will be reviewed and information will be gathered about what records are maintained, for how long, and in what quantities. The office manager asks to have someone who is familiar with the records assigned to assist, and mentions that the actual inventory will probably take less than an hour, that the department manager's assistance will probably not be required during this initial phase, and that there will definitely be no interference with the department's operations.

The actual inventorying is started by numbering every file drawer or open shelf used to store binders of records with the pressure-sensitive file folder labels prepared previously.

The analytical data required during a records inventory can best be gathered if a simple card form is used (Fig. 6-1). In conducting the inventory the *record series* concept should be used—that is, all records normally filed together and referred to together are treated as a single category or unit. For example, accounts payable files, subject files, employees' medical history files, project history files—each of these is treated as a single record, and a common retention period for all records contained in each category is established, rather than attempting to individually schedule retention of each form, report, or classification of correspondence contained in the file. This technique greatly expedites and simplifies the inventory.

Retention periods for particular records cannot be developed until the total inventory of all departments has been completed, since the interrelationships between the records kept by various departments become evident only when the distribution, filing, and retrieval of all copies of a record in all departments are known. Attempting to set up schedules too soon could well result in inadequate or inappropriate retention periods.

Once the inventory of all office files has been completed, the inventory of files in the various *inactive records storage areas* can begin. Here a similar procedure is followed. Each individual container used to house records (such as a box or transfile) is labelled with a numbered file label. A form similar to that shown in Figure 6-1 is used to record

DEPARTMENT	LOCATION	RECORD TITLE AND NUMBER

DESCRIPTION OF RECORD'S CONTENT AND USE

LEGAL STATUTES				RECORD FORMAT ☐ TAB RUN ☐ MANUAL		BASIC STORAGE UNIT	
RECORD DATES	ROW	UNIT	CUBIC FEET OCCUPIED	FREQUENCY OF REFERENCE		ACTION	

RECORDS INVENTORY MRC 2	RECOMMENDED RETENTION	OFFICE	STORAGE	DESTROY

Figure 6-1. Records Inventory Form

information about these records. It is unnecessary to write down much of the information called for on this form, however, since such data often will already have been noted during the inventory of current records in the office files. It is important to record, however.

The name of the department that sent the boxes to storage
The name of the record
The volume and frequency of reference
The identification numbers of the boxes in which the records are stored

Naturally if a record was not turned up during the office inventory because it is no longer produced or maintained in office files, all data called for on the inventory form will be listed at this time.

Once all storage areas have been reviewed and the inventory has been completed, the next aspect of records retention scheduling begins—the appraisal phase.

Appraisal

Records appraisal is concerned primarily with the development of realistic retention periods that permit the earliest possible destruction of each record series while still ensuring that records are retained as long as they are needed.

The object of records appraisal is to determine

The current and future internal reference value of the records for administrative, statistical, research, and archival purposes

The necessity of retaining the records for use in internal audits

The necessity of retaining the records for specified periods to meet federal or state regulatory requirements

The necessity of retaining the records to safeguard the organization against legal action by its suppliers, customers, stockholders, or other third parties

DETERMINING INTERNAL REFERENCE VALUE

Data gathered during the inventory will reveal the freqency with which departments refer to certain records both while the records are maintained in active office files and while they are in storage. This information will have been recorded on the inventory form.

Appraisal of the internal reference value of a records series result in definition of two different retention periods, one specifying the length of time the record must be retained in office files to ensure ease and rapidity of reference, and the other specifying the length of time the record will be retained in inactive records storage before being destroyed. As a general rule of thumb records should be retained in office files from their receipt or creation until they are referred to less than once a week. At that point, if they must still be retained they should be repacked and transferred to a records storage area until they are finally disposed of.

Exceptions to this rule occur when the volume of the records is so large that their in-office storage poses a problem or so small that transferring them to storage is simply not justifiable. In addition, project, case, or personnel files that are created over a period of months or years generally are not transferred to inactive storage until the project or relevant employee is terminated and the frequency of referral declines.

Experience has indicated that in the case of most transaction records (such as receiving reports, test reports, checks and drafts, and correspondence), the greatest number of referrals (80% on the average) will be made in the first thirty days following their creation or receipt. By the end of six months such records will have all but outlived their current-file reference usefulness. After one year or eighteen months referral usually becomes so negligible that most transaction records can be destroyed or, if they must be retained for audit, legal, or regulatory purposes, transferred to inactive storage for continued retention for whatever period is necessary.

In the case of nontransaction records such as ledgers, research notebooks, and medical case files, there generally is a long-term reference requirement that will preclude early destruction and probably make it infeasible to transfer these files out of office storage until one to two years after the termination of the project or the employee.

Short and medium-term reference value can usually be readily and accurately determined; determining long-term value is much more difficult. Ordinarily only employees who consult the records regularly will be in a position to indicate whether the records have any long-term value for purposes such as statistical analysis, future research, or developmental studies. The office manager will play the devil's advocate when anyone claims that a record series has long-term value, and he or she has to be totally convinced before accepting such a claim. In a typical organization fewer than 10% of all record series retained for two-years have enough long-term value to warrant retaining them ten years or longer.

INTERNAL AUDIT REQUIREMENTS

As a general rule, internal auditors usually need to have readily available all records that document compliance with specific company policies. Documents such as purchase requisitions must be retained in office files until after the next balance sheet audit, voided checks and drafts until the reconciliation of each month's bank account, and telephone and telegraph toll charges pending their audit. A quick check with the organization's internal audit department will indicate which records they will require for audit, as well as the length of time these records must be retained. The length of time records need to be available for internal audit is usually very short, and this requirement will have little if any impact upon recommended retention periods, other than possibly retaining certain records in office files for a longer period than they would normally be if the rule of thumb of transferring them to inactive storage whenever reference drops below once a week were strictly followed.

INDEPENDENT AUDIT REQUIREMENTS

Independent audits are audits performed by outside auditing firms. Retention periods must meet the needs of the external auditors and also be in accordance with company policies as well as with any industry requirements.

GOVERNMENT REGULATORY REQUIREMENTS

To this point, determining the value of each record has been a rather simple, subjective matter. The only requirement was to ask the persons who must work with the records how long they wished to retain them. Determining which records must be retained, and for how long, to satisfy various federal and state regulatory agency requirements is, on the other hand, quite a complicated matter. Every federal and state regulatory agency imposes specific mandatory record keeping requirements on organizations subject to their regulation, and any decision to destroy records must take these regulations fully into account.

Federal regulatory requirements
These requirements are of two types. Some are so broad that they apply to every business organization regardless of its size, location, or principal industry. Others apply strictly to one industry.

The regulations of federal agencies in the first category require the retention for minimum periods of time of records documenting the basic operational and financial position of the company. The following regulatory agencies fall into this category:

The *Internal Revenue Service* (IRS), under the Internal Revenue Code (26 CFR L.6001-1), requires the retention of various detailed records (such as invoices or cost records) to support general and subsidiary ledger accounts for three years—the period of time during which the IRS may file a claim against an organization for the assessment of additional sales or income taxes.

The Internal Revenue Code has another catchall section that requires the retention of summarizing records (such as general and subsidiary ledgers, depreciation records, and financial reports) for "so long as the contents thereof may be material to the administration of any internal revenue law." Most organizations find it advisable to schedule such records for retention for twenty years or more to ensure their availability in the event of IRS inquiry.

The *Interstate Commerce Commission,* as described in 49CFR (Chapter 49, Code of Federal Regulations) imposes a two-year statute of limitations on the initiation of claims by common carriers against customers for the recovery of charges. This in effect imposes a minimum two-year retention upon such shipping documentation as bills of lading, claims for damages, freight bills, and way bills.

The *Department of Labor's Wage and Hour Division,* through its enforcement of the Fair Labor Standards Act (FLSA) and the Age Discrimination in Employment Act imposes further requirements that necessitate the availability of payroll and personnel records for periods of from one to three years.

The *U.S. Postal Service* requires in 39CFR that organizations using postage meters keep a meter record book (Form 3602-A) "showing register readings of metered mail on each day of operation of the meter for at least one year from the date of last entry."

The *Equal Employment Opportunity Commission's* mandatory record-keeping requirements have a direct bearing upon various records "having to do with hiring, promotion, demotion, transfer, layoff or termination, rates of pay, and selection for training or apprenticeship," requiring the retention of such records for six months from the date of creation or of the personnel action reflected in the record, whichever is later.

Of the regulatory agencies in the second category—those with responsibility for a specific industry or activity—some regulate so stringently that their regulations prescribe detailed records retention schedules that must be complied with by all organizations subject to their regulation. Other agencies have less stringent regulations and usually do not specify detailed records retention schedules.

Examples of federal agencies that prescribe detailed schedules are

The Securities and Exchange Commission (17CFR240-17A-4)
The Federal Communications Commission (47CFR73)
The Federal Power Commission (18CFR)
The Interstate Commerce Commission (49CFR)
The Civil Aeronautics Board (14CFR)
The Department of Defense (Armed Services Procurement Regulations: 32CFR7)
The Atomic Energy Commission (41CFR)
The National Aeronautics and Space Administration (41CFR18)

Publications describing the record-keeping requirements of these agencies can be obtained at a nominal charge from the Superintendent of Documents, U.S. Government Printing Office, Washington, D.C.

Most other Federal regulatory agencies do not publish itemized retention schedules. Their requirements are stated in broad terms in their regulations, and the determination of which records must be retained to satisfy these requirements is left pretty much to the individual organization that maintains the records.

An excellent quick-reference source describing the general records retention requirements of all of the federal regulatory agencies may be found in Title I, Appendix A of the *Federal Register,* "Guide to Records Retention Requirements." This inexpensive publication, which is updated annually and may also be purchased from the Superintendent of Documents, delineates the records retention requirements of every federal agency and contains a valuable index that indicates, by various industrial descriptions, the regulations to which specific industries are subject. This reference book is a must for anyone developing or maintaining a records retention program.

State regulatory agency requirements
The regulatory power of these agencies, like the federal ones, may be either broad or very specific in its application. Examples of agencies

whose regulatory powers extend across industry lines are state labor departments, the health departments, the taxation departments, and the human rights commissions. Examples of state agencies concerned with specific industries are the insurance departments, banking departments, and the public utilities commissions.

The records retention requirements of the state regulatory agencies tend to parallel those of their federal counterparts. In fact, some states, such as Connecticut and Virginia, have adopted *in toto* the minimum records retention requirements of the Federal Power Commission, the Interstate Commerce Commission, and the Federal Communications Commission. Compliance with federal regulatory agency requirements will ordinarily ensure compliance with state regulations.

DETERMINATION OF LEGAL VALUE

The final criterion to be considered in appraising the value of each record series is how long the record must be available to protect the company against legal action brought by such third parties as stockholders, customers, and suppliers. The key factor involved here is the various statutes of limitations on initiating action to recover damages. The advice of the organization's legal counsel should be obtained with respect to the statute of limitations on initiating claims to recover

Unpaid minimum wages or overtime wages
Damages resulting from nonperformance of written contracts
Stockholder losses resulting from misinformation furnished by corporate offices
Damages for personal injury
Real property
Losses resulting from the purchase or sale of goods and services on open account

The statutes vary from state to state, and unfortunately no recent compendium of them is available.

Once the reference value of each record series has been determined, one can proceed to the next phase of records retention scheduling—the actual selection and negotiation of retention periods.

Negotiation

Data gathered during the inventory and analyzed during the appraisal phase are now ready to be used in formulating records retention schedules and presented to the managers concerned for their review and approval.

While there are numerous ways in which recommended records retention schedules may be presented for review, experience has shown that the format must include, in a concise, readily understandable form, all the data that the managers will require to determine the appropriateness of a recommended retention period. The form shown in Figure 6-2 will meet this requirement.

LEGAL REVIEW

The initial review of all recommended records retention schedules should be made by the legal department, which will examine each recommended retention period on the basis of only one criterion: "Does the recommended period ensure compliance with all legal and regulatory requirements?" The legal department should not concern itself with the possible need of the tax or accounting department to retain the records; those needs will be separately determined at a later review by those departments.

I have found from experience in working with scores of clients that obtaining legal approval first—while an unusual procedure—is very worthwhile, since it immediately puts to rest the main worry of most department managers—that by destroying records too early they might be violating a regulation or law or leaving the company powerless to refute unjust claims or reply to legal actions. By having the legal department establish exactly what the legal and regulatory requirements are for each records series, this doubt is quickly laid to rest.

Naturally the legal department will have the option of recommending the lengthening or shortening of any records retention period if they feel such changes are warranted on legal grounds. After review and approval (or recommendation of changes) the legal counsel signs each page of the records retention schedule in the space provided for legal approval and, after entering the date, forwards the schedule to the tax department for its review.

RECORDS RETENTION SCHEDULE
SQ 1674 6/76

DEPARTMENT

LOCATION

SCHEDULE NUMBER

EFFECTIVE DATE

PAGE ___ OF ___

ITEM NO.	RECORD TITLE	FORM NUMBERS	RETENTION PERIODS			APPLICABLE STATUTES	PRE-DESTRUCTION CLEARANCE		
			OFFICE	CENTER	DESTROY		DEPART-MENTAL	LEGAL	TAX

APPROVALS (SIGNATURES & DATE)

DEPARTMENT MANAGER	LEGAL	TAX (IF REQUIRED)	RECORDS MANAGER

Figure 6-2. Records Retention Schedule

Tax Review

The tax department's review is made to ensure that any records required for tax audit purposes will be available. The tax department examines each records series to determine

Whether the records series will be required in the event of state or federal tax audit

Whether the recommended retention period for each record series is adequate for auditing purposes. Like the legal department, the tax department has the option of recommending that any retention period be lengthened or shortened if such revision appears necessary.

Once all retention periods have been reviewed and all recommended revisions indicated, the tax managers sign the records retention schedules forms in the appropriate space and forward them to the department managers.

Operating Review

Now that all tax, auditing, and legal requirements have been identified, the department manager's task becomes very simple. He or she must merely determine whether the recommended retention periods will satisfy the needs of the department. The retention period for each of the department's records series must be long enough to avoid problems in retrieval. After noting any desired revision in either the total retention period or its office/center distribution, the department manager signs each page of the records retention schedule, dates the form, and returns it to the office manager.

Office Manager's Review

The office manager reviews each records retention schedule upon its return and sets aside any that require further action (such as those that contain recommendations for revised retention periods or those that require additional information). These must be processed individually, by the office manager. All other schedules (those that were approved by the legal, tax, and operating departments) are ready for to be issued.

In reviewing the schedules that have been questioned, the office manager first examines those in which revisions have been recommended for legal or auditing purposes. All such recommendations calling for longer retention periods must be approved. Any that call for reduced retention periods must be examined individually in the light of other requirements (such as the operating department's reference needs) to ensure that the reductions are absolutely essential. The same scrutiny will be given to any department manager's recommendation that a records series be held beyond its legal or audit requirements. The consequences of such an extension will be discussed with both the legal counsel and the tax manager to ensure that it will have no undesirable legal or audit side effect. Once all discrepancies have been resolved and the retention periods have been established for all record series, the records retention schedules may be issued and implemented.

Implementation

When a records retention schedule is issued to the departments, it should be accompanied by instructions to each department manager to implement the schedules affecting his or her department within thirty days and, if necessary, to either destroy the records affected or transfer them from office files to a storage center. The office manager should follow up at the end of this period to ensure that such implementation has occurred.

Inactive Records Storage

Establishing a facility for storing records that are not frequently referred to but that must be retained to comply with various requirements is an essential part of any cost-effective records management program. The effective use of such a facility, as noted earlier, can lead to cost reductions of up to 80% compared to office storage. Such savings, however, are dependent upon

The use of low-cost, space-saving equipment, supplies, and physical layout

A storage system that ensures an orderly arrangement and control
  of records
Procedures and forms that ensure prompt, accurate, and efficient
  handling of records

SELECTING A SUITABLE BUILDING

Certain minimum specifications should be taken into account when selecting a building in which to house the inactive-records storage facility:

The floor should be capable of sustaining a minimum load of 300
  pounds per square foot.
No paint or other flammable materials should be stored in the same
  building.
The building should be well lighted. Industrial-type flourescent fixtures should be suspended over the area and must be capable of
  providing minimum levels of 25 foot candles of light in the record
  storage area and 50 foot candles in the administrative work area,
  at 3 feet above floor level.
There should be both a loading dock and a temporary storage area.
To control access and impede unauthorized entry, there should be
  a minimum number of exits, and all ground-level windows should
  be screened or barred.
There should be no evidence of rodent infestation.
Fire detection and extinguishing systems should be provided. Generally speaking, water sprinkler systems should be avoided if
  possible, since water damage is generally more destructive to
  tightly packed paper records than is fire or smoke—fire rarely
  does more than singe tightly packed records, it seldom burns
  them.
There should be adequate room for expansion.

STORAGE EQUIPMENT

Containers
The key to selecting economical, efficient records storage equipment is
the proper storage container. All other equipment relates to this. The

two most useful types of storage containers are the transfile and the standard cubic-foot box.

Transfiles. Each transfile is designed to hold the entire contents of a standard letter- or legal-sized file drawer. Constructed of either corrugated material or steel, the transfiles have two parts: an outside sleeve and an inside drawer. A fully loaded transfile weighs approximately sixty pounds. To provide for easy in-and-out movement of the drawer in its sleeve, drawers in the better grade of transfiles have nylon rollers.

Transfiles are designed to be stacked squarely on top of each other and are held fast by a series of metal clips, so that an assembled group resembles a honeycomb and is usually so described. The honeycomb can extend from floor to ceiling, since it is quite strong and is capable of withstanding severe pressure without damage. A pulpit-type ladder is used to reach the higher transfiles. Ideally each ladder should be equipped with locking feet and have a work tray at waist height on the top shelf.

The major problems encountered in using transfiles are that

There are no stops to prevent a drawer from sliding completely out of its sleeve and falling onto the floor or causing injury to the referencer.

The honeycomb created by erecting transfiles is relatively inflexible; once it is in place, rearranging it becomes a major project.

A fully loaded transfile is quite heavy and awkward to handle.

Due to the size of the transfile, it is awkward to return an entire container for reference.

Transfiles represent a sizeable investment compared to the alternative container—the standard cubic-foot box.

Standard cubic-foot box. This is a corrugated box measuring 15 by 12 by 10 inches and is designed so that letter-sized records can be filed parallel to the 12-inch side and legal-sized filed parallel to the 15-inch side. Smaller records can be filed parallel to either side, as appropriate, in one or more rows, with cardboard dividers in between. A cubic-foot box holds approximately one-half the contents of a standard file drawer. Compared to a transfile it is relatively light when loaded (about thirty pounds) and has handholds on each of the 12-inch sides, making it fairly easy to lift and carry from one place to another. Extremely inexpensive (costing $1 or less apiece in quantities of 2,500 or more), these boxes are designed to be used on steel shelving.

Steel shelving

Steel shelving is very important in an inactive-records storage operation. The shelving permits cubic-foot boxes to be stacked close to the ceiling while remaining accessible. In my experience, steel shelving is superior to and in the long run cheaper than wood shelving. Buying wood for shelving may be cheaper than buying knocked-down steel components for shelves, but the costs of erection, painting, and periodic repainting to prevent rot and insect infestation generally offset the higher purchase price of the steel shelving.

Steel shelving is more mobile than wood. Should it be necessary to rearrange or relocate the storage area, this could be an important consideration. It is wise to buy a good grade of steel shelving. Cheap steel may buckle and sag under the heavy load of records. Whenever possible, shelving units should be reinforced by fastening adjacent units back to back and side to side, ensuring greater rigidity when fully loaded. It is also desirable to install additional braces from the tops of the steel uprights and shelves to adjacent posts and walls.

Ladders

Pulpit-type ladders are the most suitable for use in inactive-records storage facilities. The ladder should be high enough to permit comfortable access to the boxes on the uppermost shelf. It should provide a rigid work tray upon which boxes can be placed during filing or retrieving. For safety, the ladder should have wheels that lock when body weight is placed on them.

Work tables

A sturdy roll-around cart, approximately two feet wide by three to four feet long, will prove extremely useful for moving records from one location to another and for holding boxes during reference.

PHYSICAL LAYOUT

The existing physical features of the area will prove to be the principal inhibiting factor in the layout of the storage facility. Location of doors, pillars, and windows will influence the number and placement of shelving units. There are three basic arrangements:

Single-unit layout. This is generally used against walls. Each unit is bolted to the next at the sides, and access is from the front.

Double-unit layout. This arrangement requires less space for shelving and access aisles and is suggested for open areas in which access is available from both sides of the shelving units. Each unit is bolted back to back to another unit. These double units are then bolted side by side. Access is from the front. There is no aisle between.

Triple-unit layout. This arrangement is not normally used due to the difficutly in getting at boxes stored in the center unit of the three units; joined back to back. However, because of the space-saving factor, it is suitable for storing very infrequently referenced records.

For maximum economy use a combination single-, double-, and triple-unit arrangement. This will afford the greatest return in storage area per square foot of floor space.

To facilitate access to the records, adequate aisles must be provided. Allow 30-inch aisles between shelving units, and provide a 4-foot main aisle to allow for the movement of hand trucks and ladders and for temporary storage of boxes awaiting shelf space.

LOCATOR SYSTEM

To facilitate reference and to permit a random storage operation, a system must be devised to quickly and accurately determine the location of any box stored in the facility. A random storage system has two distinct advantages over one that groups together all records belonging to a particular department: it permits more efficient utilization of space, and it reduces the likelihood that unauthorized persons will be able to locate particular records, since the key to finding any individual record is not readily apparent.

While several locator systems are in use, one of the best is a two-part "significant numbering system" in which the first number designates the number of the individual box (which is sequentially assigned starting from number 1) and the second number designates the assigned shelving location. The latter is derived by sequentially numbering each shelving unit in the facility and then each shelf within each shelving unit. Once assigned, an identification number becomes permanent and is used only for the particular box involved. It is never reassigned.

The box number and the location number are marked on the end panel of the box, facing the aisle. These are the only markings that appear on the box. The security that such a locator system provides is indeed formidable. So long as the detailed listing of contents is kept under lock and key and not markings other than the locator number appear on the box, it will be very difficult for an unauthorized person to locate a given record.

Preparing Records for Inactive Storage

To ensure rapid, accurate retrieval of records transferred from office files to inactive storage, the records must be carefully prepared for transfer.

Boxes are not to be packed too tightly, but are filled to within one inch of capacity, leaving adequate room for the ready removal and replacement of records.

Since reference to boxes with scrambled contents is both costly and time-consuming, records are not accepted for storage unless the contents are packed in a neat and orderly manner. Because of the rigidity of the steel shelving units, the boxes must not bulge, and the covers must close easily. Records are not sent for inactive storage filed in hanging-type file folders since the metal hanger will prevent the covers from closing smoothly.

Whenever possible all records in a given box will have the same destruction date. This eliminates the necessity of reviewing the contents individually and selectively removing and destroying obsolete records.

A list giving key information about the contents is prepared as each box is packed. At minimum, this list gives the name of the department transferring the records; a description of the records sufficiently detailed to facilitate future retrieval; the dates of the records; and the date after which they may be destroyed.

When a particular record is recalled for reference, the requisitioner furnishes the identification number of the box in which the record will be found. Using this number as the reference, an employee in the storage area then determines the location of the box, removes it from the shelf, locates and removes the requested record, inserts a charge-out card in its place, and returns the box to its assigned location before sending the records to the requisitioner.

Employees requesting records should be encouraged to make extensive use of the telephone when requesting information. An average of five minutes per request can be saved each time information from the records is furnished to requisitioners by telephone instead of forwarding the documents for review.

Another time and cost saver in processing reference requests is to use photocopies of requested records. Fully six minutes per request can be saved by supplying a photocopy rather than the original record itself. Eliminating the need for processing charge-out cards and refiling the original record more than pays the cost of the photocopy. Such copies should be marked *"Destroy after reference."*

OFFICE COPYING SERVICES

Today over 240 different models of office copiers are marketed by more than 40 manufacturers. Some of these copiers use coated papers, others plain bond. Some enables users to produce a copy that is smaller than the original if desired. Still others offer microprocessor control features to assure proper monitoring and control of the copier's functions. Such variety makes the decision to select an office copier difficult.

At the same time, the costs associated with office copying are rising. A portion of such increases may be attributed to normal inflation but a goodly percentage is the result of misuse and pure waste.

This combination of factors—a multitude of equipment from which to choose, employee misuse and waste, and increased costs—gives the person who is managing a company's office copying services the responsibility of ensuring that the copying needs of various departments are satisfied in the most cost-effective manner while minimizing misuse and waste.

Providing for User Needs

Generally, two types of photocopies are required:

Convenience copies: copies that are required for an employee's own reference and operating needs. Convenience copies usually do not require collation, reduction from the original, or a high degree of resolution. Rarely are more than two copies required from the same original.

Distribution copies: these are copies that will be reproduced and distributed within the organization or to clients, suppliers, governmental agencies, or the media. Such copies usually must have a better appearance and typically involve the production of more copies of any one original than with convenience copies. Collating, and preparing reduced copies of oversized originals, are often necessary.

Satisfying these requirements generally necessitates establishing a *copying service network* composed of

Low-priced, simple-to-operate, low-volume desk-top copiers. These copiers, located in the offices so that they are readily accessible, are used primarily for preparing convenience copies. Although controlled by the office manager, who also ensures that they are routinely maintained and serviced, such convenience copiers are operated by any employee who wants to use them, the employee merely walks up to the nearest convenience copier and produces the required copies.

Higher-priced, faster, more sophisticated office copiers designed for producing fewer than twenty copies of each original. Such office copiers are attended by a trained operator. The person who needs copies simply delivers the originals to the operator and states how many copies are required.

Expensive, state-of-the-art, microprocessor-controlled high-speed copiers for producing twenty or more copies of each original.

Such equipment is attended by a skilled operator. The office manager is responsible for coordinating the maintenance and servicing of these last two types of copiers.

Determining the Network's Configuration

Deciding which copiers are required, how many, and the location of each, requires an analysis of the organization's current and projected copying requirements. This can be most readily accomplished by making a month-long survey involving the use of copy logs. As each employee makes a copy on the office copier, he or she records the following data on the copy log:

Purpose of the copies (convenience or distribution)
Type of material copied (letters, books, etc.)
Number of originals copied
Number of copies made from each original
Whether collating was required
Whether reduction was required

At the end of the month the copy logs are collected and summarized. This provides a concise profile of the organization's current copying requirements—the type of material being copied, the ratio between originals and duplicate copies for both convenience and distribution purposes, the percentage of requests that involve collating or reduction, and—an important figure—the total number of copies produced during the month.

By interviewing a representative sample of users, the office manager can find out

How frequently users must reproduce pencil originals, black-and-white photos, and color photos
How often a "perfect" copy is required (that is, one that is virtually indistinguishable from the original)
What percentage of the reproduced copies will subsequently be written on, and whether this writing will be done in pencil or ink
Whether, in comparison with the previous year, more, fewer, or about the same number of convenience and distribution copies

are being prepared on office copiers, and what the estimated percentage of the increase or decrease is

Whether it is expected that the volume of copies made in the next year will increase, decrease, or remain the same compared to the current year, and what the estimated percentage of the increase or decrease is

With this information in hand the office manager can proceed to select the office copiers. The various product surveys periodically produced by such trade publications as *Administrative Management* and *Modern Office Procedures* can greatly simplify the selection process. These surveys summarize key features and cost data for each of the office copiers marketed in the United States today. By comparing these features to the users' requirements as derived from the copy logs, one will quickly be able to eliminate numerous models (if, for example, the organization requires "perfect" copies the choice will be restricted to copiers that use plain bond rather than coated papers).

In calculating the costs of a copier one must consider the original price of the equipment, the cost of supplies, and the cost of servicing. Once these are calculated and reduced to a cost per copy one can ascertain the relative cost for the purchase and use of each machine.

The selection of one or more models of office copiers for the convenience copying stations and for the centralized, attendant-serviced distribution copying facilities will require making a tradeoff between capabilities and costs, on the one hand, and user requirements and available funds on the other. Rarely will a perfect match occur.

The question of how many of each model of office copier selected is required may be answered by dividing the monthly volume of copies the company requires by the manufacturer's estimate of the output for each copier reduced by a 15% "fudge factor." Thus if 210,000 convenience copies are prepared each month and the adjusted rated output of the particular copier under consideration is 10,800 copies per month, an office would need 20 of that model.

The location of the individual copiers should be dictated by the location of the major users. Ideally, no one should have to walk further than 200 feet to reach a convenience copier or travel more than one floor up or down to reach a distribution copier. Actually, however, these standards cannot often be met, since the sizes, shapes, and occupancy rates of the office areas will probably determine the location of the copiers.

Reducing Misuse and Waste

The following suggestions for reducing misuse of copying services and waste were made by office managers who attended a recent American Management Association seminar in office management:

Charge back the costs of copies to the departments. This will minimize unnecessary copying. Use copy controllers (or meters) to count and record the number of copies each user makes.

Locate the convenience copiers in each department within sight of the department manager. The psychological impact of this placement will reduce the use of copiers for personal, nonbusiness purposes.

Deactivate the multiple-copy dial of the convenience copiers so that it is less convenient to make more than one copy.

Lock the copiers at night and on weekends to prevent unauthorized after-hours use.

Rewire the copiers' power supply so that the copier can be activated only by a remote switch located on a nearby supervisor's desk. This procedure can cut costs by over 30%, one manager reported.

Use less expensive private-brand toner and copying papers, but be careful to avoid "bargains" offered by "paper pirates" (as described in Chap. 11).

Purchase and use recycled (reclaimed) toner.

TELEPHONE SERVICE

According to a recent survey by J. Porter Henry, a well-known management consultant, "For most offices, the telephone bill is the second or third largest item of expense. First come salaries, and after that either rent or telephone."

Surprisingly, most companies have done very little to control their telephone expenses, reasoning perhaps that compared with other communications alternatives, such as business letters, personal visits, or telegrams, the telephone provides two-way conversation at a fraction of the cost and time and often allows a matter to be resolved in a single contact. Management, therefore, may think of telephone expenses as something so necessary to operational efficiency that any time and effort spent to reduce them by the office manager may be regarded as wasted. This is a fallacy. Telephone expenses are too high to ignore, and, since they can easily be lowered, they present a great opportunity for cost reductions.

At one time companies could do little to significantly reduce telephone expenses—they were at the mercy of their local telephone company and AT&T Long Lines. Today it is truly a whole new ballgame. The 1969 Carterfone decision by the Federal Communications Commission (FCC) opened the door to significant cost savings by allowing telephone users to purchase their own equipment and connect it to the telephone company's lines. This, coupled with the subsequent development of private long-distance telephone networks, gave many companies the opportunity to reduce and subsequently minimize the annual rate of increase of their telephone expenses for the first time.

The office manager need not be a telecommunications expert to provide cost-effective telephone services for his or her organization. He or she need not become involved in such technical matters as computer-controlled private telephone systems or the transmission of data or graphics over voice-grade telephone lines (elements that many large organizations group together with telephone services into a telecommunications management program headed by a highly trained communications engineer). The program described here is not highly technical. It involves four major elements: equipment acquisition; long-distance networks; auditing the accuracy of telephone charges; and controlling telephone expenses.

Acquiring Equipment

The conventional service provided by local phone companies includes the monthly lease of each telephone instrument and the various optional features included on that instrument, such as buttons, lights, and keysets. The monthly rental charge continues as long as the organization continues to use the instrument and its various features, creating what has been likened to paying monthly apartment rental charges without ever acquiring ownership.

The FCC's Carterfone decision, rendered in 1969, changed all this by ruling that any telephone user could legally connect other manufacturers' equipment to his or her local telephone lines. As a result it is now possible for both individuals and businesses to purchase any telephone equipment that they feel will best meet their operating requirements and attach the equipment to their local telephone company's lines. After doing so the telephone user no longer pays the local telephone company's equipment rental costs, but he or she does assume responsibility for maintaining the equipment. Invariably, in business, such service is provided under contract by the company from whom the telephone equipment is purchased. Payment terms with periods ranging up to ten years are usually provided, so that the out-of-pocket expenses incurred for the customer-owned equipment approximate the formerly incurred rental charges during those years.

The general experience seems to be that the larger the number of telephone extensions and the greater the number of optional features included as part of the original equipment, the greater will be the savings from the installation of customer owned and serviced equipment and the shorter will be the pay-back period.

As in all rapidly growing industries, the national and regional companies that sell and service telephone equipment vary in terms of financial stability, reliability of equipment, features offered in the equipment, quality of service, and pricing and payment schedules. In deciding which company to buy from it is essential to consider all of these factors.

FINANCIAL STABILITY

Because the sale of customer owned and serviced telephone equipment is a rapidly expanding business, many domestic and foreign companies have entered the market. Subsequently many of them withdraw when they fail to meet their marketing objectives, if undercapitalization prevents them from reaching the desired level of promotion and manufacturing, or if profits are too low. When such a company leaves the market, its customers suffer, since additional and replacement equipment, and possibly prompt service, may no longer be available. In choosing equipment the office manager therefore needs to assess the financial stability of the company that manufactures and services the equipment. The questions to ask include:

How many installations has the company sold?

What has been the percentage of increase or decrease in the number of installations during each of the past three years?

Has the company expanded its sales and service organization (in terms of locations *and* personnel) within the past two years?

Any company that appears to be on the decline or leaves any doubt in one's mind as to whether it can remain in the market should be eliminated from further consideration.

RELIABILITY OF EQUIPMENT AND QUALITY OF SERVICE

The benefits of owning one's own telephone equipment will be rapidly cancelled if the equipment does not function properly or if it takes too long to get service. One needs to know

What type of problems tend to occur

How often they occur

How quickly the manufacturer provides service for problems

The average time required to correct a problem

The only way to ascertain this is to request from the company a list of all the companies in the vicinity that use its equipment. One can then call several at random to learn of their experience. Any equipment whose reliability or quality of service is less than perfect is eliminated from further consideration.

FEATURES OFFERED

It is important to analyze the various features of each manufacturer's equipment, and the options offered, to ensure that the company's current and future communications needs will be met by a new system or to discover any possible improvements that could be made in the current system. While such an analysis rarely leads to the elimination of a manufacturer from the list, it often results in one or more manufacturers being identified as most desirable.

PRICING AND PAYMENT SCHEDULE

The remaining manufacturers are then requested to submit a bid for (1) providing the required equipment and (2) servicing it on a contractual basis. Such a proposal should spell out the various payment options and should state what charges will be involved if the customer

Wishes to upgrade or modify the equipment during the purchase period
Moves to new offices and wishes to move the equipment, either during or after the purchase period
Wishes to upgrade, modify, or relocate the equipment after it has been paid for

At this point the projected costs of the customer owned and serviced equipment are compared with the charges imposed for similar equipment and service by the local telephone company. If no cost savings are apparent, it will probably be best to continue renting equipment. If there would be cost savings, the office manager should rank the various customer owned and serviced equipment on the basis of the evaluative criteria discussed above. After observing the two top-ranked systems in actual use and scrutinizing the applicable data processing reports on their performance, one will be able to select the equipment that best meets the organization's unique requirements. Before signing a contract, however, it would be wise to obtain one final bid from the local telephone company, since, in response to competitive pressure, some now sell service equipment to their customers.

Long-Distance Networks

Another recent development that offers a potential for reducing telephone costs is the use of privately operated long-distance networks rather than AT&T's standard Long Lines facilities. These privately operated networks are all similar in concept and operation. Subscribers may access the network from any push-button telephone within their call origination area by dialing a normal seven-digit local telephone number. The subscriber then dials his or her assigned account number, followed by the area code and telephone number desired. Depending upon the network, the call is transmitted via satellite or relay station.

The use of privately owned long-distance networks usually permits savings of between 20 and 25% over AT&T Long Lines' rates, but there are a number of disadvantages:

> Not all locations within North America are served. By reviewing telephone company toll statements of several months, one can determine the extent to which the private long-distance network will service the organization's calling areas.
>
> Dialing up to twenty-two numbers to initiate a call is time-consuming and an annoyance to many people.
>
> Frequent complaints arise about noisy and unclear circuits.
>
> Since the account number is the entry to the long-distance network, unauthorized use is more of a problem than with AT&T Long Lines.

Auditing the Accuracy of Phone Bills

According to several telecommunication consultants, it is not uncommon for telephone bills to contain errors that lead to either overbilling or underbilling. The overcharging may relate to either equipment and service charges or to charges for toll calls.

Equipment and service charges. Occasionally, when a customer adds or removes a telephone instrument or one of its options or when a particular type of service (such as WATS or FX) is added or deleted, the local telephone company's records are not updated to reflect that fact. Consequently the charges for equipment and service are either too high or too low. To avoid this the office manager can request from the local telephone company business office a current inventory of equipment and services being supplied to the organization. After comparing the inventory to the organization's current equipment and services, one can refer any errors to the telephone business office for correction.

Toll calls. It is also common for calls to be either incorrectly charged to a company's telephone number or fraudulently charged to its credit card number. To avoid this all direct-dial and credit card toll calls can be logged as made, and this log can be used to reconcile the accuracy of the monthly phone bill by comparing it to the detailed statement of toll calls.

Controlling Telephone Expenses

Telephone costs, although small for many individual calls, are staggering in composite. According to telecommunications consultant Harry Newton, misuse of the telephone by employees can account for 20 to 40% of an organization's telephone expenses.

To reduce such misuse and abuse, some of these measures may be helpful:

Install *call screening,* a computer-based technique by which individual telephones are limited to calling only specified area codes. The area codes reached by each phone are determined on the basis of the employee's job responsibilities.

Install locks on all telephones to prohibit unauthorized after-hours use.

Charge all telephone expenses back to the user departments. This can be done with the aid of one of the computerized systems that breaks down the organization's local and toll calls by originating extension, number called, time of call, length of call, and total cost. Such a chargeback system gives the department manager an incentive for reducing telephone expenses.

Install screening devices to prevent calls being made to Dial-A-Joke, weather, time, and other consumer-oriented recorded services offered by the local telephone companies.

Instruct employees to make only direct-dial, station-to-station calls, to avoid the higher surcharges and tariffs involved in operator-assisted and person-to-person calls.

When calling commercial suppliers, airline reservation offices, and similar companies, check first to see if they have an "800" number. If so, place calls with the 800 number rather than through regular long distance.

Instruct all personnel who have credit cards furnished by the company not to use their credit cards when making calls from their home phones. Instead have them bill any business calls made from home to their home phones and submit an expense voucher to receive reimbursement for them. This, according to noted telecommunications consultant Frank K. Griesinger, can produce a 35% reduction in the cost of credit card calls.

Furnish three-minute egg timers to all employees to help them to realize the length of their calls.

Educate all employees so that they understand that WATS calls are not "free." According to an attitude survey that I conducted, nearly 40% of the employees in one company thought they were and therefore saw little wrong with their personal use of this service or with making excessively long business calls via WATS.

WORD-PROCESSING SERVICES

Word processing is a technique that reduces the costs and time required to create, transcribe, and revise correspondence, reports, and other written materials through the use of automated input and output equipment.

Word processing input equipment includes individual and centralized dictation systems and optical scanning equipment. *Word processing output equipment* includes any equipment that through integration of standard typewriting concepts with telecommunications or data processing technology is capable of (1) recording all transcribed key strokes in a magnetic media format for (2) subsequent output in the original or a revised version with minimal operator intervention. Briefly, the procedure for generating written materials by word processing techniques is as follows.

Input Subsystem

The originator, acting either on his or her own initiative or in response to a request from another person, decides that a written communication is required. He or she then prepares a brief outline detailing the points to be included in such a communication, their sequence, and any necessary amplifying statements. Using his or her desk telephone, the originator dials an access number to reach a voice-activated dictation system located in a centralized word processing output department. Referring to the previously prepared outline the originator then dictates the text of the communication to be transcribed.

There are three other optional input methods:

The originator may dictate into a desk-top or portable dictation unit and then transmit the recorded cassette to a secretary or to the centralized word processing department for transcription.

The originator may prepare a handwritten draft, which is in turn forwarded to a secretary or the centralized word processing department for transcription.

The handwritten draft may be transcribed by a secretary or by the word processing department using a typewriter equipped with a font that can be read by an optical scanner to produce a magnetic media recording that can be processed by word processing output equipment.

Output Subsystem

Listening to the dictated input through headphones or referring to the handwritten draft, the operator enters the text into the word processing output equipment by typing on a modified typewriter keyboard. As this occurs the various keystrokes are recorded in a digital code on the output equipment's magnetic media. The keystrokes are recorded simultaneously in ordinary alphanumeric characters either on a CRT screen contained as part of the word processing output equipment or as ordinary hard copy output. Unlike ordinary typewriting, however, the input may be revised after initial entry in order to correct errors, add or delete data, insert or remove punctuation, or even rearrange the material. Such revisions are simultaneously recorded in two formats: (1) on the magnetic media and (2) on the CRT or in the hard copy. Once the input has been keyboarded to the operator's satisfaction and is correct in both content and format, the operator may initiate the *print* command, producing hard copy. The hard copy is then returned to the originator, while the magnetic tape is retained for use in case the output requires revision.

The originator then reviews the output and enters any revisions directly on the hard copy, which is returned to the word processing operator for reworking.

Upon receipt of the revised hard copy, the word processing operator locates the corresponding magnetic tape, inserts it into the word-processing output equipment, and activates the *print* command. The text is automatically transcribed until the point is reached where revision is necessary. There the operator stops the equipment, manually enters the revision, and resumes automatic transcription until revision is once again required, when the cycle is repeated. As in the original keyboarding, revisions are made simultaneously to both the magnetic media and the CRT or hard copy-based text. Once all revisions have been made, the *print* command is given, and revised hard copy is prepared.

This output is again returned to the originator, who can, if he or she so desires, again revise the text, in which case the revision cycle is repeated.

Advantages of Word Processing

Word processing has several distinct advantages over traditional non-automated methods of preparing written materials.

It increases both the originator's and the transcriber's productivity. Where revisions are involved, increases of 45% in output are not uncommon.

It reduces personnel and material costs.

It reduces the time required to revise a given piece of writing.

The Office Manager's Role

The office manager's task is to assess his or her organization's word processing requirements and ensure that those needs are met in the most economical manner. The assessment involves determining the type of transcription services that the various departments require and then providing the organizational structure, personnel, and equipment that will supply that level of service.

A detailed study must be made of the types of materials transcribed within the company and of their format, volume, frequency of revision, and turnaround requirements. This will show which departments have a continuing need for word processing and which require it infrequently.

Unless one or more of the following conditions exist within the company, the cost of word processing cannot be justified:

Twenty percent or more of all transcribed materials are revised and retranscribed prior to issue.

A variety of pattern paragraphs, "boiler-plate," or form letters are generated.

At least one-third of a secretary's day is spent typing.

If one or more of these conditions is not met, manual typewriting methods should be continued.

The analysis of work load will indicate whether there is a need for decentralized word processing or whether a centralized system will be more effective. If a decentralized system is preferred, desk-top, portable dictation equipment will usually be needed, and separate word-processing output units, each containing its own keyboard, processor, and printer, must be purchased. If a centralized system is preferred, the equipment will probably include centralized telephone-accessed (or "dial-up") dictation equipment and shared-resource output equipment in which several keyboards share the same processor and printer, generally a more economical set up.

Decentralized operation requires that secretaries be retrained in word processing operations—a task that, due to cost and the continuing need for it, usually involves developing an in-house training program. Centralized operation requires the hiring of production-oriented, highly competent word-processing operators.

The decision to install a word processing system is not lightly reached, since the possible ramifications are significant. Whatever type of system is selected, the office manager must be thoroughly involved in its choice and familiar with how it works, so that he or she can monitor its use and the changing needs of the various user departments, making suggestions for revisions as they become necessary.

CHAPTER 7

Office Layout and Design

The importance of office layout and design to individual productivity and to interpersonal communication within the office is often not fully recognized by office managers. Recently, human engineers have proved that there is a direct correlation between an individual's work environment and his or her overall productivity and efficiency. In addition, they have successfully identified the key physical and emotional characteristics of a well-planned, well-designed office facility. Experience has conclusively shown that such an office will

Provide an environment that promotes high individual productivity
Facilitate interpersonal communication and effective supervision
Promote efficient workflow
Allow for subsequent modification of the office facility at minimal cost

Three factors are involved in office layout and design:

Space requirements: ensuring that adequate space is provided to permit efficient workflow, interpersonal communication, and effective supervision and to provide various support functions; and finding the best arrangement for the space

Physical environment: providing for the basic temperature and humidity, lighting, and acoustical controls required for comfort

Emotional requirements: satisfying individual workers' various psychological and occupational requirements for privacy, status, and interpersonal communication

DETERMINING SPACE REQUIREMENTS

Determining the space requirements of the various departments in an organization necessitates figuring out how much room will be needed for

People space: the working space required by the employees assigned to each department or unit

Support space: the space required for such support services as mail and supply services, cafeterias, and word processing services, as well as for reception areas and conference rooms

Circulation space: the corridors, aisles, and lobbies located throughout the office facility that are used by employees and visitors for both inter- and intra-departmental travel.

Determining space requirements is normally a team rather than individual effort. Team members are drawn from an in-house or consultant group responsible for office layout and design, as well as from the various departments. In this way maximum manpower can be brought to bear on the task while as an added benefit the participation of people who are intimately familiar with each department or unit's requirements for manpower, equipment, interaction, and privacy is assured.

Determining how much space will be needed is essential to the success of the overall office layout and design effort. The survey must be both accurate and comprehensive. The following four-phase approach can help to assure that it is.

Data Gathering

In this phase information is obtained concerning (1) current and projected personnel and equipment assigned to each department, (2) intra- and inter-departmental communication requirements, (3) privacy requirements, and (4) specialized equipment requirements. These data can be readily accumulated.

Current staffing data can be obtained from the management of each department or unit. Such data includes the title and number of each currently authorized position and the type of duties performed by the incumbents of each position.

Future staffing needs can be estimated on the basis of projections of anticipated work loads. Such projections will be made for each of the five years following the survey.

Current equipment can be ascertained by making a physical inventory in each department to determine (1) models; (2) dimensions, condition, usable and available capacity (if used for storage of records, supplies, etc.); and (3) persons to whom they are assigned (if applicable).

Future equipment requirements can be estimated on the basis of an evaluation of future work load and staffing needs.

If either current or future equipment is highly *specialized* in nature (i.e., if it presents unique space or environmental requirements) this can be readily determined through interviews with knowledgeable personnel.

Inter- and intra-departmental communication requirements, which will largely govern the physical positioning of employees within each department and of one department with respect to another, can be ascertained in a variety of ways, such as by (1) tracing the flow of work through its various processing steps; (2) having employees record the names and departments of all employees with whom they interact during a one-month period; (3) interviewing each employee; and (4) making random observations.

Privacy requirements can be ascertained by reviewing the tasks performed by each employee to determine whether the confidentiality of information involved in a position justifies a private office or whether the employee must counsel other employees on their performance.

Summarizing the Data

The data will then be summarized:

Current and projected staffing needs are tabulated by department and also by job title. This gives an estimate of the number of persons for whom office space must be provided at present and in the future.

Present and future equipment needs are tabulated by department and by type of equipment, providing guidance as to the quantity of equipment that must be housed.

Intra- and inter-departmental communication requirements (commonly referred to as *adjacency requirements*) are detailed either tabularly or graphically, providing a basis for positioning individuals and departments or units in relation to each other.

Privacy requirements are summarized by department, indicating the employees who need privacy and estimating the frequency and amount of time for which private facilities are required.

Any current or projected requirements for special equipment are detailed by department or unit to ensure that such needs are properly met.

Efficiency Measures

During this phase innovations are considered that will decrease the amount of space required and meet other important design requirements. For example,

The need for people space can be reduced by adding a second shift to the word processing, data-entry, and other production staffs, rather than by merely hiring additional personnel for the normal 9 A.M. to 5 P.M. shift.

Two and three-drawer file cabinets can be replaced with more space-efficient four and five-drawer models, reducing floor space requirements.

A common conference area and private carrels can be provided to eliminate the need for private offices.

Modern techniques such as facsimile transmission and teleconferencing can be used to facilitate communication among departments or units that for some valid reason cannot be located near each other.

The storage of all but working inventories of office supplies can be centralized, reducing the number of supply cabinets required in office areas.

A records retention schedule can be developed (see Chap. 6) for destroying obsolete records and transferring records that are seldom consulted to low-cost warehouse space, minimizing the number of file cabinets that must be housed in office areas.

Material such as personnel files that must be retained in active files for long periods can be put on microfilm.

Consideration should also be given to establishing *workplace standards* to prescribe the quantity and type of space that must be provided for the employee in each position, as well as the equipment and type of office furniture to which he or she is entitled. Workplace standards may be liberal or restrictive depending upon the availability of space and the atmosphere and character of the office. As a rule, relatively procedurized jobs that require little in the way of specialized and free-standing equipment have restrictive workplace standards. The opposite is usually true of complex jobs.

Generally, workplace standards should provide, at a minimum, for 215% more space than is occupied by the employee's office furniture and free-standing equipment, to allow for both access and circulation space. For example, if an employee has a 5-by-3-foot executive desk, a swivel chair, and a letter-sized filing cabinet (occupying a total of 23 square feet of floor space), a minimum of 59 square feet of floor space should be provided.

Developing Recommendations

Once some of these efficiency measures have been decided on, the allocation of space to the various departments and units can begin. Such allocation becomes a rather mechanical operation.

People space is determined by multiplying the total number of employees to be housed, both currently and in the future, by the applicable workplace standards. If workplace standards have not been developed, people space is calculated by totaling the space needed for current and projected office furniture and free-standing equipment and multiplying the sum by a factor of 215% or more. The space allocated is based upon future projections rather than current staffing levels if available space permits. This will eliminate much of the time and cost involved in rearranging office space to accommodate staff additions or reductions.

Support space requirements are calculated in the same manner, on the basis of staffing and equipment requirements.

Circulation space for corridors, stairways, and hallways can be provided by adding 10 to 15% more space to the people space and support space. It will be recalled that the people space already includes an allowance for the space needed for intradepartmental circulation.

By adding these three totals, one arrives at the figure for overall floor space.

The next task is to provide for adjacency requirements. As a rule, every attempt should be made to locate departments or units and individuals as close as possible to those with whom they routinely interact in their work.

Meeting privacy requirements is the next task. If common conference rooms are to be used, they should be located conveniently for the individuals who will use them; if possible, such rooms should be removed from the hustle and bustle of the general office area.

Finally, space to meet any special equipment requirements, such as subdued lighting for microfilm readers or hard wiring for electronic office equipment, must be provided. Equipment manufacturers are the best source of information about such requirements and how they can be economically and effectively provided for.

ARRANGING OFFICE SPACE

Having defined the space requirements, one is now ready to decide how the office space will be arranged. There are two alternatives: (1) the traditional or *closed plan* and (2) the open plan. No blanket statement can be made about which is preferable; each has its own advantages. The office manager's task is to compare such advantages and to select the alternative that will satisfy the organization's unique requirements at the lowest cost.

Traditional Arrangement

The traditional, or closed, plan is characterized by the extensive use of private offices and by the physical separation of departments or units into separate rooms. Visual and acoustical privacy is provided by either walls or partitions extending from floor to ceiling. Clerical work stations are located symmetrically, side by side or one behind the other, in open areas.

The primary advantages of the traditional arrangement are that

Maximal visual and acoustical privacy is assured.
A more status-oriented impression is conveyed.
Noise and distractions are less than with the open plan.

Open-Plan Arrangement

As the name suggests, the open plan calls for placing most employees in semiopen and open space rather than in private offices. Visual privacy is maintained through the use of partitions and screens no more than six feet high, rather than by walls and ceiling-height partitions. Acoustical privacy is maintained through the use of sound-absorbing materials on the surfaces of ceilings, walls, and floors, as well as around work stations and equipment.

The chief advantages of the open plan are that

The cost of rearranging work stations is thirty to forty times lower than with the traditional closed plan.
The absence of walls helps maintain uniform heating, ventilation, and air conditioning levels.
Communication and supervision are generally easier than with the closed plan.

Surprisingly, the space required is almost equal using either alternative. One cannot, therefore, justify using one method rather than the other on the grounds that more people and equipment will be accommodated in the same amount of space.

CONTROLLING THE PHYSICAL ENVIRONMENT

An office's physical environment has a direct bearing on the productivity of employees and the accuracy of their work, on absenteeism, and on operating costs. Such conditions as inadequate or excessive temperature and humidity levels, dusty and smoky air, improper lighting, and irritating noise levels can quickly cause physical discomfort that becomes progressively worse as the day goes on. Coupled with normal physical fatigue, these undesirable conditions invariably have an unfavorable effect on employees' physical and mental outlook, making it more difficult for them to concentrate upon the tasks at hand. Consequently the volume of work falls off, and its quality, in terms of both accuracy and content, decreases. Substandard physical conditions also cause a higher incidence of absenteeism and lost time due to colds, eyestrain, migraine headaches, and the like. The net result is higher operating costs.

The discussion in this section will focus on the various factors that must be provided in the office's physical environment to ensure maximum employee comfort, health, and productivity, proper machine operations, minimal operating and maintenance expenses, and the safe preservation of paper, microfilm, and magnetic media–based records.

Air Filtration

The two primary sources of "dirty air" in the office are airborne dust and dirt, and tobacco smoke. Allowed to circulate through the office, such dirty air could well result in

Physical discomfort to both employees and visitors
Decreased efficiency of air conditioning and ventilation equipment
Damage to microfilm records and the loss of data stored on magnetic tapes and disks
Unnecessary mechanical wear in such office equipment as tape-recorders and computer terminals
A buildup of static electricity that may cause a malfunction in word processing and computer equipment
Increased maintenance expenses resulting from more frequent dry

cleaning of drapes, washing of windows, shampooing of carpets, and dusting of walls, furniture, and surfaces

There is no effective way to prevent airborne dust and dirt from entering an office. Every time a door or window is opened or the air conditioning or heating system turns on, airborne dust and dirt are introduced into the office's atmosphere. Likewise, it is possible but not practical to restrict the introduction of tobacco smoke by banning smoking since it would be too expensive to segregate smokers from nonsmokers in the office. The most feasible, cost-effective approach is to remove undesirable substances from the air with filtration equipment.

It is generally advisable to filter both outdoor and recirculated air by using roughing-type prefilters for the outdoor air, placed in the intake ducts, and bag-type final filters following the humidifiers, placed downwind from the fan. Usually this filtration equipment removes most of the dust, dirt, and tobacco smoke. If the concentrations of such pollutants are too great to be removed effectively by these two types of filters, one should consider installing an electrostatic precipitator.

Lighting

The sharp increase in utility costs that followed the energy crunch of the 1970s, coupled with the ongoing national policy of energy conservation, has necessitated a total reevaluation of traditional methods of illuminating offices. In the days of cheap energy little thought was given to designing cost-efficient office lighting systems; the main objective was to provide levels of illumination high enough so that all employees could see very well the various written materials and equipment with which they worked. The cost of providing such illumination, since it was relatively low, was secondary. Consequently most offices were overilluminated: far more light was provided than was actually needed to perform the tasks at hand.

All this has now changed. Of necessity, emphasis on office lighting has switched from providing maximal illumination for the entire office to determining the lighting requirements of each work station and providing only the necessary light in the most economical manner.

IMPORTANCE OF PROPER LIGHTING

The importance of adequate lighting to office efficiency can best be appreciated by considering the results of a survey conducted by the Louis Harris organization for the Steelcase Corporation (reported in *Administration Management,* October 1980). This survey asked 1,004 office workers to indicate what factors make an office comfortable. Fully 85% responded, "good lighting."

"Good lighting" may be defined as an illumination level that provides enough light at a work station so that an employee is able to perform close work for extended periods of time without incurring eyestrain or other physical discomfort. Such lighting does not allow an imbalance of light distribution and also reduces glare and minimizes shadows, since such conditions contribute to both visual discomfort and physical fatigue.

Various studies have proved that good lighting is essential to high productivity. At the Social Security Administration, for example, productivity declined 28% when illumination levels were reduced from 150 footcandles to 50. A similar reduction in illumination levels in a General Electric Company's divisional data entry section resulted in productivity declines of 12%.

OBJECTIVES

In designing an office lighting system, therefore, three major objectives must be satisfied:

A level of illumination must be provided that will permit the completion of office tasks without eyestrain or other physical discomfort.

Lighting costs must be minimized.

The lighting system must generate minimum heat, to reduce the need for additional cooling in summer. This is critical, since, in many high-rise buildings office lighting imposes as much as 60% of the cooling load on the building's heating, ventilation, and air conditioning (HVAC) system.

RECOMMENDED LEVELS OF ILLUMINATION

Table 7-1 provides some guidelines for determining proper levels of illumination that were based upon the Illuminating Engineering Society of North America's recent listings. Applying the guidelines should not be difficult. For example, an inactive records storage archives, where the primary job involves the filing and retrieval of records, would require 75 footcandles of illumination; an accounts payable clerk, whose primary duties involve reviewing and approving vendor invoices (statistical work) would require 150 footcandles; the person responsible for checking engineering drawings against a change order to ensure that revisions have been made correctly would require 200 footcandles. In addition, the guidelines recommend that 20 footcandles of illumination be provided in corridors, elevators, and stairways.

ACHIEVING RECOMMENDED ILLUMINATION LEVELS

As noted earlier, it is uneconomical to rely primarily upon traditional overhead lighting. A more cost-effective approach is to

Supplement the overhead (or ambient) lighting with *task* lighting.
Use ceiling, floor, wall coverings, equipment, and office furniture, that reflect light.
Position lighting fixtures so that glare and shadows are minimized.
Properly maintain the lighting system.

Table 7-1. Recommended Illumination Levels

Type of Work Performed	Recommended Footcandles of Illumination
Mechanical, architectural, drafting	200
Statistical and accounting	150
Word processing	100
Filing	75
Reading (reports, correspondence, etc.)	75

Source: The Illuminating Engineering Society of North America

Table 7-2. Recommended Reflectance Values

Surface	Reflectance Values (%)
Ceilings	80 and above
Walls	50–70
Furniture	25–45
Office equipment	25–45
Floors	20–40

Source: The Illuminating Engineering Society of North America.

Task lighting. This type of lighting has become increasingly important since the energy crunch began. Task lighting calls for additional lighting fixtures (such as desk lamps, swing-arm fluorescent lights, and built-in lighting fixtures) to be added to any work station that requires more illumination (footcandles) than the ambient lighting can deliver.

Organizations such as Fenvessy and Schwab, Inc., that have reduced ambient lighting and added task lighting have found that they have been able to lower their electrical consumption.

Increasing surface reflectivity. By selecting highly reflective surfaces or finishes for ceilings, walls, and floors one can ensure maximum utilization of lighting sources. With such surfaces the light that falls upon the ceilings, walls, and floors is reflected back toward the center of the room, increasing the number of footcandles that are delivered to individual work stations. The opposite is also true: using surfaces that have low reflectance value reduces the amount of light that is reflected. This latter concept helps to reduce glare. By specifying desktops, equipment, and furniture that have low reflectance values it is possible to reduce the glare that might otherwise cause visual discomfort.

Table 7-2 provides the Illuminating Engineering Society of North America's recommended reflectance values for office interiors.

Positioning lighting fixtures correctly. The correct positioning of lighting fixtures will do much to promote an even distribution of light in the office and to minimize glare and shadows.

Glare is of two types: source glare, and reflective (or "veiling") glare. Source glare occurs when the lighting fixture is positioned so that it shines into somebody's eyes. Reflective glare occurs when light falls upon a desktop, typewriter, or CRT and is reflected up into someone's eyes. Either type of glare is undesirable since it can cause eyestrain, headaches, and overall physical fatigue.

Shadows result from positioning a light source so that before the light reaches the work surface it falls upon some object or person that casts a shadow upon the work surface.

To position lighting fixtures correctly,

Position task-lighting fixtures so that the light source is not at or only slightly above eye level.

Install ambient lighting so that the light is projected onto the ceiling and is then reflected down toward the various work stations. This method works especially well with perimeter lighting.

Use cover lenses over overhead fluorescent fixtures to ensure even light distribution and reduced glare.

Position ambient and task-lighting fixtures on either side of and behind workers to minimize reflective glare.

Relocate furniture, equipment, and work stations to eliminate shadows.

Maintenance. Poor light quality is caused by a variety of readily correctable situations—for instance, dusty and dirty light bulbs and lenses can easily be cleaned, and burned-out or flickering light bulbs that cause shadows and uneven light distribution can be replaced. Strange as it may seem, lighting maintenance in most offices is done with a troubleshooting approach rather than as preventive maintenance. Usually, unless someone complains about a burned-out or flickering light bulb, no maintenance is done. Consequently dust and dirt buildup and unreported defective lighting units result in a loss of illumination that can range, according to an Illuminating Engineers Society of North America study, above 25%.

Far more cost-efficient is a routine preventive maintenance program that calls for "group relamping" and periodic cleaning of bulbs, fixtures, lenses, and reflectors. In group relamping all the light bulbs in a given office area are replaced at the same time, rather than individually as they burn out. According to a study by the General Electric Company, a well-planned group relamping program will in the course of a few years reduce the labor costs involved in replacing individual bulbs as they wear out by 90%. Most group relamping programs also include cleaning of reflectors, lenses, and fixtures at the time when the bulbs are changed, further reducing maintenance costs.

Acoustical Controls

Two aspects of acoustical control must be considered in any office: *reducing noise levels to acceptable ranges.* Many people cannot function properly in a noisy environment. After a relatively short exposure to constant noise, they find it difficult to concentrate and experience physical discomfort and fatigue. Provision must also be made to preclude the possibility of conversations being heard and understood by other than the parties involved. To provide for these diametrically opposed objectives, it is necessary that cost-efficient, effective acoustical controls be implemented as part of office design.

This is no simple task, since the sources, tones, and intensity (or loudness) of the sounds typically found in an office are diverse. For example,

In general office areas one hears the sounds of people moving around, of office equipment being operated, of telephones ringing, and of conversations.

In production areas most of the noise is caused by machines. In the word-processing department one hears the staccato sound of output printers operating at speeds of up to 540 words per minute, the whirring sound of air conditioners, and the hum of electric motors.

In "Executive Row" and areas that include private or semiprivate offices the main sources of sound are the occasional ringing of telephones, periodic typing, and quiet conversation.

Each situation poses its own unique acoustical problems, and each requires a different approach if the acoustical controls are to be effective and cost-efficient. Before considering the various methods of acoustical control, however, a basic understanding of office acoustics is needed.

Sound versus Noise

First let us differentiate between *sound* and *noise* as each pertains to office acoustics:

Sound means anything that is heard both within and near the office. The intensity, or loudness, of such sound is measured in *decibels*—the higher the decibel value, the louder the sound. Depending upon the decibel rating, the various sounds that are created by normal office activities may range from inaudible (as in the case of pens and pencils writing on paper) to unpleasant and distracting (as in the case of several computer or word processing printers operating simultaneously). Sounds in the office are unavoidable and, as in the case of conversation, are often necessary to the conducting of business.

Noise refers to a condition that is created when the sounds reach such intensity that the majority of persons will find them disconcerting and, if allowed to continue unabated, painful.

The level of noise at which hearing damage occurs has been established at 85 decibels. Continued exposure to noises at or above 85 decibels will cause hearing loss. Sound levels in offices rarely reach such levels. However, depending upon such factors as the number of office machines in operation at any one time and their proximity to each other, the dimensions and physical arrangement of the room, and the sound absorbency of the materials used to cover the ceilings, floors, and walls, sustained noise levels can well range between 60 and 80 decibels, causing headaches, increased fatigue, and other discomfort.

Most employees can accept sound levels of 50 decibels or less and will experience no noticeable physical or mental discomfort if exposed to such levels throughout the working day. Persons whose duties require close concentration or careful analysis, however, are likely to find 50 decibels distracting. The maximum noise levels allowed in the various areas of an office must be matched to the degree of concentration the persons working there need to have. As a general rule, noise in the office should not exceed the following *maximum noise levels*

General office areas—such as those occupied by payroll, purchasing, industrial relations, and other similar functions—40 decibels

Areas in which large concentrations of office machines are found, such as the mailroom, word processing department, or computer room—50 decibels

Offices occupied by executive, managerial, and other professional personnel who work long hours on research or analysis or who must for other reasons be assured of an atmosphere conducive to sustained concentration—30 decibels

ACHIEVING AND MAINTAINING ACCEPTABLE NOISE LEVELS

Noise in the office can be reduced to and maintained at or below recommended levels through the use of (1) architectural controls, which utilize sound-absorbing materials, and (2) engineered controls, achieved by installing acoustical hoods over office machines, increasing the distance between work stations, and using "white noise." Generally, acoustical control can be achieved most economically through a combination of architectural and engineered controls, rather than by using either one alone.

Architectural controls. These noise controls work on the principle of the absorption of sound waves. The various sounds created in the office travel outward in all directions from their source at speeds of 1,100 feet per second until they encounter an obstruction such as a surface of the room, a desk, or a supply cabinet. Then, depending upon the hardness and porosity of the surface of the obstruction, one of the following will occur:

The sound will pass through the obstruction and continue in its outward-bound direction. This occurs when the obstruction is composed of highly porous materials that have low sound absorption capabilities, such as nylon curtains.

The sound will be reflected back toward its source, if the obstacle is composed of nonporous materials that have a low sound absorption capability—glass, concrete, plaster, ceramic tiles, and gypsum board.

The sound will be either totally or partially absorbed, if the obstacle is composed of porous materials that have sound absorption capabilities. Depending upon the degree of sound absorption, none or some of the sound will be reflected back toward the source. Examples of such materials are cork tiles, acoustical fiberglass, and tufted, jute-backed carpeting.

Applying these concepts, architectural controls call for the use of highly porous, sound-absorptive materials for walls, ceilings, floors, and window coverings. Using such materials as cork tiles, acoustically rated carpeting, and acoustical fiberglass draperies reduces noise levels in office areas. These materials reduce the amount of sound that is reflected back toward the source by the various surfaces of the rooms in which office activities are conducted.

Engineered controls. These noise controls treat individual sources of noise rather than attempting to reduce the level of all noises in the office.

One such method is to install sound-absorptive enclosures over output printers, or acoustical hoods over automated equipment. This has proved to be quite effective in all three types of office areas—general areas, areas in which concentrations of machines are found, and areas next to executive and other professional offices. Studies conducted by organizations that have installed acoustical enclosures and hoods have found that noise levels originating from office equipment are reduced by as much as 90%.

Another effective engineered control is to place sound screens, or partitions, covered with porous, highly sound absorptive materials such as cork tiles around the area that requires the reduction of noise level. This technique works as well in increasing conversational privacy in quiet or open areas as it does in reducing overly loud sounds created by employees and equipment.

The third engineered control is to merely space the various work stations further apart in order to reduce the number of different sounds coming from any one office area. The same number of sounds are present in the room, but because they are spaced further apart, they do not reach the intensity that would result if they were closer together.

The final engineered control involves using a sound masking system (or, as it is more commonly known, *white noise*). With this method, a sound producing system, generally installed with speakers mounted at ceiling height, produces a moderate, unobtrusive electronic sound that increases the overall ambient noise level to offset or mask a portion of the sounds emanating from the people and equipment in the area. As a result, people in the area in which the sound masking system is operating are not aware of the actual sound levels and are therefore not as psychologically or physiologically responsive to the noise as they would normally be.

Heating, Ventilation, and Air Conditioning

In a number of surveys of office personnel conducted since the "energy crunch" began, workers have rated "a comfortable environment" as the one factor that is most important to their productivity and accuracy. If air temperature and moisture content rise above 76°F and 40% relative humidity during the summer months, over half of the office population will feel uncomfortable, according to the American Society of Heating, Refrigerating and Air Conditioning Engineers. Unless air circulation allows the warm, humid air to move about, employees will begin to grow drowsy and feel unduly fatigued. Their work will suffer, as productivity lessens and the ability to concentrate declines.

Air quality must also be controlled in the winter when the outside air is cold and dry. Unless the inside air is warmed, moisture is added, and the air is freely circulated, people will feel too cold and uncomfortable to work productively, and illnesses from winter colds will be increased.

Inadequate environmental and climatic controls can also have bad effects on record keeping media and office machines. Microfilm, paper records, and magnetic tape all face the risk of physical deterioration from storage in uncontrolled environments in which temperatures and humidity are allowed to range above or below prescribed levels. Likewise, wordprocessing and dataprocessing equipment often malfunctions if static electricity is present or excessive temperature and humidity exist.

Such undesirable effects necessitate the installation of an effective heating, ventilating, and air conditioning system in the office. These systems (more commonly known as HVAC systems) are designed to provide a comfortable, healthy working environment by regulating the office's atmospheric conditions. Specifically, HVAC systems control indoor temperatures, air circulation, and moisture content so that they are healthy.

HVAC systems must be designed specifically for the areas in which they are to be used if they are to be truly cost-effective. Such design requires quantification of

The size and shape of the office area

The cubic feet of space in the office area

The number of people who normally occupy the area

The estimated heat, measured in British thermal units (BTUs), generated by the equipment

The type of light fixtures that will be used, and their wattage, location, and heat generated during operation

In addition, consideration must also be given to the following geographic factors:

Normal temperature and humidity ranges during the winter and summer months

Direction of the prevailing winds and their normal magnitude or speed

Orientation of the building with respect to the sun

Number of glass windows and walls in the building, and their location. (Are they on the sunny side of the building? Are they downwind from the prevailing winds?)

Once this information has been gathered and analyzed, a HVAC system geared to the individual office's requirements can be developed. So critical is this design to both employee and equipment productivity, as well as to the control of heating and air conditioning costs, that it should be left to qualified mechanical engineers. It is penny wise and pound foolish to attempt to save a few dollars by designing one's own HVAC system, since the cost of installing an inadequate or unnecessarily complex system is generally much greater than the fee that was avoided by not hiring a mechanical engineer.

PROVIDING AN
EMOTIONALLY SATISFYING ENVIRONMENT

The third factor involved in office layout and design—the emotional requirements—is probably the most often overlooked. Consequently even though some offices are well designed in terms of space allocation, acoustics, lighting, and environmental controls, they still fail to achieve the projected benefits of increased productivity, improved communication and supervision, and efficient workflow. Invariably the cause is failure to properly identify and provide for the psychological needs of employees. This may be because the features that make an office's environment emotionally satisfying appear at first to be of too little significance to justify more than a perfunctory analysis. However, this is not at all the case. Let us now examine the features that must be evaluated and provided for if one is to design an emotionally satisfying office environment.

Background Music

A human's psychological and physiological reaction to music is very predictable. Depending upon the tempo of the music and the types of instruments used, an individual will be stimulated or relaxed, made happy or put in a subdued frame of mind, even though the music is playing very softly or the person is not actively or consciously listening to it. Thus music not only has charm; it also has significant power.

Commercially available services that provide "background music" utilize music's ability to influence human behavior in order to relieve employees' tension and fatigue while increasing the quality and quantity of work produced and reducing unnecessary conversation. The music is specially selected to achieve specific behavioral responses. In the early morning, when employees are still refreshed, light, airy selections are generally played, since fatigue has not yet set in. As the morning progresses, however, the selections become faster and more stimulating to counter the growing fatigue. The same pattern is followed in the afternoon.

Background music must never be distracting. It is designed for subconscious rather than active listening. For this reason brass instruments and solos are avoided.

Maximum benefits are obtained when the music is played intermittently during the day, rather than continually. The results of using programmed background music are truly impressive:

A mail-order house reported that errors were reduced by more than 20% after background music was installed in its data entry department.

Productivity increased over 10% after a textile manufacturer implemented a background music system in his general offices.

Over 75% of the office employees at a major foundation, responding to an attitude survey conducted six months after the introduction of background music, reported that their jobs were more pleasant as a result.

Use of Color

It will undoubtedly surprise many office managers to learn that in addition to affecting the aesthetic atmosphere of the office, the proper selection of colors also (1) reduces fatigue and eyestrain, (2) decreases heating, air conditioning, and lighting costs, (3) fosters greater productivity and (4) provides an atmosphere that is conducive to reflective thought, detail work, and prolonged concentration.

The conscientious office manager cannot afford to leave the selection of a color scheme for the office walls, ceilings, floor coverings, draperies, and furniture to chance. To do so would be to risk ending up with an environment that could decrease productivity and the quality of output, increase energy costs, and adversely affect employees' mental outlook.

Let us examine the selection of colors from three aspects: aesthetic qualities; psychological and physiological effects; and, finally, operating costs.

Aesthetic Qualities

Colors have the ability to make an office appear larger or smaller, as well as to make its shape appear squarer or more rectangular. Color selection can therefore compensate for unattractive physical proportions of an office area. When there is a need to use color in this way, two basic facts must be kept in mind:

Dark colors absorb light, make an area seem smaller than it actually is, and give the impression of confinement.
Light colors reflect light, create the impression that an area is larger than it actually is, and suggest spaciousness.

These effects of color can be used advantageously to compensate for aesthetically undesirable situations. For example,

An overly long, rectangular corridor or office can be made to look squarer by painting the end walls a dark color and the side walls a light color.
A small area may be "enlarged" by using light colors on all surfaces—walls, floors, and ceilings.
An office that looks barnlike and empty, because it is large or lacks furniture and occupants, can be made to appear smaller if dark colors are used.

USE OF COLOR TO SIMPLIFY TRAFFIC FLOW

Many organizations, such as J.C. Penney Co., use colors to facilitate intrabuilding travel. Each wing of the building is assigned a color (for example, north wing, red; south wing, blue), and the carpeting throughout that wing is the same color. All offices in the wing are identified by color, floor, and room number (for example, red-5-106), greatly simplifying travel and locating individual offices.

USE OF COLOR TO INDICATE ORGANIZATION

Through the use of differently colored carpets, partitions, and chair coverings, it is possible to organize the office by color. To illustrate, the credit department's work area may have a charcoal gray carpet and beige-colored chair coverings, while the purchasing department's carpets are brown and their chairs are covered in yellow. One may see at a glance where credit's and purchasing's work areas and personnel are located.

Human Reactions to Color

Human beings react in very predictable ways to color. They find

Warm colors (yellow, orange, and red) invigorating;
Cool colors (blue, green, and violet) relaxing;
Pale tints of cool colors (light blue, light green, and light violet)
depressing; and
Neutral colors (gray, beige, and ivory) mildly stimulating.

By keeping these reactions in mind when selecting colors for the various areas of the office, one can select color schemes that will produce the reactions that are suitable for the work done in particular areas. For example:

Employee lounges, break areas, and cafeterias can be done in cool colors to create a relaxed atmosphere.

Office areas occupied by people who do creative work (such as advertising copywriters) can be done predominately in neutral colors, with touches of warm colors to provide suitable stimulation.

General office areas can be done in neutral colors to provide a mildly stimulating environment.

In sales and production areas (such as the word-processing section) warm colors can be freely used, particularly on the walls facing employees' desks.

Naturally, colors that people find depressing (the pale tints of cool colors) should not be used in any office color scheme.

Numerous studies have established the impact of color upon productivity, fatigue, and overall mental attitude by testing the effects of color schemes on employees. For example, the walls in a given work area might be painted a pale tint of a cool color, such as light blue. Employee productivity and absenteeism would then be measured over a period of several weeks. The walls would then be repainted in a warm color such as bright yellow and productivity and absenteeism would again be recorded. Such studies have found that productivity is higher and absenteeism is lower when warm colors are substituted for the pale tints of cool colors. Two other results typically occur: the incidence of fatigue and eyestrain is less when warm colors are used, and employees feel warmer even though the inside temperature remains unchanged and the outside temperatures have not varied very much.

USE OF COLOR TO REDUCE ELECTRICITY COSTS

The use of color, as noted in the discussion of lighting, can significantly affect an organization's electricity costs. By selecting light-colored paints, floor coverings, furniture, and equipment with high reflectance values, one can ensure efficient utilization of available light. If dark colors are used, a greater proportion of light will be absorbed, and a less efficient utilization of available light will be realized.

Status

Status is a primary emotional requirement for most individuals. It is an accepted practice in American business and government, educational, and nonprofit organizations of every size and type to provide office facilities and amenities on the basis of rank. As an employee advances from one organizational level to the next higher, his or her office will generally be in a more desirable location; he or she will be allotted more floor space and will be provided with more expensive furnishings. So ingrained has this practice become that a good office is one of the perquisites of high rank in many organizations. Just as siblings mentally assess each other's Christmas presents in terms of number and value, so too employees compare their offices to those of others at the same hierarchical level to ensure that no one's office is better situated, larger, or more opulently furnished than theirs.

The office manager can recognize and provide for this emotional need by establishing clearly defined standards so that the process of assigning and furnishing offices involves as few variables and decisions as possible. The most cost-efficient method for doing so involves developing a series of "workplace standards" that prescribe for each functional title within the organization such factors as

Square feet of space allotted

Whether the work station will be located in an open area or in a
    private office

The type of office furniture authorized, including dimensions, col-
    ors, and materials (for example, double-pedestal executive desk,
    60 by 30 inches, with walnut finish)

Any accoutrements and special equipment, such as carpeting,
    video-display devices (more commonly known as CRTs), paint-
    ings, lithographs, or other artwork

If workplace standards are set, it becomes a simple matter, when someone is assigned to a different position, to ascertain quickly and accurately the type of work area to which he or she is entitled and to eliminate a very real cause of internal dissension.

Satisfying the Need for Privacy

The discussion of acoustics addressed the question of ensuring privacy
of conversation. Visual and physical privacy are also important.

Many managers feel a need for a walled office with a door that they
can close on occasions when they do not wish to be disturbed, are
holding meetings of a confidential nature, or are reviewing or preparing
reports and presentations they wish to safeguard against unauthorized
viewing.

A study by SLS–Environetics (one of our nation's largest office interior design firms) indicates that the average manager who has a door on
his or her office will leave it open nearly 90% of the time in order to
facilitate communication with a secretary, observe the people passing
by the office, or avoid the feeling of being isolated. This study suggests
that it is feasible to seek alternate means for providing visual and physical privacy than resorting to the walled-office/door layout, since such an
arrangement restricts open access and impedes both effective supervision and communication between the manager and his or her subordinates. Two such alternatives are to provide conference rooms for use by
any manager who needs privacy, and to position portable screens
around the manager's work station.

Office layout and design is a complex, detailed subject. It is unlikely that the typical office manager will possess enough skills to handle all aspects of office design alone. However, a working knowledge of the disciplines that affect office design is an excellent resource to acquire, since it will help the manager to deal intelligently with the various vendors and consultants who become involved in designing the office.

CHAPTER 8

Payroll
and Petty Cash

The importance of payroll and petty cash systems to the operation of any organization cannot be overstated. No single factor will prove as detrimental to employee morale or affect relations between labor and management more negatively than an employer's inability to promptly and accurately pay employees the wages due to them and reimburse them for out-of-pocket expenses incurred on the employer's behalf. The office manager must constantly monitor the organization's payroll and petty cash systems to ensure that they are operating cost-effectively and accurately.

PAYROLL SYSTEMS

Basic objectives. Any payroll system, regardless of whether its operation is manual, semiautomated, or computerized, must be able to accomplish four principal objectives if it is to comply with applicable laws and labor agreements and serve the organization's auditing, operating, and managerial requirements. Specifically, the payroll system must

Include source records that list the hours each employee has
   worked in a given payroll period
Make it possible to accurately and quickly compute the wages due
   to each employee for a given pay period, taking into account
   such factors as regular and overtime hours worked, shift differ-
   entials, pay rates, authorized deductions and tax withholding,
   and garnishees
Ensure that individual paychecks or cash payments (as applicable)
   and the various accounting entries to document employees' net
   earnings, deductions, and witholdings are accurately prepared
Provide for the analysis and distribution of payroll expenses among
   the organization's various cost centers

Available systems. A variety of alternatives are available for computing
the payroll, preparing payments, and creating and updating the records
and reports that document the transactions:

Manual systems using handwritten forms and manually prepared
   reports
Semiautomated systems using one-write pegboard form sets to create the paychecks and the necessary reports and records
Automated systems using the organization's own data processing
   equipment
Automated systems using the computers of a service company

Each of these alternatives will be examined in detail.

Manual System

Six steps are involved in setting-up a manual payroll system:

An employee payroll master record must be established.
The regular and premium hours each employee works during every
   pay period must be recorded and reported.
The gross earnings, deductions and withholdings, and net earnings
   for each employee must be computed.
A paycheck or cash payment equal to those net earnings must be
   prepared and delivered to each employee.

The payment must then be documented.

Reports that are required by various government agencies as well as by the organization itself must be prepared to record these payroll transactions.

ESTABLISHING A MASTER PAYROLL RECORD

This step consists of assembling in a readily accessible format all information that is needed to compute a given employee's gross earnings, deductions and withholdings, and net wages. The following information is required:

The employee's name, address, and social security number

The employee's identification or clock number

The department and location assigned

The job classification and wage rate

The number of exemptions the employee claims for tax withholding purposes

The deductions that the employee has voluntarily authorized be made from his or her wages.

This information can be readily obtained from three sources:

The federal Form W-4 ("Employee's Exemption Withholding Certificate") that everyone must file with his or her employer in order to establish the number of withholding exemptions claimed for tax purposes. This form, which remains effective until superceded, gives the employee's name, address, social security number and number of tax exemptions claimed.

The organization's own "personnel action notice," or whatever form is used to add personnel to a department's roster or to revise the status of a person already assigned to a given department. This form usually gives the employee's identification or clock number, the department and location assigned, the job classification, and the wage rate.

The company forms that are used to authorize voluntary deductions from the wages of individual employees for union dues, purchases made in the company store, repayment of salary advances, thrift plan contributions, and charitable contributions. The information of importance to the payroll department on such forms is the inclusive dates of the authorized deductions and the purpose, amount, and frequency of the deductions.

Usually when a payroll is prepared manually, the master payroll record is combined with a *year-to-date record* of each employee's gross earnings, deductions and withholdings, and net wages in the form of a *consolidated earnings ledger* using standard accounting columnar paper, one page per employee. The data that are necessary to calculate payments to the employee, along with his or her name, address, and social security number, are entered in the space provided across the top of each sheet; information relating to hours worked, gross earnings, deductions and withholdings, and net earnings appear under each column, with the amounts from each pay period entered on the same line.

RECORDING AND REPORTING HOURS WORKED

The procedures for recording and reporting the hours each employee works in a given pay period are to a large extent based upon the Fair Labor Standards Act (more commonly known as the "Wage and Hour Law"). This legislation stipulates that every employer shall ensure that all employees "subject" to the act (broadly speaking, full and part-time employees who work in other than an executive, administrative, professional, or outside sales capacity) record their daily attendance, including the times they started and stopped working, and that such attendance records be maintained for at least three years to permit audits by the FLSA.

To comply with this requirement, two attendance reporting formats have been developed:

A manually entered *timesheet* on which each employee enters daily the times he or she started and stopped work

A mechanically prepared *clock card* (sometimes referred to as a *time card*), which when used in conjunction with a device known as a *time clock* (or *time recorder*) automatically prints the time of day when the employee began or stopped work

Unlike the timesheet, which may provide for all employees in a
given department to enter their starting and stop times on a single record, each employee has his or her own clock card, which
is generally used for the entire pay period.

At the end of each pay period, the department head or, in larger
organizations, the unit supervisor gathers up the timesheets or clock
cards, reviews them for accuracy and completeness, adds up each employee's standard hours (up to 40 per week) and any premium (overtime) hours, and signs each record as approved. The approved
timesheets or clock cards are then forwarded to the payroll department
or, if the organization is too small to justify a formal department, to the
employee responsible for computing and issuing the payroll.

Since executive, administrative, professional, and outside sales personnel are exempt from the requirements of the Fair Labor Standards
Act, a work-simplifying and cost-reducing payroll procedure is to use a
different form of recording attendance for these employees. Instead of
having them report their attendance on a *routine* basis, they can document their attendance on an exception basis. If the employees are at
work, no report is made; if they are absent for all or part of a day, their
absence is reported to the payroll office on a simple interoffice memorandum. Since such employees do not receive overtime pay and since the
purpose of their reporting is to ensure that they do not exceeed established vacation and sick leave allowances, this reporting procedure will
suffice and save processing costs.

Computing Employee Earnings

Upon receipt of the timesheet or clock card by the payroll division, the
standard and overtime hours worked by each employee are entered on
his or her individual consolidated earnings ledger sheet (the record recommended earlier that combines into a single record each employee's
master payroll record and his or her year-to-date earnings, and deductions and withholdings). The standard and overtime hours are multiplied
by the applicable pay rate, indicating the individual's *gross earnings*.
Statutory withholdings (for FICA, federal, state, and local taxes, and
state unemployment insurance and pension contributions) are then cal-

culated and entered in the appropriate columns on the ledger sheet. Any voluntary deductions for such things as union dues, United Fund contributions, and safety shoes are ascertained and entered to the ledger in the spaces provided. By subtracting the applicable deductions and withholdings from gross wages, each employee's *net earnings* are calculated. The amount is then entered in the space provided on the ledger sheet.

PREPARING AND DISTRIBUTING PAY

After each employee's earnings have been calculated and verified, the payroll is prepared for distribution. There are three forms in which payrolls can be distributed:

Cash
Checks made payable to employee
Deposits made directly to the employee's checking account

If cash payments are involved, the payroll department calculates the total amount that must be paid out and either (1) requests that the organization's bank issue cash in denominations that will enable the payroll department to pay each employee the amount owed to him or her, or (2) forwards to the bank a listing of the amount due each employee and has the bank make up the payroll inserting in each employee's pay envelope bills and coins equal to the amount due. If the latter method is used, the bank imposes an additional charge and the office manager must find out whether the additional cost of using the bank to do this work is cost-justified.

When payments are made in cash, each employee is required to verify the receipt of his or her money, ordinarily by signing a pay receipt that is part of the pay envelope. Such pay receipts are then retained by the payroll department for audit purposes and to refute any mistaken claims of nonpayment of insufficient payment.

If payment is made by check, the recommended practice is to require that the check be authorized by someone outside the payroll department, to reduce the possibility of fraud. Ordinarily the payroll department prepares the checks and forwards them to the treasurer for review and signature.

Most auditors with whom the author has consulted advocate the use of a check-writer to further reduce the possibility of fraud. The check-writer is a small machine that makes it virtually impossible to alter the amount written on the check, since the machine either embosses or perforates the amount onto the face of the check.

Several auditors suggest that the people assigned to deliver the checks or cash payments to the employees not be employees involved in computing the payroll or preparing the checks or cash payments. This further subdivision of responsibility will prevent an unauthorized person who has falsified the time worked or amount due or used a fictitious name from receiving the cash or forging a signature and cashing a check.

A third control procedure is to issue all checks with a preprinted serial number and assign someone not involved in preparing the payroll the responsibility of seeing to it that all checks numbers have been accounted for by either the checks distributed or incorrectly drawn checks that were voided. The numbers used are controlled through a numerical control register.

Every auditor whom the author consulted advocated paying by check rather than by cash, in order to minimize the chance of robbery or loss of the payroll prior to distribution. If cash must be used to pay wages, the auditors all advised that physical safeguards, including armed guards, be provided for.

JOURNALIZING PAYROLL TOTALS

The next step involves posting summary totals to the various general ledger accounts. Most manual payroll systems perform journalization in two-steps:

A payroll journal worksheet is prepared using standard columnar accounting paper. The names of the various ledger accounts to which postings will be made (reflecting departmental cost centers to be charged and cash, deduction, and withholding accounts such as FICA contributions and federal taxes withheld to be credited) are each entered at the top of a column. Individual amounts are posted from the consolidated earnings ledger sheet

to this worksheet, and a total amount is calculated for each
ledger account.

These totals are then posted directly from the worksheet to the
general ledger.

PREPARING REPORTS

Federal law requires that every employer create and maintain records of
the amounts earned by, withheld from, and paid to each employee and
that such data be reported periodically to the employee and to the
government. Specifically, the employer must

Make deductions from each employee's wages for such mandatory
purposes as tax withholding, FICA contributions, pension payments, and unemployment insurance premiums

Compute and report each employee's gross taxable income by de-
ducting payments for such nontaxable items as sick pay and
clothing allowance

Maintain a cumulative earnings record for each employee so that
deductions for FICA contributions will terminate when the employee's year-to-date earnings have reached the legal limit for
that calendar year

Submit periodic payroll tax returns and reports to various federal,
state, and local agencies

Furnish each employee, at least once annually, with a statement of
FICA taxable wages and contributions

The employee year-to-date earnings record recommended as part of
the consolidated earnings ledger makes it easier to compile this data,
since such a record assembles in a single, readily accessible summary
form all information relating to a given employee's cumulative year-to-
date earnings, deductions, and withholdings. From this single record
the following mandatory reports can be prepared:

Form 941: employer's quarterly federal tax return, a quarterly listing filed with the U.S. Internal Revenue Service indicating the
dollar amount of income tax withholdings and FICA contributions deducted from each employee's wages during the preceding
three months

Form W-2: withholding statement, an annual report each employer must file with the federal, state, and local tax authorities (with a copy to the employee) reporting each employee's annual gross and FICA earnings and amounts withheld for federal, state, and local taxes

State unemployment insurance reports, filed quarterly by each employer, used to report and transmit money withheld from employee wages and that contributed by the employer for unemployment insurance premiums

In addition to these mandatory reports, any manual payroll system must be capable of generating reports for the organization, on both a one-time and a continuing basis, relating to such things as personnel utilization, overtime worked, and turnover rates. In the manual payroll system the consolidated earnings ledger will supply this information.

Semiautomated System

This term is a misnomer; a more accurate term would be a *one-write payroll system.* Semiautomated payroll systems use special sets of forms (known as the *pegboard* system) that make possible simultaneous preparation of a variety of payroll records and forms (paychecks, check registers, and earnings records), greatly simplifying the manual process described previously.

The pegboard system (available from such vendors as Histacount Corporation of Melville, N.Y., and Safeguard Business Forms of Philadelphia, Pa.) has two components: a pegboard, and form sets. The pegboard is a hard, flat writing board with evenly spaced metal pegs positioned along one or more sides. The paper form sets are punched at the margins to conform with the peg arrangement; the forms in each set are collated and interleaved with carbon paper so that any data entered on the top form are simultaneously entered on the forms below. The form set is held securely by the metal pegs so that all the pages stay in place during use.

The pegboard-based semiautomated payroll system is similar in operation to the manual system with respect to the first three steps (establishing an employee payroll master record, reporting hours worked, and computing earnings). It is in the remaining three phases—preparing the paychecks, journalizing the payroll, and preparing the various reports and records—that the differences occur.

In the semiautomated payroll system all three of these latter steps are combined. A precollated carbon-interleaved form set consisting of a paycheck and earnings statement (top form), a check register, and an earnings record is mounted on the pegboard. When the paycheck is written, the data contained in it (employee name, gross earnings, amounts deducted and withheld, and net earnings) are entered simultaneously on the check register and on the earnings record (although often different headings are used for these), eliminating the need to prepare such records individually. These records, in turn, serve as the source for the various reports required by governmental tax authorities and by the organization's own management.

To be truly effective, pegboard systems, require skillful forms design. For this reason the office manager should seek the assistance of the companies that sell the systems when designing a pegboard-based semiautomated payroll system.

Computer-Based System

The payroll system is usually the first system that organizations convert from manual to computer processing. There is a valid reason why this is so. The payroll system meets every criterion for cost-effective computer-based processing:

A large number of transactions are involved.
The processing of the transactions is repetitive.
Common source documents are involved.
Mathematical computations must be performed.
Accuracy is important.
Other applications (such as figuring labor distributions) feed off the payroll system.

The computer-based payroll register differs significantly from either the manual or the semiautomated payroll system. Let us review the steps involved in setting up a computer-based payroll system to see where the differences lie.

Establishing a Payroll Master Record

With a computer-based payroll system, each employee's payroll master record is set up and maintained in a magnetic media format (that is, on magnetic tape or disks) rather than on paper. The same records that serve as the source for setting up the manual system's master record will suffice for the computer-based system.

Recording and Reporting Hours Worked

There is no change in the manner in which employees record and report their hours—timesheets or clock cards are as cost-effective with the computer-based system as with the manual payroll system.

Computing Employee Earnings

This is the area in which the significant changes occur. With a computer-based system, data relating to the hours each employee worked are converted from the ordinary writing (alphanumerics) appearing on timesheets or clock cards to machine readable data stored on magnetic tape or disks. Data entry may be done by keypunching, optical scanning, or directly from a data entry terminal.

The data relating to hours worked by each employee in a given period are maintained in order of employee identification numbers in a separate transaction file. This file is compared with the payroll master record by a computer to determine the employee's actual earnings; the regular and overtime hours reported in the transaction file are multiplied by the employee's pay rate contained in the payroll master record, and gross earnings are calculated. The amounts to be deducted and withheld are subtracted from these earnings, and each employee's net earnings are thus determined.

Preparing and Issuing Pay

As a by-product of calculating each employee's wages, the computer system is also capable of writing each employee's paycheck or of preparing a bank deposit form if the employee's wages are to be deposited to his or her bank account.

If wages are to be paid in cash, the process is the same as in the other payroll systems. The payroll department must either requisition the required currency and prepare the pay envelopes or else ask a bank to prepare the envelopes.

JOURNALIZING PAYROLL
TOTALS AND PREPARING REPORTS

Once payroll data have been encoded onto magnetic tape or disks, the data can be readily manipulated to produce many different types of useful reports and information. The ability to manipulate and reformat the data greatly facilitates the two remaining procedures in the computer-based payroll system—posting the data to the general ledger accounts and preparing reports and records for government agencies and for management. The program that directs the computer to perform the various processing steps involved in preparing the payroll can also instruct the computer to automatically summarize all the data and compile from it charges against or credits to the various general ledger accounts involved. In addition, the program can be written so that a cumulative year-to-date earnings record is automatically prepared as a by-product of the payroll processing and is maintained on magnetic tape on disks. The latter step is important, since the federal government now permits employers to submit form 941 (employer's quarterly federal tax return) and form W-2 (withholding statement) on a magnetic tape rather than on paper as long as certain standards concerning arrangement and identification of data, density of data, external and internal labeling, and the like are met.

Commercial Computer Services

Companies that do not have a computer can still avail themselves of the cost and operational benefits of a computer-based payroll system by using a commercial computer service. Such a service enables any company to obtain computerized processing without having to invest in computer hardware, software, or personnel. Computer services develop general-purpose computerized payroll systems that meet the needs of most companies in their immediate market area. Many organizations have found that commercial computer services are able to process their payrolls at less cost than and just as fast as they can do it themselves using any payroll system.

PETTY CASH

Most organizations have established a policy of depositing all money received as income in a demand deposit checking account and making all payments by check. While this will suffice in most cases, there are still times when currency will be required (for example, when small payments must be made for office supplies, postage due, or local travel). To meet this situation a special-purpose petty cash fund can be established.

The petty cash fund operates as follows:

An imprest fund is established in the amount of so many dollars. This means that at any one time the amount of unissued cash on hand in the petty cash fund and the receipts for cash payments already made from petty cash must equal the amount that has been imprest.

A petty cash fund is established by the cashier, who requests that a check be drawn that is equal to the full amount of the imprest fund.

The issuing of this check is recorded in a petty cash journal.

Upon receipt, the requested check is cashed and the currency placed in a special drawer (petty cash drawer) to await issue.

As disbursements are made from the petty cash fund, they are posted in the petty cash journal, and each recipient furnishes suitable supporting documentation (sales receipts, petty cash vouchers, etc.) for the amounts requested. The supporting documents are kept in the petty cash drawer until it becomes necessary to replenish the petty cash fund.

When it is necessary to replenish the petty cash fund, the cashier assembles all sales receipts and other documentation supporting disbursements, adds up the amount they represent, and requests from the accounts payable department a check equal to the amount of cash that has been disbursed.

After verifiying the accuracy of the totals, the accounts payable department perforates the supporting documents (to prevent re-use or alteration) and issues a check equal to the amount disbursed. The amount is recorded in the petty cash journal.

The cashier exchanges the check for currency, which is placed in the petty cash drawer to await issue.

There are a number of controls that every office manager should initiate to minimize the possibility of improper disbursement and fraud.

All supporting documentation should be made in ink to reduce the possibility of undetected alteration of dollar amounts.

As noted previously, all supporting documentation should be perforated by accounts payable to prevent its reuse and should be attached to the check request (or whatever form is used) for replenishing funds.

Periodically someone other than the cashier involved should audit the petty cash drawer, to make sure that the currency on hand plus the dollar value of the supporting documentation in the drawer equals the total amount of the imprest fund. For maximum effectiveness, such an audit should be performed unannounced and at highly irregular intervals.

The office manager would be well advised to maintain a close watch over the payroll and petty cash systems to ensure that each not only performs the organizational function it has been designed for but that it also does so in a manner that fosters improved employee morale and increases labor-management cooperation.

CHAPTER 9

Labor Unions and the Grievance Procedure

In recent years various labor unions and employee associations have had notable success in organizing professional, technical, and clerical office workers—the groups that historically have resisted attempts to organize them. Within the past two decades these groups have entered into office unions in such diverse fields of work as education, publishing, manufacturing, government, public utilities, and warehousing. The reasons are many: cost-of-living adjustments, paid to unionized coworkers but not to office workers, which are essential if salaries are to resist erosion by inflation; the threat of job loss due to automation, corporate relocation, or mergers; and sharp disagreement between top management and the rank-and-file office staff over how best to ensure the latter's future security.

Buoyed by their success, labor unions and employee associations have intensified their efforts at organizing previously nonunionized of-

fice employees in such industries as banking, insurance, and stock brokerage; in such service industries as computer and word processing
companies; and in such organizations as commercial airlines, which are
presently undergoing difficult economic times and frequent reductions
in force. Indeed, the office staff has been called by at least one
knowledgeable labor expert "a plum ripe for the picking."

IMPACT UPON THE OFFICE MANAGER

Unionization of the office staff has three primary effects on office management.

First, the *work rules* defined in the union contract may severely limit
the office manager's ability to organize and staff the organization's various support services to achieve maximum cost and operational efficiency. Indeed, in situations where the union or employee association is
particularly strong, the office manager may find that without that
union's or association's approval and cooperation he or she will be
unable to consolidate duplicated functions, eliminate unnecessary jobs,
make changes to improve productivity, or replace people with
machines.

Second, in order to ensure uniformity of policy and to prevent misinterpretation of the labor contract the office manager may have to take
much of the responsibility for interacting with the organized employees,
the shop steward, and the local, district, and national hierarchies of the
union or employee association. Few operating managers, the author has
noted, feel comfortable in dealing with labor relations, and as a result
they are eager to transfer this responsibility and authority to the office
manager.

Third, a common complaint among organizations that have become
unionized is that under the terms of their labor contract the union or
employee association is able to control many of the economic aspects of
the business. Such inflexibility may prove troublesome to the office
manager who wishes to adopt some change to meet changing operating
needs, but is prevented by a resistant union or employee association
from doing so.

Given such situations, it is crucial that the office manager acquire a
working knowledge of labor relations, even if his or her organization is

not currently unionized or is not the target of a union's or employee association's attempt at organizing.

LABOR RELATIONS

Labor relations is a management function concerned with

Addressing the efforts of unions and employee associations to organize the organization's employees

Ensuring that personnel policies and practices are in accord with the various provisions of any labor contracts that may be in effect

Negotiating new and revised labor contracts with the union or employee associations selected by employees to be their bargaining agent

Providing a mechanism through which employees can air their grievances, receive an impartial and timely review of them, and obtain relief or redress if it is determined that the grievances are justified

A viable labor relations program is as essential for a nonunionized organization as it is for one that is unionized. It has been proved many times that companies that voluntarily establish a labor relations program to compare their own personnel policies with those in unionized organizations and, if economically possible, maintain parity with such policies, may be able to thwart unionization attempts.

In addition, by acquiring a working knowledge of labor relations, particularly with respect to collective bargaining and grievance processes, and providing a standby labor relations program before it is actually needed, the company will be in a position to respond quickly to any initial organizing attempts by a labor union or employee association. Such a fast reaction will increase the possibility of successfully thwarting the organizing attempt.

LEGAL BACKGROUND FOR LABOR RELATIONS

Unions and employee associations exist for one purpose—to represent their members in dealings with their employers in such matters as hiring, promotion, and discharge policies, compensation and fringe benefits, working hours, rest and break periods, and safety and health conditions. This concept—employees using the services of a third party to represent their interests in dealing with employers—is known as *collective bargaining*.

Acceptance by American management of the right of employees to use collective bargaining was hard-won. Blood was spilled, the economy was imperiled by nationwide work stoppages, and deep schisms were created among our nation's various economic and social strata. Given such a deleterious environment, it became necessary for first the federal and later the state governments to interject themselves into labor–management dealings to both fill the need for an impartial, third-party arbiter and regulator and to minimize the impact of labor–management unrest upon the general safety and welfare of the rest of our nation.

As a result the concept of collective bargaining as it exists today has been structured largely by federal and state legislation and regulatory requirements, as well as by judicial and regulatory agency interpretation of such legislation and regulations. Today, at both the national and state levels, the collective bargaining rights, obligations, and limitations of employers, employees, and labor unions and employee associations are clearly defined.

Federal Legislation

Three federal laws provide the major legal basis for labor–management relations:

The Wagner Act of 1935, which stipulates that employees have the legal right to organize into labor unions or employee associations and to use such organizations as their collective bargaining agents in dealing with employers on matters concerning wages and working conditions; established the National Labor Relations Board (NLRB) to administer and enforce the various provisions of the Wagner Act

The Taft-Hartley Act of 1947, which was enacted to restore what Congress viewed as an imbalance of labor relations laws and reg-

ulations in favor of the unions by imposing a series of prohibi-
tions on the unions' dealings with both employers and employees
The Landrum-Griffin Act of 1959 (whose formal title is "The Labor-Management Reporting and Disclosure Act of 1959") was the
result of the McClellan hearings, a Senate investigation into un-
ethical and illegal practices by certain unions and their officers.
This law imposes standards of conduct on American labor unions
and their leadership and safeguards the rights of both employers
and employees in their dealings with the unions.

A variety of other federal laws have affected labor–management relations, though to a far lesser extent. The *Welfare and Pension Funds
Disclosure Act of 1958* includes provisions requiring the secretary of
labor to oversee the structuring and administration of employee welfare
and pension plans. The *Byrnes Anti-Strikebreaking Act of 1938* prohibits the interstate transporation of persons to interfere with peaceful
picketing or to otherwise impede the collective bargaining process.

State Legislation

In addition, many of the states have adopted laws relating to labor relations, including "right-to-work laws" (enacted by twenty states), which
basically remove all requirements of union membership as a condition
of employment, and fair employment practices laws (enacted by almost
every state), designed to provide all persons with the opportunity to
gain employment within the framework of existing labor relations laws
and regulations.

Federal and State
Regulations and Administrative Rulings

In addition, the various federal and state regulatory agencies from time
to time issue administrative regulations and quasilegal interpretations
that are mandatory for those organizations and individuals subject to the
agencies' jurisdiction. Until challenged and set aside in either federal
and/or state courts or reversed by the NLRB, these regulations have the

force of law and must be adhered to. Examples of such administrative regulations are those issued by the NLRB with respect to when and where employees may distribute organizing literature and what constitutes unlawful interference with the collective bargaining process.

Conflicting Laws or Regulations

The U.S. Constitution stipulates that when federal and state laws or regulations conflict with each other the federal version will prevail. With this in mind one may assume that it is prudent to follow federal laws and regulations rather than conflicting state versions.

Judicial Interpretation

A significant force in the establishment of collective bargaining "do's and don't's" are the various federal and state courts. Such groups, by their very charter, are given the responsibility of determining the constitutionality of specific laws, regulations, and lower court decisions within their jurisdiction, as well as of the legality of specific actions. As a result they exercise a dominant influence over labor relations law and practice.

LEGAL REQUIREMENTS OF
FEDERAL AND STATE LABOR LAWS

The following summary describes the effect of the various federal and state labor laws upon the three parties (the employer, employee, and labor union or employee association) to the collective bargaining process.

Employees are guaranteed the right to

Form, join, or assist labor unions or employee associations
Bargain collectively with their employers through representatives
of their own choosing

Participate in lawful strikes involving their own union at their place of employment

Present grievances to their supervisors either directly or through their union representatives and have union representation at the time the grievance is heard

Terminate their affiliation with a specific labor union or employee association by a procedure known as *decertification*

Employers are subject to the following requirements:

They must not interfere (by coercion or other means) with attempts by their employees to form, join, or assist a labor union or employee association.

They cannot refuse to bargain collectively and in good faith with the labor union or employee association selected by the majority of eligible employees as their bargaining agent.

They must comply with the environmental and physical safety and health standards mandated by the U.S. Department of Labor and by the various state and (if applicable) local government agencies.

They must neither dominate nor assist any labor union or employee association by, for example,

Providing *direct* financial support in the form of loans, free use of the organization's facilities, equipment, or supplies, or by permitting union operation of vending machines on the organization's premises

Providing *indirect* support by promoting the attributes of the union or employee association to employees or by falsely crediting the union for newly awarded wage increases and improved fringe benefits

They cannot discriminate against any employee in hiring, promoting, job assignment, or termination as a result of labor or employee association membership or involvement (except in those instances in which membership in the labor union or employee association within a specified period of time after hiring is defined in the labor contract as a condition of initial or continued employment)

They must not take retaliatory action (such as discharge or harrassment) against any employee for filing a grievance or testifying against the organization in a regulatory hearing.

Labor unions and employee associations are subject to the following requirements:

They cannot refuse to bargain collectively and in good faith with their members' employers.

They cannot force an employee to join a union as a condition of employment or force an employer to discriminate against any employee who chooses not to join the labor union or employee association unless such membership is a stipulated condition of employment as defined in the labor contract.

They cannot influence or attempt to influence an employer in his or her choice of the person who will represent the employer's interests in the collective bargaining and grievance processes.

They cannot attempt to gain recognition from an employer as a bargaining agent for certain employees when another labor union or employee association is *currently* certified as such.

They cannot promote or precipitate a strike in order to force an employer to favor their union over another in a jurisdictional dispute.

They must have a consititution and by-laws and a members' bill of rights.

They must establish and adhere to standards for trusteeships and elections.

They must take steps to identify possible conflicts of interest on the part of their officers.

They must periodically file reports with the U.S. Secretary of Labor concerning the labor union's or employee association's financial transactions and status, policies and procedures, trusteeships, and conflict-of-interest monitoring.

TYPES OF UNIONS
AND EMPLOYEE ASSOCIATIONS

American labor unions and employee associations can be classified in two ways: (1) by the craft or industries from which they draw their members, or (2) by their affiliation or nonaffiliation with the AFL-CIO.

Craft vs. Industrial Unions

American labor unions and employee associations are classified as either *craft unions* or *industrial unions.*

A *craft union* is one in which all members are engaged in the same occupation but do not necessarily work in either a single or related industry. The International Association of Machinist and Aerospace Workers (IAM) is typical of craft unions. Its over one million members are employed as machinists in such varied industries as transportation, chemical and food processing, heavy manufacturing, and machine tool and die industries.

An *industrial union* is one in which all members are employed in a single industry but not in the same occupation. The United Auto Workers (UAW) is a typical industrial union. Its membership is drawn from organizations that manufacture automobiles, trucks, and buses, but the members do not perform the same duties or work in the same occupation. Some UAW members work as assemblers, others paint vehicles, others help to make the vehicles and still others help to make the vehicle's components.

An employee association may be either a craft or an industrial union, or even a combination of the two. The Civil Service Employees Association (CSEA) is typical of an employee association organized on an industrial basis: all of its members work for government agencies but not in the same job. The Major League Baseball Players Association (MLBPA) and the Screen Actors' Guild (SAG) are typical employee associations that are organized on both a craft and an industrial basis. The former grants membership to professional baseball players who are actively employed by a National or American League team; the latter grants membership to actors and actresses who work in the film industry.

The rationale for organizing on a craft or an industrial basis is purely theoretical. Unions that choose the craft organization do so in the belief that their members bargaining interests can best be served by threatening employers, if necessary, with the total loss of all persons skilled in a particular craft. Proponents of the industrial organization concept feel that the threat of closing down an entire industry gives them a stronger bargaining position.

AFL-CIO Affiliation

The second category of labor unions and employee associations is based upon their relationship with the AFL-CIO—the giant national confederation of labor unions.

An *affiliated union* is one that has voluntarily chosen to join the AFL-CIO, a national organization composed of labor unions and employee associations that band together for centrally coordinated political and economic action while still retaining much of their organizational and operational autonomy. In this respect the AFL-CIO has been likened to the U.S. Chamber of Commerce.

An *independent (or nonaffiliated) union* is one that is not a member of the AFL-CIO. The Brotherhood of Locomotive Engineers (BLE) is an example of an independent union.

ORGANIZATIONAL STRUCTURE

The typical labor union or employee association consists of a three-level hierarchy.

At the top is the national headquarters or, if the union charters local unions outside the United States, the *international headquarters,* which is responsible for developing and delivering such varied services as these to its membership:

Providing skilled negotiators to assist in the collective bargaining process

Establishing and distributing a strike fund to help ease the financial burdens during a work stoppage

Lobbying for the interests of its membership at the national, state, and local legislative levels

Training local leaders in arbitration, grievance, and negotiation techniques

Providing statistical data and research to help local leaders justify their members' wage and fringe benefit demands during the collective bargaining process

Publishing a newspaper to keep members aware of current and developing issues affecting them, as well as to foster a greater esprit-de-corps

Establishing and administering college scholarships for members' children

Providing skilled organizers to assist interested employees to obtain certification of the labor union or employee association as their collective bargaining agent

In the middle level of the hierarchy is the *district headquarters,* organized and staffed to serve the requirements of members in a particular geographic area. Usually this level is found only in larger unions, in which the geographic distance and number of locals involved make it difficult or unduly expensive for the national headquarters to provide all services. The district headquarters may be compared to the regional sales office of a corporation that is responsible for establishing, overseeing the activities of, and supporting a network of local sales offices.

The *local headquarters* of the labor union or employee association operates at the grassroots level, interacting on a routine basis with both its membership and their employers in matters relative to wages, benefits, and working conditions. In addition, the local headquarters is responsible for helping its members prepare and present any grievances that result from an employer's alleged violation of a current labor contract.

THE UNION ORGANIZING PROCESS

The National Labor Relations Board (NLRB) has established a highly structured procedure to govern the union organizing process or the manner in which employees are given the choice of joining or forming a labor union or an employee association. As a key member of the organization's management team, the office manager must be familiar with this process, since he or she will undoubtedly be deeply involved in the organization's efforts to resist such efforts.

Certification

The initial idea of attempting to organize a given organization's employees may originate either from employees of the organization or from the labor organization. In the first case one or more employees contact the particular labor union or employee association involved and indicate an interest in attempting to work towards having the labor union or employee association certified as the collective bargaining agent for themselves and their coworkers. In the second case the labor union or employee association on its own initiative decides to attempt to organize the workers in a particular organization.

Once the decision is made to attempt to organize, the labor union or employee association dispatches a *field organizer,* whose task is to convince at least 30% of the company's employees that it would be in their best interests to sign an *authorization card* naming the union or employee association as their bargaining agent. If the field organizer is successful in obtaining this percentage of signed authorization cards, a petition may be filed with the NLRB requesting that a *representation election* be held. All employees who would be represented by the labor union or employee association requesting certification are entitled to vote for or against certification.

The NLRB is empowered to determine which employees in a given organization are entitled to vote in a representation election by defining the composition of the *bargaining unit.* The following classes of employees are routinely excluded from a bargaining unit: supervisory and managerial personnel; temporary personnel; secretaries and administrative assistants who would be privy to confidential information relative to industrial relations policies; employee-stockholders who sit on the organization's board of directors; and plant protection personnel. The latter, by law, must belong to a bargaining unit that is composed solely of other plant protection personnel.

After the bargaining unit has been defined, the NLRB might require the employer to provide the labor union or employee association with the current names and mailing addresses of all persons included in the bargaining unit, so that the union or association can send to their prospective members any mail or information that is necessary to plead its case.

During the period prior to the representation election both the employer and the union or employee association can present their arguments for or against certification to the persons included in the bargaining unit. However, the NLRB has established very stringent rules that must be followed under penalty of having the election results set aside if there are violations:

Neither the employer or union or association may make an election speech to groups of employees assembled on company time within the twenty-four hours preceding the opening of the polls.

The employer must post conspicuous signs on the premises advising when and where the election will be held.

Neither party may present information that is designed to pit one group of workers against another (for example, racial or sexist inflammatory statements).

Employers cannot threaten employees with retaliation if the union is victorious nor provide rewards if it is defeated.

No electioneering may occur within a 100-foot radius of the polling place.

Sample ballots cannot be marked in any way that suggests a vote for or against the union or employee association.

The representation election will be scheduled by the NLRB to ensure maximum participation by all eligible persons. If the employees affected work two shifts, the polls will be open at times that will be equally convenient to each shift. As a rule the NLRB will try to hold the representation election on the employer's premises and in many cases will authorize the use of mail-in ballots for those persons who due to vacation or illness are unable to vote in person.

Both the employer and the labor union or employee association may designate one or more *election observers*. Such persons are free to challenge voters' identity or the eligibility of a given person to vote and may help the NLRB representative tally the ballots. The law stipulates that all election observers be nonsupervisory and nonmanagerial personnel, unless each party agrees to the contrary.

After the polls are closed the NLRB representative, assisted by the election observers and overseen by the employer's managerial and supervisory personnel and members of the employees' organizing committee tallies the votes that have been cast. The decision to certify rests solely upon this tally, and only a simple majority is required. If a majority of votes are cast in favor of the labor union or employee association, the NLRB issues a certification of representation, which designates the labor union or employee association as the collective bargaining agent. If the vote is against certification, the NLRB issues a notice stating that the majority of eligible employees who cast their ballots chose not to select the labor union or employee association to be their collective bargaining agent.

The certification process may be shortened in two ways:

If authorization cards have been signed by 30% or more of eligible employees, and the employer may agree to recognize the labor union or employee association as the employees' bargaining agent.

If 50% or more of the eligible employees sign authorization cards, the NLRB can certify the labor union or employee association as the collective bargaining agent, eliminating the need for an election.

Once certified, the labor union or employee association will begin to prepare to negotiate a *labor contract* (also referred to as a *bargaining agreement*), a document that specifies the conditions of each member's employment, wages, fringe benefits, and hours, and specifies safety rules. A formal organizational structure will be established for the bargaining unit. Depending upon its size it may be chartered by the labor organization's national headquarters as a new local, or it may be assigned to an existing local. A *bargaining committee* will be established, and a list of demands and proposals relating to wages, benefits, and other contractual matters will be prepared. The bargaining committee and the employer then proceed to negotiate the labor contract under which the members of the union and the employer will operate during the life of the agreement.

Decertification

Decertification is the process by which a majority of the members of a bargaining unit withdraw the authority previously granted to a labor union or employee association to serve as their collective bargaining agent. The initial action for decertification may be taken by an individual member of the bargaining unit or by a group of members; it cannot, however, be taken by the employer.

The decertification process, which can be initiated twelve months after the original certification, provides that another NLRB-conducted election be held, and that if a majority of members vote against the union or association it will be decertified. A new collective bargaining agent may then be selected, or if the majority so desires the collective bargaining unit may be dissolved.

The NLRB has very strict regulations concerning decertification. The action must originate with and be developed by members of the bargaining unit *only*. Employers may neither suggest or encourage decertification in any way.

THE GRIEVANCE PROCEDURE

A key provision of every labor contract is the grievance procedure, a process by which (1) an individual member of the bargaining unit, or (2) the labor union or employee association, or (3) the employer can obtain adjudication on its claim that a provision of the labor contract has been violated. Normally the grievance procedure involves a claim against management. It is filed by either an employee or the union or employee association. The procedure for processing a grievance varies somewhat from one organization to another, but this is the typical sequence of events:

An employee who is a member of the bargaining unit feels that a condition of employment, as defined in the bargaining unit's labor contract or in past practice (which constitutes part of the labor contract), has been violated.

The employee presents the complaint to his or her immediate supervisor, explaining in what way he or she believes that the labor contract has been violated, and requests immediate correction.

If the employee is not satisfied with the supervisor's response, the shop steward is contacted and the situation discussed. If the shop steward agrees that there has been a violation of the labor contract or of past practice, he or she meets with the employee's supervisor to attempt to resolve the situation.

If the Shop Steward is dissatisfied with the supervisor's answer, the matter may be presented to the local union's grievance committee or its chief steward (as applicable). They review the situation and take one of the following actions:

Proceed with the grievance, if there appears to be a clear violation of the labor contract.

Obtain further information, if adequate facts upon which to judge the validity of the employee's claim are not available.

Urge the employee to drop the grievance if it appears unfounded or if there is little likelihood of a favorable judgment.

It should be noted that most unions, while eager to respond to legitimate grievances of their members, will discourage any that lack validity or that are unfounded. Prescreening employee grievances is one of the most valuable services performed by the grievance committee or the chief steward.

If it is decided to proceed with the grievance process, a formal complaint is prepared that provides details about the alleged violation of the labor contract. The shop steward signs the complaint and forwards it to the employee's supervisor, who reviews it and either acknowledges or rejects the complaint, adds a brief justification for the decision, and signs and returns the grievance to the shop steward.

If the employee and the shop steward (acting alone or in consultation with the local union's grievance committee or chief steward) decide to appeal the supervisor's ruling, the grievance is referred to the executive to whom the supervisor reports. After calling in the complainant and the supervisor and consulting with the office manager to obtain clarification of the labor contract, this executive reaches a decision as to whether a violation of the labor contract has occurred. As in the case of the supervisor's review, the reasons for the judgment are noted, and the statement is signed and returned to the shop steward.

Should the ruling be in favor of the employee, the unfair practice is stopped and, if applicable, restitution is made. Should the ruling be against the employee, there are two higher levels of appeal—

one to senior management and, if unsuccessful, to an independent arbiter whose ruling is binding upon all parties.

It is crucial that both the office manager and his or her associates
develop a good rapport with the local shop steward, as well as with the
local grievance committee and chief steward. They should, for their
mutual benefit, establish a working relationship, since they are presum-
ably resonable people who are just as anxious to right a wrong as to
prevent a devisive, counterproductive, unnecessary labor dispute.

The grievance process, if fairly and properly administered, can be a
powerful means to foster harmony between labor and management
and improve employee morale. For this reason all office managers
should actively support its operation.

CHAPTER 10

Incentive Programs

For more than a century incentive programs in which each employee's earnings are based upon his or her individual job performance have been used to increase the quality and quantity of work produced by factory, warehouse, and other blue-collar workers. Surprisingly, however, the concept of tying an individual's wages to his or her productivity has not gained the same degree of acceptance in the office environment. Consequently most office workers are compensated simply on a straight-time basis—a method that does not recognize and reward better than average job performance. Under this system motivating office employees to increase their productivity becomes extremely difficult. Indeed, in the opinion of knowledgeable office productivity consultants, it is virtually impossible to induce office personnel to work harder to produce more, higher-quality output without providing them with the financial incentive to do so.

In view of this, office managers seeking a way to increase the quantity and quality of work produced within their organization would be well advised to consider the feasibility of establishing an incentive program for those office activities in which it is applicable.

GENERAL OVERVIEW

Any office job may be included in an incentive program provided that it is possible to establish a definition of what constitutes a *standard level of performance*. Such a standard may be expressed in a variety of ways: dollar volume of business sold, number of transactions processed, or number of units produced. Employees in any office job, from the most structured (that of a file clerk) to the most creative and unstructured (that of a computer programmer or salesperson), can each be paid according to their individual productivity.

Reduced to basics, all incentive programs are similar in approach:

A *standard level of performance* is established for each job included in the incentive program. This level may be established in a variety of ways:

By a time study, if the job is routine, procedurized, and readily measureable

By past performance data, if they are available

By empirical standards (arbitrary setting of what are judged to be attainable performance goals) based upon the organization's best estimates. This approach is generally employed where sales, public contact, and professional and creative work are involved.

Standard performance may therefore be expressed in terms of dollar sales per month, pages typed per week, or telephone interviews completed per day, and so forth.

Productivity data are then recorded on a continuing basis for each employee, indicating the volume of work produced, using the measure of standard performance

Each individual's productivity is then divided by the standard level of performance that has been established for that particular job. The result is the *percentage of efficiency* at which each employee is working.

The percentage of efficiency rating is then used to determine the incentive payment that will be given to each employee.

INCENTIVE PROGRAMS
AND CORPORATE PROFITABILITY

Productivity studies conducted by a variety of companies and government agencies have reached the following conclusions about the productivity of office personnel:

If no program exists to measure each employee's daily output and to compare his or her productivity to a standard level of performance, the average office employee will function at between 60 and 65% of efficiency.

If each employee's daily output is measured and subsequently related to a standard level of performance, the average office employee will function at a level of efficiency that ranges from 80 to 90%.

If, however, a well-designed, well-administered incentive plan is established that properly and effectively ties monetary rewards to individual or group productivity, the average office worker will continually function at a performance level that ranges from 120 to 130% of standard.

This increased productivity affects overall profitability in two ways:

It leads to greater utilization of available equipment and personnel, obviating or at least reducing the need to increase such equipment or personnel in order to achieve greater output levels.

It leads to a decrease in unit labor costs *until* the 100% efficiency level is reached. Beyond that, most incentive programs return no additional decreases in unit labor costs, since the value of the additional effiency typically is returned to the participating employees in the form of incentive payments. Still, it should be noted that savings in unit labor costs that result from an incentive program usually are so significant that they fully justify the program.

One further benefit deserves mention; following the implementation of an incentive program, employee absenteeism and turnover generally decline. As a result the costs of paying overtime or hiring temporary help also decline.

IMPLEMENTING AN INCENTIVE PROGRAM

Setting Goals

The initial step in planning for an incentive program is to decide what goals the program is designed to accomplish. The goals may be either tactical or strategic.

Tactical goals are designed to improve the organization's general functioning. Some typical tactical goals are to

Improve the relationship between workers and management, improve morale, and decrease animosity

Attract better qualified employees

Retain qualified employees (reduce turnover)

Motivate personnel to maximum productivity, thereby freeing supervisors and managers from supervisory duties and allowing them to devote more of their workday to planning and organizing

Provide an atmosphere that will lead employees to resist any attempts to organize a union

Strategic goals are designed to give the organization an advantage over its competitors. Some typical strategic goals are to

Increase the organization's market share

Increase overall productivity

Increase profitability

Increase returns on investment

Increase product quality and reliability

Once it is determined what the goals of the incentive program are, the office manager needs to decide whether the goals are attainable. The following questions must be considered:

Are the goals realistic and attainable given the current and near-term financial and operational situation? The office manager and the organization's top management must realize that an incentive program is far from a panacea. It usually will raise employee productivity and reduce per-unit output costs, both of which will be steps toward realizing many of the possible goals of the program, but it will not in itself overcome problems that are caused by poor supervision, inadequate or improper equipment, or undercapitalization. It is extremely important to be as objective as possible in assessing whether the goals that prompted consideration of the incentive program can be met by it.

What are the general feelings of the employees towards management? Realistically, if the employees are generally distrustful of the management and their attitude cannot be changed, there is little possibility that any incentive program will succeed.

Is there any indication that influential employees have had a bad experience in dealing with incentive programs under previous employers? As with the preceding factor, the presence of a well-liked, influential, or vocal critic of incentive programs is a danger that must be neutralized if an incentive program is to suceeed. It may be possible to mitigate some of this criticism by enlisting one or more of the critics to help plan and implement the efforts.

Is the workforce motivated by the opportunity to earn perhaps 20 to 30% more as a result of working harder? Strange though it may seem, many people are not motivated by the opportunity to increase their earnings unless the increase is truly significant. Again, the office manager must make a judgment as to whether a potential increase in earnings of 20 to 30% will motivate the office employees to accept the incentive program and work to maximize their productivity.

Determining Which Jobs to Include

As was noted earlier virtually every office job can be included in an incentive program, since it is possible to quantify the output of most office jobs. Most office managers with whom the author has spoken advocate a two-stage approach to bringing jobs under the incentive program. They suggest starting with the routine jobs that are readily measured (such as data entry, transcription of dictated or handwritten input, filing, mail sorting, and operation of reprographics equipment). Then when the problems have been worked out and the program has gained acceptance, the less routine jobs (such as customer service, cashier operations, and sales) can be added. The ultimate goal is to bring as many jobs as possible into the incentive program.

Selecting the Plan

The next task is to select the type of incentive plan that will be used. The three general categories of incentive plans are: (1) one-for-one; (2) increasing bonus as performance increases, and (3) decreasing bonus as performance increases.

One-for-one plans. These are the most common of all incentive plans, as well as the easiest to understand and the most economical to administer. Under a one-for-one plan, employees receive a bonus of 1% of their pay for each 1% increase in productivity they attain over the standard level of performance (which is 100% efficiency). Therefore, if an employee who earns $6.50 an hour achieves a productivity of 110% of standard, he or she would receive an additional 65 cent bonus, or a net wage of $7.15.

One-for-one incentive plans give employees the opportunity to increase their earnings to a level substantially above the going rate for the job.

Increasing bonus as performance increases plans. These, as the name suggests, provide for the base bonus rates to increase as the employee's productivity increases. For example, the plan can allow the employee to receive a three quarters of 1% increase in earnings as a result of every 1% increase in productivity between 101 and 110% of standard, a seven-eighths of 1% increase between 111 and 115% of standard, and so forth, on a graduated scale. Such an arrangement rewards better than average productivity while still promising greater rewards for superior individual performance. For that reason many office managers favor this type of incentive program.

Decreasing bonus as performance increases plans. These, in the opinion of most observers with whom the author has spoken, are counterproductive, since they destroy rather than foster maximum individual productivity. Incentive programs of this type, as one would rightfully conclude from their name, have a downward sliding scale; the more productive the employee is, the lower the bonus rate that he or she receives. For example, the employee may receive a 1% increase in earnings for every 1% increase above standard performance between performance levels of from 101 and 109%. Between the levels of 110 and 119% this bonus rate may drop to three-quarters of 1% per 1% increase in productivity. With such an arrangement it is only logical that employees will peg their production at the point where they receive maximum earnings for their effort.

Incentive programs that use bonus payments of this type are generally those in which management distrusts the accuracy of their standards and in which the standard level of performance is estimated or developed by empirical means rather than by time study or an analysis of historical performance data.

In selecting the type of incentive plan that will work best for his or her organization, the office manager considers all aspects—the costs of each type of plan, the ease with which the plan can be administered, and the ease with which employees can understand the details. Again, unless one has very serious reservations about the possibility of developing realistic standards, one will avoid incentive plans that provide for the bonus rate to decrease as the level of performance increases.

Establishing a Budget

Incentive programs may be funded with the savings or profits generated by the participants' increased productivity, or by allocating a specific, often arbitrary amount for payment of bonuses. The decision to select one alternative over the other will be based largely upon two factors: the organization's cash flow situation, and the office manager's perception of top management's attitude toward the incentive program.

If cash is continually tight or if the office manager knows that top management is unfavorably disposed toward an incentive program, it will be politically sound to recommend that the program be funded out of actual savings and profits that are realized by the program. In this case there will necessarily be a lapse of time between the earning of the incentive bonus and its payment. The delay could discourage the participating employees and the labor unions that represent them.

If, however, the organization's top management is bullish on the incentive program and if the cash flow situation permits, it would be wise for the office manager to recommend that an arbitrary amount (say 12% of the annual base salaries of the participants) be set aside to provide for the timely payment of incentive earnings. In this way there will be no lengthy delays between the earning of the incentive bonus and its receipt, a factor that will greatly increase the acceptance of the program by the participants and their unions.

Relationship Between Salary and Bonuses

To ensure the success of an incentive program, a firm policy about the relationship between guaranteed base earnings and incentive earnings must be established. One approach is to treat each as a separate factor in overall compensation. A base salary is assigned to the particular job, taking into account prevailing wages paid by other organizations for similar jobs in the local area. The purpose of this base (guaranteed) salary is to enable the organization to attract and retain qualified workers with a given skill. Any incentive earnings reflect an employee's increased productivity and value to the company and do not in any way affect the basic guaranteed wage that the employee receives for his or her labor.

On the other hand, one can view the base salary and the incentive earnings as two components that taken together comprise the employee's actual earnings. With this arrangement the guaranteed salary will probably be less than that paid in the area by other employers without an incentive program, but if incentive earnings are added, the participant's total earnings will be greater than the going wage. Such an arrangement, proponents point out, helps in recruiting and retaining the more productive type of office worker—people who have sufficient confidence in their own ability to take less in guaranteed wages in order to earn more in the long run.

Either arrangement has its advantages and limitations. Such factors as the existence of an office union, the availability of skilled workers, and the level of productivity that must be achieved before the employee's base salary and incentive earnings bring him or her to the prevailing wage level will affect the decision to recommend one or the other alternative to top management.

Determining the Basis for Participation

Incentive programs may be designed so that employees participate as individuals, but an alternative is group participation.

Individual participation. With this arrangement, each participant is in a matter of speaking in business for him- or her-self. The employee's own output—and his or her's alone—will determine the amount of incentive earnings he or she will receive. Even if others in the department who perform the same tasks achieve greater or lesser levels of productivity, this particular participant's incentive earnings will not be affected in any way.

Group participation. With this arrangement each participant is assigned as part of a team consisting of employees who all perform the same job or task. The individual output of each team member is calculated, averaged, and compared to the standard level of performance that has been established for that particular job or task. If the team's average productivity exceeds the standard level of performance, all members of the team share equally in the incentive bonus, regardless of their productivity or performance level.

A variation of the group participation plan, frequently used when individual workers are closely supported by one or more assistants or support personnel, is to group all such personnel into a team. Again, the individual worker's productivity determines the total amount of incentive earnings paid to the team. The earnings are then distributed among the individual workers and assistants or support personnel, according to a predetermined formula. For example, if the bonus rate provides for a payment of 1% of earnings for performance above the standard level, the individual worker will receive three-quarters of 1%, and the supporting team members will share in the remaining one-quarter of 1%. This arrangement, known as the *Bedaux plan,* recognizes the fact that in many jobs productivity or performance depends upon the joint efforts not only of the person who performs the job but also of one or more support or subordinate personnel. Therefore all should share in the rewards.

This approach is not unlike that taken in restaurants, in which all employees, from kitchen help to waitresses, commonly share in the customers' tips. The rationale is that each has contributed to some degree to the customer's satisfaction.

As the reader has probably concluded, however, group plans do favor the less productive and average participant at the expense of the highly productive employee. Naturally many highly productive workers oppose the group plan. The group plan does have one major advantage over the individual plan, though; in addition to providing a way of including support personnel in the incentive program, the overall productivity of groups is generally higher than would be achieved if the participants' individual productivity were the sole basis for determining bonuses. Group participation does in fact foster a spirit of cooperation that, coupled with the normal pressure of keeping pace with the rest of the group, usually leads to increased productivity by all the participants.

In addition to the persons who actually perform a given task or job and their support and subordinate personnel, it is common practice to include in the incentive program the supervisors of persons who are paid the bonuses. Doing so, it has been found, invariably further increases overall productivity, since the supervisor has a direct financial interest in the group's productivity and will make sure that the conditions necessary to achieve maximum output are provided—that equipment is properly serviced workers have adequate supplies of materials, and that deficient performers receive timely corrective or on-the-job training.

Establishing Performance Goals

In considering performance goals the office manager will need to decide (1) what should be measured; (2) how it should be measured; (3) how to adjust standards to allow for unusual circumstances and the likelihood of errors.

What to measure. In every job or task there are one or more outputs that typically complete a given processing cycle. In filing, such outputs include records being placed in a file cabinet, retrieved for reference, and refiled. In reprographics, outputs include the preparing of masters and the reproducing of duplicate copies. Counting such outputs will provide a figure for the number of transactions processed by a given employee.

The office manager's task is to review the workflow for the job or task to be included in the incentive program and subdivide it into one or more processing cycles, each concluding with a specified output. He or she might find it advantageous to flow chart the various job or task elements as was described in Chapter 4. With the aid of the flow chart, identifying the various outputs becomes a relatively simple matter. These outputs may then serve as the measureable items.

How to measure. A unit of measurement should reflect some element that is common to the processing steps being measured. If, as in the case of a data entry operation, the volume of data to be encoded varies from one transaction to the next, it would be incorrect to attempt to measure output in terms of total transactions; rather, measurement in terms of the *number* of characters encoded would be much more reasonable. Likewise, if a unit of measurement is to be established for a customer service operation, the most meaningful unit would be "customer contacts completed." A little ingenuity is really all that is required to ensure that the most appropriate unit of measurement is selected.

Adjusting for special situations or errors. In establishing performance goals, one must be alert for instances in which various tasks have widely varying degrees of difficulty. For example, in a word-processing function the time required to transcribe a statistical report that includes both columns of figures and narrative text is generally considerably longer than the time required for a simple narrative letter. It is good practice to assign weights to each type of output in accordance with the degree of difficulty of the task. Determining relative degrees of difficulty requires taking a sample of the time needed to produce each output and determining the average time. Then, using the simplest transaction as the base and assigning to that transaction a weight of 1, each output is assigned a weight that reflects the increased time it takes to complete the task in relation to the simplest output. When output is reported, these assigned weights will present a truer picture of each individual's productivity and performance.

Each employee's output should also be adjusted to reflect errors that require total or partial redoing of the job. The employee's output is reduced by a factor that reflects the time required to correct the error or defect. Such adjustments are of course arbitrary rather than absolute, although in a number of companies a formal chargeback system that credits the account of the person who corrects the work and debits the account of the employee who made the error allows for accurate adjustments. Adjusting productivity ratings to reflect less than perfect quality helps to guard against the development of slipshod work habits by employees who are striving for maximum output.

Developing a Payment Schedule

There are no firm rules as to when incentive earnings should be paid. Some organizations pay them in the first paycheck issued after they are earned, others on a monthly or quarterly basis; still others accumulate incentive bonuses and pay them out once annually. Usually the less the guaranteed salary paid to the participant the more frequently will the incentive earnings be paid out. In general, word processing operators are paid bonuses once a month or more frequently, while salespersons are paid quarterly, semiannually, or annually.

Other factors such as the company's cash flow situation and the cost of money affect the frequency with which incentive earnings are paid out.

Documenting the Plan

The final step before presenting the plan for review by top management is to state its features and rules in writing. This is a key ingredient in gaining management and employee acceptance. It has been shown time and again that unless an incentive plan is written down in a format and style that will be readily understood by all participants, as well as by supervisors and managers, it will rarely function as hoped for. The written description must be clear and must include, at a minimum, a full description of the type of plan, the methods for calculating incentive earnings, the payment schedule, and the circumstances under which the standard levels of performance can be revised.

The documentation of the plan should form a portion of the package that is submitted to top management. After the incentive program has been approved and its salient features are known, the documentation should be revised and issued as a reference source to all concerned—participants, their union representatives, and managerial and supervisory personnel.

Testing and Debugging the Program

As a precautionary step it is a good idea to test and refine the incentive program before it is actually implemented. This can be done either by simulation using theoretical data, or by using live data. During the dry run many of the problems that may occur during the early stages of the program as well as the uncertainties that may need to be ironed out will be uncovered at a time when they can cause no damage.

After the incentive program has been tested, debugged or refined, it can be announced to the employees. It is wise to enlist the support of the labor union (if any) in announcing and supporting the program. Such tacit support will go a long way toward increasing the degree of acceptance and the possibility of success.

Resistance to Incentive Programs

When an employee group or a union resists an incentive program, the cause can frequently be traced to one or more of the following situations:

The employees distrust management and do not believe that the incentive program will work to their benefit.

The features, goals, and rules of the incentive plan have not been properly explained. The employees and their union representatives are unsure about the operation of the incentive program.

The bonus rates and standard levels of performance are periodically changed by management without any reason or justification for the change being given to the employees affected.

The employees' opportunity to substantially increase their earnings by increasing their productivity is limited by the program's bonus rate schedule.

Reassessment and Revision

The ideal incentive program is one that is dynamic, one that can periodically be reviewed and if necessary revised to reflect the changing interests and requirements of both the participants and the organization. This means that to be truly effective the incentive program must be periodically examined to make sure that

All procedures employed in performing any measured job or task have been simplified as much as possible, that time- and labor-saving equipment and forms are used, and that all employees are both knowledgeable about and well trained in the application of such procedures (Chapter 4 details methods for improving the operational and cost-effectiveness of such procedures.)

All performance standards reflect current job requirements and the degree of difficulty involved. Whenever a change in procedure, equipment, or forms occurs, the standard level of performance is reviewed and if necessary revised.

The features of the incentive program reflect to the maximum extent possible the current interests and requirements of both the participating employees and the organization.

The incentive program is honestly and accurately conducted, management periodically verifies the accuracy of employee productivity data, and participants and their supervisors accurately record and report such data.

Reporting Program Accomplishments

The office manager periodically summarizes and reports the effects of the incentive program to both top management and the participating employees. This helps to convince both parties of the benefits to them of continuing the program. The report indicates the percentage of increase in productivity that was attained as a result of the program and details the average incentive pay earned by the participants. The report to top management also details the increased profits that were realized as a result of the program, as well as discussing the effect that the program has had on such factors as employee turnover, absenteeism, quality and accuracy of output, and the organization's competitive position.

CHAPTER 11

Office Supply Management

The old adage "Watch the pennies and the dollars will take care of themselves" may aptly be applied to the purchase, stocking, and issuing of office supplies of every type. Although comparatively low in unit costs, office supplies are used in such large quantities that even a small cost savings in one item can be translated into a significant cost reduction overall.

In recent years the percentage of the typical organization's operating budget allocated for office supplies has increased markedly. According to an informal survey, conducted February 1982, of one hundred organizations of varying sizes, office supply expenses account for 6% of total office expenditures—more than double the estimated average percentage of five years ago. In the collective opinion of the respondents to this study, there are five primary reasons for such a sizable rate of increase:

The prices of many office supplies have increased at rates that substantially exceed the rate of inflation. This is especially true of office supplies that are made from petrochemicals (such as sheet-plastic protectors and toner of office copying machines), paper (such as typing bond, report binders, and file folders), and steel (such as file cabinets).

Increasingly more office supplies are designed to be disposable—used once, then discarded. Ball-point pens, word processing and computer printer ribbons, and precollated paper and carbon second sheets fall into this category.

The lack of standardization of products precludes the maximum use of planned procurement programs. This in turn, reduces opportunities for cost reduction.

Waste, pilferage, and overstocking appear to be increasing.

Many organizations do not exercise the same care in purchasing, stocking, and issuing office supplies that they use when other categories of purchases are involved.

Prices of office supplies will continue to rise in the future; there is nothing that the cost-conscious office manager can do about that. Such price increases need not mean a corresponding increase in overall expenditures for office supplies, however. Through the implementation of a concept known as *office supply management,* the office manager can reduce the costs of purchasing, stocking, and issuing office supplies to a point at which the price increases are totally offset.

OBJECTIVES

Office supply management has three major objectives:

To minimize the costs involved in purchasing, stocking, and issuing office supplies

To reduce the frequency of requisitioned supplies being out of stock or otherwise unavailable

To decrease pilferage, waste, and overstocking

The office supply management concept draws upon a variety of materials management techniques to achieve these broad objectives. *Materials management* includes the processes of (1) purchasing, (2) inventory management, and (3) value analysis. Such techniques can readily be learned and applied without any prior knowledge of materials management.

For ease of discussion, we will focus on three aspects of office supply management: (1) purchasing, (2) stocking, and (3) issuing of office supplies.

PURCHASING OFFICE SUPPLIES

In considering how the cost of office supplies can be reduced, the following facts must be borne in mind:

Most office supply vendors offer volume discounts: the larger the quantity of a given item that is ordered, the lower the unit cost.

Off-the-shelf (standard) office supplies generally are less expensive than those that have been customized or modified to meet the buyer's unique specifications (for example, imprinting the buyer's name on pencils).

Competition among office supply vendors almost always results in lower prices for the astute buyer; therefore, the greater the number of suppliers capable of providing a particular item, the greater the opportunity for price reductions.

Many office supplies are available in several different quality grades; the higher-quality grades will invariably be more expensive than the lower-quality grades.

Each of the techniques suggested below for reducing the unit purchase prices of office supplies reflects one or more of these four facts.

Standardization

Unless a conscious effort is made to avoid it, most organizations will purchase and stock many more varieties of a given office supply than are actually needed. To illustrate, the sales office of a company that manufactures agricultural implements was found to be stocking twelve different types of ball-point pens (black, blue, red, and green ink in each of the following writing points: fine, medium, and thick). Analysis of need found that only four combinations were actually required: black and red, in fine and medium points. Such practices lead to higher costs in all phases of office supply management:

Purchase costs, since the company did not receive the volume discounts that would have been available if the same quantities had been purchased in fewer types

Stocking costs, since the company had to provide shelf space and keep records for each individual type of pen

Issue costs, since it takes more time to pick the requisitioned pens from among twelve storage bins than from four.

Another common practice that unduly increases per-unit costs is purchasing office supplies for which there are only a limited number of suppliers. Examples are ribbons for certain models of word-processing printers and electronic typewriters, corrugated containers with attached lids that are used for long-term storage of inactive records, and certain sizes and colors of computer labels. It is relatively safe to assume that if the supplier base is broad, competiton will be keener and unit prices for such items will be lower.

The first step in any office supply management program, therefore, is to develop standards and specifications for each type of office supply required. The purpose of this step is to (1) reduce the number of variations of a given type of office supply that is used, in order to increase the quantities ordered and obtain a more favorable volume discount, and (2) to eliminate the unique features that limit the number of potential sources of supply.

These two broad objectives may be achieved by making a "functional analysis," in order to see what are the basic categories of supplies needed to perform the functions of the office. To make the functional analysis the office manager assembles one sample of every office supply that is currently either stocked by the central supply room or ordered and stocked by the various departments. As the various items are received, they are classified into one of the following six primary categories:

Writing implements and accessories (pens, pencils, erasers)
Copying and reprographics supplies (toner, ink, paper)
Filing supplies (file folders, labels, ring binders)
Desk accessories and supplies (rubber cement, stapling machines and staples, letter trays, tape dispensers, desk calendars)
Typing and word processing supplies (print wheels, ribbons, correction fluid, word processing media)

Stationery, other than forms (precollated second sheets, envelopes, carbon paper, lined pads)

It will be noted that no provision has been made for such items as business forms and stationery with preprinted letterheads; office furniture; data processing equipment, media, and supplies; or micrographics equipment media and supplies. Standardization of such items should not be attempted as part of an office supply management program; they require a separate study.

Once the various office supplies have been categorized, it becomes a simple, straightforward task to develop a profile of the individual types of supplies in each category. It is helpful to have a worksheet similar to the one shown in Figure 11-1. A separate worksheet would be completed for each category (such as filing supplies) and type (file folders and file folder labels) to be analyzed.

Examination of the completed worksheet will indicate when two or more variations of the same type of supply are being stocked. Then, in consultation with users and the various office stationers, one can investi-

STATIONERY SUPPLIES REQUISITION

This form to be used to requisition stationery supplies from stockroom.

DATE	DEPT. CODE	REQUISITIONER – PRINT LAST NAME

STOCK #	ITEM DESCRIPTION	UNITS	QUANTITY

REQUISITION ORIGINATED BY	DELIVER TO LOCATION
REQUISITION APPROVED BY	DELIVERY RECEIVED BY

SQ 4898 9/81

(Courtesy, E. R. Squibb & Sons)

Figure 11-1. Stationery Supplies Requisition Form

Office Supply Management

gate whether it would be possible to designate one variation as the standard, eliminating the need to purchase and stock the others. The key to an effective standardization effort is to make sure that no item that is really needed is eliminated.

The next step is to consider whether any unusual specifications of any of the items remaining on the purchase list limit the number of potential suppliers. The idea here is to eliminate, to the greatest extent possible, dependence upon one or a few vendors and to avoid situations in which there is no competitive pressure upon the suppliers to offer reasonable prices.

Working with one or more suppliers, the office manager reviews each worksheet and notes (1) whether any items are available from three or fewer suppliers, and (2) the reasons why this is so (for example, perhaps a ribbon for a particular word processing output printer can be obtained only from the manufacturer, since no other supplier offers the type of cartridge required by the printer). The next task is to determine whether it will be possible to revise the specifications of the limited-source-of-supply item in order to provide a wider supplier base. This will ordinarily necessitate examining the operating procedures in which this office supply is used. If the equipment or procedure unequivocably requires the limiting specification, no further action is possible. If the limiting specification is not essential to the operation of the equipment or the completion of the task, a less restrictive specification can be substituted, increasing the potential supplier base.

Value Analysis

Value analysis is a cost reduction technique that was first introduced into manufacturing operations during the late 1950s. In value analysis, every aspect of a given product is analyzed to ensure that the product performs the function it is intended to perform in the most cost-efficient manner. By uncovering unnecessary frills and overly elaborate features, value analysis has enabled American businesses to save millions of dollars annually.

From the standpoint of office supply management, value analysis involves (1) choosing the least expensive products that will perform the necessary office functions satisfactorily; (2) eliminating items with unnecessary features whose cost exceeds the operating benefits they offer; and (3) avoiding, insofar as possible, cutomized products.

To apply the value analysis concept to any given office supply, one must first determine the purpose that the item serves (for example, a paper clip or a staple is designed to hold loose papers together). Bearing the purpose in mind, the office manager then seeks to answer the following questions:

What is the per-unit cost of the item?
Does the use of this item contribute a value that is at least equal to the cost of the item?
Does its use require all the features that it contains?
Is there a less expensive, equally satisfactory way to accomplish the desired result?
If this item is not a standard product, could such a standard product be substituted?

To illustrate, let us assume that the office manager is evaluating a serrated (or, as it is commonly known, a "nonskid") paper clip. The purpose of all paper clips is to hold loose papers together without actually fastening them to one another. This is done by compression: when the papers are inserted between the prongs of a wire paper clip, the prongs press against the papers and hold them. Serrated paper clips are more expensive than plain, nonserrated clips, and, as tests have shown, they rarely prove superior in use. Eliminating the serrated "nonskid" feature would thus result in a cost saving, while continuing to provide an effective way to hold loose papers together.

Economic Order Quantity

The economic order quantity (EOQ) concept involves identifying the quantity of a given item that should be purchased to ensure *lowest overall costs*—a particularly perplexing problem to many office managers. Ordering a large quantity of a given item will nearly always reduces the unit price, but it will also tie up funds that could be used for other purposes and require additional storage space and equipment. In addition, overbuying may cause supply obsolescence.

Many organizations attempt to solve this problem by establishing arbitrary standards for the size of purchases, such as ordering a six months' supply of writing implements and stationery, a three months' supply of copier papers, and so forth, at a time. Others order on the basis of pricing schedules: to achieve quantity discounts, they order copier toner and chemicals in case lots and pencils and ball-point pens by the gross, regardless of projected use. Neither approach will generally prove to be as economical and efficient, from either a cost or a space utilization viewpoint, as using a modified version of the economic order quantity (EOQ) concept.

There are two categories of costs involved in the management of office supplies:

> *Procurement costs:* those expenditures that are incurred in obtaining the required supply of a given item. Procurement costs include
>> The purchase price of the item
>> The costs involved in (1) issuing a purchase order for the item, (2) receiving and inspecting the item upon delivery, and (3) processing and paying the vendor's invoice
>
> *Carrying costs:* the costs involved in stocking the item prior to use, and the value of any supplies made unusable by obsolescence, damage, or deterioration, or lost by pilferage

Naturally, the fewer the orders placed annually for a given item, the lower the overall procurement costs. Carrying costs, however, will be higher than they would be if smaller orders were placed. The converse is also true. However, there is a point at which the *combined* procurement and carrying costs will be at a minimum—the economic order quantity. Buying at or as close as possible to this point will ensure the office manager that he or she has achieved minimal overall costs.

The following equation will provide the EOQ for any given office supply. Any hand-held calculator that can figure square roots can be used to calculate the EOQ, using the following equation:

$$EOQ = \sqrt{\frac{2SE}{KC}}$$

where

> SE = estimated annual usage
> K = carrying costs expressed as a percentage of inventory value
> C = unit costs

Here is an illustration. Assume that black-ink, fine-point ball-point pens, used in quantities of 5,000 annually, cost 30 cents each to purchase. Cost studies have established that current procurement costs for the pens are running $8 per order and that carrying costs are running 15% of the average value of the inventory on hand. If the entire year's requirement (5,000 pens) were ordered at a single time, procurement costs would be minimal—$8. The average inventory would amount to 2,500 pens, having a net value of $750 (resulting from the 5,000-pen beginning inventory decreasing to zero over a twelve-month period). The carrying costs for the pens would amount to 15% of their average value, or $112.50. Therefore the total cost of purchasing and carrying the entire year's requirement of these pens would be $8.00 + $112.50, or $120.50.

If, however, we were to *increase* the order frequency, both the quantity of pens ordered and the carrying costs would *decrease*. At some point, though, the total combined costs would begin to rise, since the increase in procurement costs would exceed the decrease in carrying costs.

Table 11-1 lists the various costs involved in ordering 5,000 pens at frequencies ranging from once a year to every second month. Notice that the most desirable combination of procurement costs and carrying costs occurs when the pens are ordered four times a year in quantities of

Table 11-1. Costs of Ordering Pens at Various Intervals

Number of Orders per Year	Quantity per Order	Invoice Amount per Order	Annual Procurement Cost	Average Inventory Value	Carrying Costs (15% of Inventory Value)	Total Combined Costs
1	5,000	$1,500.00	$ 8.00	$750.00	$112.50	$1,620.50
2	2,500	750.00	16.00	275.00	56.25	1,572.25
3	1,667	500.00	24.00	250.00	37.50	1,561.50
4	1,250	375.00	32.00	187.50	28.13	1,560.13
5	1,000	300.00	40.00	150.00	22.50	1,562.50
6	834	250.00	48.00	125.00	17.75	1,565.75

1,250 pens per order. If we ordered more or less frequently than quarterly, total costs would be higher.

It is not necessary to develop such a decision table for each procurement, since one can simply use the EOQ equation. Applying the equation to the preceding example produces the following result:

$$EOQ = \sqrt{\frac{2SE}{KC}}$$

$$EOQ = \sqrt{\frac{2 \times 5,000 \times \$8.00}{30¢ \times 15\%}}$$

$$EOQ = \sqrt{1,777,778}$$

$$EOQ = 1,333 \text{ pens}$$

The reader will note that the calculated EOQ corresponds very closely to the quarterly order suggested by the decision table.

The advantage of the EOQ concept over other methods of determining optimum order quantities is that regardless of the quantity involved, the type of office supplies ordered, or the purchase price, the use of this concept will make the sum of the procurement and carrying costs consistently lower than when any other system of inventory management is employed. The reason for this is that the EOQ system always achieves one or the other of these results:

A balancing or equating of the procurement, overhead, and inventory carrying costs

A reduction in one set of costs (either procurement or carrying costs) without an offsetting increase in the other

Contractual Buying

VALUE OF CONTRACTUAL BUYING

Contractual buying is a purchasing cost reduction technique in which the office manager, acting on behalf of the organization, enters into a contract with an office supply vendor providing for the purchase of one or more specified office supply items at a stipulated price for a specified period of time. A single purchase order is issued (referred to as either a *blanket purchase order* or a *systems contract*) containing the minimum quantity of goods (if any) that the organization guarantees it will requisition during the period covered by the purchase order and also specifying the unit price at which the vendor agrees to furnish the item. A price adjustment is usually made at the conclusion of the contract if the organization either exceeds or falls short of requisitioning the guaranteed quantity. In such cases the unit price may be adjusted either upward or downward and a final settlement made.

A six- or twelve-month contract period is the norm; the term generally depends upon the stability of prices for the items ordered and upon their general availability. As a rule the term for items that are volatile in price or often in short supply is a maximum of six months, while the term for supplies that are less likely to fluctuate in price and supply is twelve months.

Contractual buying benefits both the customer and the supplier. For the customer it offers the following advantages:

It reduces the need to issue a purchase order more than once during the life of the contract.

Correspondingly, it reduces the clerical work load and the costs involved in preparing and issuing requests for quotations, receiving and analyzing vendor responses, and preparing and issuing the actual purchase order.

It protects the organization against price increases during the life of the contract.

The vendor benefits as well:

Selling and estimating costs are reduced, since only a single bid is made during the life of a given contract.

By knowing in advance the quantity of a given item that must be supplied, the vendor can maximize its own profit by stockpiling or combining two or more customers' orders to achieve more favorable pricing from its suppliers.

MAKING A BLANKET PURCHASE ORDER

The procedure for making a blanket purchase order is relatively simple. The steps are as follows.

Developing a profile of purchases. By reviewing records such as purchase orders issued for office supplies, requisitions upon the central supplies department for office supplies, and inventory records (if available), the office manager determines for each item

The total quantity ordered from all suppliers in each month during
the preceding year
The prices paid for each quantity ordered
The supplier with whom each order was placed
The number of each item requisitioned by and issued to the various
departments each month

This information provides a profile of the office supplies used within the organization. From it one can determine how many of each item are ordered and issued in a given month, as well as whether there are any seasonal price fluctuations, and also whether the prices of the items are relatively stable or subject to continuous increases or fluctuation. Finally, one will have a reliable indicator as to whether specific items are competitively priced or whether some vendors charge prices that seem to be unaffected by competition.

Selecting the items to be purchased. The next step is to review the various items and select those that are ordered in sufficient quantity to justify the time and cost involved in reducing their per-unit costs by developing a blanket purchase order, or those that are highly volatile in price and often in short supply. One attempts to select standard items in order to increase the quantity of items purchased at one time and realize volume discounts.

Obtaining price quotations. A request for quotation is then prepared and is issued not only to current suppliers but also to others who could conceivably provide the products. The Yellow Pages is a good source for finding potential suppliers. As part of the quotation each vendor should be required to submit

Names of current customers and office managers in other organizations who can vouch for the vendor's reliability and the quality
of the product

Details regarding the procedures the vendor uses for filling requisitions against the blanket purchase order

Information about any other services the vendor provides that would simplify the overall office supply management function

Evaluating the quotations. Naturally, each reference will be carefully checked, and the quotation and supplemental information evaluated in detail. One should not be unduly influenced by price. Price is important, of course, but it is just one of a number of criteria that must be taken into consideration. One must consider the references that the vendor has received from customers and determine whether or not the vendor's promises are reflected in the customers' experiences. In addition, it is important to examine the procedure the vendor uses in dealing with customers. If the vendor imposes a complex procedure, the result could be errors and consequent service problems and inconveniences that could negate the cost savings realized from the contract. A high score should be given to any vendor who agrees to allow authorized customer personnel to requisition supplies against a blanket purchase order by telephone rather than by submitting a written release form. This simple procedure alone can result in time and cost savings that could well approach the costs of developing the blanket purchase order. One should also consider with favor any vendor who offers a "stockless procurement" option. Under this arrangement, which will be examined in detail later in the chapter, the vendor maintains the inventory of the contracted item subject to requisition by the customer. Stockless procurement has a double advantage:

It eliminates the need for the customer to devote time, space, and personnel to maintaining inventories of supplies.

It assures the customer that items will be available on short notice and that the organization will not be billed for any items stored on its behalf until the customer has actually requisitioned them.

Selecting the vendor and issuing the blanket purchase order. The final step is to select the vendor who will be awarded the contract and issue the blanket purchase order to him or her. At this time the office manager should also forward to each department in the organization a memorandum giving the key details of the blanket purchase contract (for example, the items purchased, the vendor's name and address, the minimum order quantity, the normal lead time between the receipt of the requisition and the filling of the order, the unit price, and the effective dates of the contract). In addition, each department should be given a set of instructions about how to order against the contract.

Organizations whose annual requirements are insufficient to justify entering into contract buying may find it advisable to join together with one or more other companies in their vicinity to form a buying cooperative. The aggregate requirements of the participants may well be enough to justify such an effort to the mutual benefit of all concerned.

Stockpiling

Stockpiling is a technique that many office managers have used successfully to minimize the effects of inflationary price increases and temporary shortages of a given office supply. With this method, if one becomes aware that the price of an item is likely to increase or that supplies are likely to be short, one places an unusually large order for the item. The effect is to protect the organization against both increased prices and shortages.

Stockpiling has been used with considerable success for the purpose of

Anticipating a disruption in delivery schedules of office supplies due to possible strikes or other labor unrest

Offsetting the increases in the prices of office supplies that invariably occur whenever the OPEC nations increase the price per barrel of crude oil

Postponing the impact of an announced price increase in an office supply by placing a *stockpiling order* before the effective date of the increase

Purchasing Private and Independent Brands

An increasing number of office supplies are being independently or privately branded—that is, they are being produced and packaged by established manufacturers and resold under another company's brand name. This can be compared to the "no-frills" products in the local supermarket.

Private and independent brands offer savings that often run as high as 25% compared to the costs of national brands. However, there is an inherent risk in their purchase and use: there is no guarantee that a private brand produced by a given manufacturer will be equal in quality and reliability to the national brands. It is best to test any independent or private brand items *under actual use conditions* before placing an order, so that one can become aware of any inadequacies in the product and be in a better position to decide whether these inadequacies will offset the potential savings resulting from the lower purchase cost.

Recycling Supplies

Some office supplies can be partially or even totally recycled after their initial use and then resold at costs that are significantly below those of nonrecycled items. Recycled office supplies are of two categories:

Those that are totally reclaimable: developing solution for microfilm processing equipment and toner for office copiers typify this category. The "spent" solution or toner may by reclaimed, returning it approximately to its original condition, after which it may be repackaged and sold.

Those that contain both reclaimable and nonreclaimable components: word processing printer ribbons are a good example of office supplies that fall within this category. After use the carbon ribbon may be removed and discarded, while the cartridge itself may be reloaded with a new, unused carbon ribbon; the recycled item will be sold at price below that of an identical but nonrecycled printer ribbon.

Again, since there well be some loss of quality each time an item is recycled, it is a sound practice for the office manager to first pretest and then carefully monitor the performance of any recycled office supplies.

"Bargain" Supplies

Occasionally, by following newspaper ads and by expressing an interest to various suppliers, the office manager may be able to obtain unused office supplies at a price that is below normal market prices. For example, a company may be changing from an office copier that uses coated paper to one that uses plain bond paper and may therefore be willing to sell its unused coated stock at a discount. Another company may be changing from standard upright files to lateral files and have quantities of unsuitable file folders and labels that they would like to sell at less than their cost. The astute office manager will be alert to such cost-saving opportunities.

One word of caution: not all offers to sell office supplies at prices that are below current market value are legitimate. Within recent years an organized scam has developed, in which persons claiming to be employees of established office supply manufacturers such as IBM or the Xerox Corporation, or of local, well-known office supply dealers or of phone business, government, educational, and non-profit organizations call an office manager and offer to sell name brands of typewriter ribbons, lift-off tapes, copier supplies, or similar items at well below current market prices. The caller states that he or she is a supplier who is drastically overstocked because of a cancelled order and needs to free the storage space. If an order is placed, the purchaser will probably find that he or she has not received the particular brand of typewriter ribbon, copier toner, or other item offered. Further, the quality and reliability of the brand will invariably be below that of the name brand promised. Rather than realizing a bargain, the unsuspecting purchaser will have paid more for the inferior item than if the item had been purchased from a normal source of supply.

A variation of this scam also exists: the caller claims to be from a company that is going out of business and says that the company wants to liquidate whatever office supplies it can at whatever price it can get. Again, the results are invariably the same: inferior merchandise at inflated prices.

Both the Federal Trade Commission (FTC) and the Better Business Bureau (BBB) have issued warnings about these scams and have prepared educational materials that every office manager should read. These may be obtained by writing to the

Office of the Secretary
Federal Trade Commission
Washington, D.C. 20580

and asking for information pertaining to "WATS Line Hustlers," or to the

Council of Better Business Bureaus
1150 17th Avenue, N.W.
Washington, D.C. 20036

enclosing a self-addressed, stamped envelope, and asking for a copy of the BBB's pamphlet "Paper Pirates."

As noted earlier, bargains can be found, and the office manager should be alert for them. However, if the offer to sell comes from an unsolicited source or seems too good to be true, caution should be exercised. Obtain the caller's name and the name of his or her organization and then check with the FTC or BBB to see if they have any negative information about the caller or the organization. If the caller claims to be an employee of an established office supply manufacturer or dealer or of an organization that is liquidating its office supply inventory, hang up and call the manufacturer, dealer, or organization to verify the truth of the caller's story.

STORING OFFICE SUPPLIES

Maintaining inventories of office supplies is a particularly expensive, labor-intensive operation. According to published studies conducted by both government and industrial organizations, the various costs that are involved in (1) receiving and recording incoming deliveries of office supplies, (2) storing supplies pending issue, and (3) monitoring their stock status to ensure timely replenishment typically account for between 20 and 25% of the purchase costs of the items stored. If these costs are adjusted to reflect pilferage and damage, the figures could well increase by as much as an additional 5%.

Therefore it is important that the office manager evaluate the organization's office supply storage operation to ensure that it is as most cost-effective and operationally efficient as possible. There are three basic types of storage for office supplies: (1) centralized storage, (2) satellite storage, and (3) vendor storage.

Centralized Storage

This is the traditional business approach, patterned after the materials storeroom and tool crib operations found in most factories. The organization establishes an attended central supply room for the receipt, storage, and issuing of forms, typing and word-processing supplies, desk accessories, and the like. The individual departments requisition the various items that they require on an as-needed basis, generally by using a "supplies requisition form" (similar to that shown in Figure 11-1). The supply clerks, using the supplies requisition form, locate the requested items and either forward them to the requisitioner by interoffice mail or special messenger or hold them for subsequent pickup by the requisitioner or an associate.

Satellite Storage

The concept of satellite storage became popular with the advent of the open office plan (described in Chapter 7). In this storage arrangement, both centralized and decentralized office supply storage facilities are used. Office supplies move from the various vendors' warehouses and drop-shipping points, to the purchaser's central supply room, to the "satellite" storage areas in the individual departments. The central supply room serves as a holding area in which the bulk of the inventories of office supplies are maintained. The various satellite supply rooms maintain much smaller inventories—usually quantities that are adequate for filling two to four weeks' requisitions. Each of the individual departments is assigned to one of the satellite supply rooms. Depending upon the controls used, requisitioning items from the satellite facilities may require submission of a supplies requisition form or may be undocumented. The requisition request is filled from the working inventory maintained in the satellite supply room. As the working inventories are drawn out, the person responsible for maintaining the satellite supply room sends a replenishing order to the central supply room, which fills it either from existing inventories or else by placing an order with a vendor.

Vendor Storage

This concept, commonly referred to as *stockless procurement,* is an extension of the contractual buying techniques described previously in this chapter. In addition to contracting for the sale of specified quantities of a given office supply at a guaranteed (fixed) price during the contract's term, the vendor also agrees to serve, in effect, as the customer's central supply room, filling requistions received either by telephone or mail from his or her own inventories and forwarding the requisitioned items directly to the department requesting them. Consequently the customer does not need to establish or maintain any supply rooms; each department maintains a current working supply of the office supplies they require right in their immediate work areas (generally in one or two file drawers). Since weekly replenishment orders are involved under this arrangement, there is no need to requisition or maintain more than a one-week inventory in the offices.

The customer is billed once a month on the basis of the quantities of office supplies requisitioned by and delivered to the organization during the preceding 30 days. Thus inventory carrying charges and the possibility of obsolescence are minimal.

Which Alternative Is Best?

The choice of an office supply storage arrangement should be made on the basis of an evaluation of the projected costs and operational benefits projected for each alternative. The benefits vary from one organization to the next because of such variables as the number and location of departments served, the availability and cost of floor space and storage equipment, the organization's philosophy regarding the use of outside vendors, and the adequacy of stock controls. Once such cost and operational benefits have been quantified, it is fairly easy to ascertain which storage arrangement is best for the particular organization.

ISSUING OFFICE SUPPLIES

The office manager's primary objective with respect to issuing office supplies is to reduce waste, pilferage, and overordering—factors that will add significantly to the overall costs of office supplies. The following methods have proved to be effective in reducing the frequency and volume of waste, pilferage, and overordering.

Supply Rationing

As the name suggests, supply rationing is a technique that limits the quantity of office supplies that a specified department may requisition within a given period of time. Beyond that quantity, any additional requisitions require the approval of the executive to whom the department manager reports.

Rationing supplies necessitates determining the quantities of each office supply that a particular department requires in a given period. Generally this can easily be achieved by averaging the number of each item requisitioned in the preceding twelve months and then adjusting the results up or down as necessary to reflect increases or decreases in current staffing and work load compared to the average of the preceding twelve months.

Supply rationing has proved to deter overordering and hoarding of office supplies. In addition, rationing usually leads to a tightening of controls over the issuing of supplies within a department, thereby reducing pilferage. Experience has shown that following the implementation of supply rationing, reductions in consumption of office supplies of from 10 to 15% are not uncommon.

Chargeback System

As was explained in Chapter 1, a chargeback system has been found to be an effective way to control office operating costs. Such a system should definitely be implemented with respect to office supplies. Each individual department should be required to budget its office supply expenditures across the fiscal year. As individual supply requisitions

are filled, their costs are to be charged back to the requesting department and applied against the department's budget allocation for such
items. Thus the department head is responsible and ultimately accountable for any excessive requisitioning of office supplies. As a result, he or
she will probably be on the watch for waste, pilferage, and overordering, since an inability to stay within the budget will reflect unfavorably
upon his or her managerial performance.

Restricting Access to Supply Rooms

It has been proved conclusively that when employees are allowed to
"browse" in the central or satellite supply rooms, they draw out far
more office supplies than if they merely prepared their requisitions at
their desks and telephoned or mailed them to the supply room. With this
in mind, the office manager would do well to close the various supply
rooms to all but those persons who have been assigned responsibility for
maintaining them and require that users transmit their requisitions by
telephone or interoffice mail.

Reducing the Units of Issue

Many office managers follow the practice of issuing office supplies in
whatever quantities the manufacturers package them in. For example,
they issue typing paper in minimum quantities of one ream, pencils by
the dozen, and forms in quantities of fifty or one hundred. This is a
wasteful practice, since most users require less than the quantities packaged by the vendor, and the result is overordering. The way to avoid
this is to examine the various units of issue for the items stocked and
reduce any units that seem to be too large.

CHAPTER 12

Interacting with Top Management

Although a key member of the organization's management structure, the office manager will rarely be included among its top-level management. Typically, however, the office manager is at the level within the organizational hierarchy that reports directly to a member of top management. In addition, the broad scope of the office manager's responsibilities generally necessitates frequent interaction with virtually all of the organizations top management personnel. To a great extent the office manager's effectiveness will be determined by how well he or she deals with such personnel. If in their contacts with the office manager top management are of the impression that their office manager is a knowledgeable, capable individual who can be relied upon to research any situation thoroughly and accurately before recommending a course of action, they will give him or her a freer hand than if these managerial skills are less evident.

As a rule, the office manager's personal access to members of top management is limited in terms of both time and frequency. Top management, by necessity, is forced to deal in terms of written rather than verbal communications. Their day is simply too short to be able to handle impersonal meetings and all the matters that require their attention. Most of their business must of necessity be conducted through written reports and correspondence and followed up as necessary by brief meetings and telephone calls to clarify or expand any relevant issues.

To function effectively with top management, the office manager must become proficient in communicating through written reports and correspondence. In this chapter we shall explore the question of what top management needs to know, in terms of the office manager's areas of responsibility, and how the office manager can prepare and present this information to facilitate its usage by top management.

THE ROLE OF TOP MANAGEMENT

In order to better understand the information that top management requires in its interactions with the office manager, let us first consider the function that senior managers serve in any organization. Reduced to basics, their role is the same as the office manager's (as described in Chapter 1), only on a much larger scale. Top executives are responsible for using the various resources at their disposal—manpower, money, and materials—to accomplish a given set of objectives that have been established by the board of directors or board of trustees. Examples of such objectives might be to increase the organization's market share, to make more profits, to open a new market, or to attain increased community acceptance. Management accomplishes these objectives by bringing to bear upon the organizational elements reporting to them their expertise in the areas of planning, organizing, controlling, and motivating—the same managerial skills that the successful office manager uses to achieve maximum cost efficiency and operational effectiveness in his or her own areas of responsibility.

To do so effectively, however, top management must be provided with three categories of information:

Information that will assist them in establishing objectives
Information that will enable them to attain the objectives
Information that will help them to measure the results of their efforts

Regardless of the operations for which various senior managers are responsible, their informational needs are the same—a fact that the office manager should keep well in mind in dealing with them.

One further point should be made with respect to these informational needs. Top management not only needs to know *what is happening* but also, and more importantly, *why it is happening*. In order to provide the latter answer the office manager will frequently have to evaluate and interpret the facts that are available to him or her, since top management needs *interpreted* facts or information.

In his or her interactions with top management, therefore, the office manager's objective must be to provide information required for decision making and control purposes, at the time it is needed, in the most useable format, and at the lowest cost. Each of these factors will now be considered individually.

PREPARING REPORTS

Supplying the Correct Information

An informal survey conducted by the author among senior management personnel attending an American Management Association seminar revealed a common complaint: these executives felt that they did not receive all the information they required to effectively manage the organizations for whom they were responsible. Many indicated that they frequently received incomplete, misleading, or incorrectly interpreted information and, as a result, were often hindered in reaching decisions. In the author's experience such situations occur because the persons who are responsible for preparing reports fail to first identify the exact information that top management requires. Consequently the information that is supplied is often irrelevant.

To illustrate, consider the case of an office machine manufacturer who issued a product recall to correct a potential safety hazard in one of his models—a poorly grounded connection that posed the risk of electrical shock. The management personnel who issued the product recall were interested in obtaining as great a response as possible and planned to increase their efforts to obtain customer compliance if response was found to be lagging. Top management therefore advised the office manager to monitor the return and repair of the models and to report on the status of the recall effort weekly. The office manager and the persons coordinating the product recall diligently tallied the number of units that were received each day, as well as the number that were repaired. Each week, they summarized this information and forwarded it to top management. It was not long before management realized that this information, while interesting, was in itself of very limited value. To ensure a successful product recall, they needed to know not only how many units had been turned in and repaired but, more important, how many of the originally sold models were still being used in an unsafe condition.

In most instances in which reports fail to supply top management with the information they require, the person preparing the report has (1) failed to ascertain the purpose for which the information is required, and (2) failed to ensure that the information supplied will help fulfill that purpose. This latter factor, which the layman calls "deciding and supplying what's important" and the information professional refers to as "identifying and reporting the critical factors," is the key to providing top management with the correct information.

Every task has a *critical factor*—that single step or series of steps that if not done well will doom the task to failure. These are the factors that must be identified and reported on to top management if senior officers are to be furnished the information they require to do their job well. In general, the operations that fall within the office manager's area of responsibility have three common critical factors: costs, schedules, and performance. Failure to control any of these factors in virtually every area of activity (whether it is reprographics, space utilization, or office procedures) will result in an operational failure. Thus in his or her dealings with top management the office manager should be sure to provide information about costs, schedules, and performance, as well as any supplemental information that he or she is able to identify.

Approaching information selection from the standpoint of identifying and reporting the critical factors provides one other major benefit—it reduces the amount of nonmanagerial information that would otherwise be included in the reports. Nonmanagerial information—that is, information that is not essential to decision making or control purposes—is the bane of every manager's existence. If the report does not focus on the critical factors, the manager must waste time reading through information that will not facilitate his or her decision or action. By focusing on the critical factors, the office manager can compress the information, reducing the time that top management must spend reading the report and taking appropriate action.

Assuring Timely Reporting

From top management's point of view, the information required for decisionmaking and control purposes is valuable only if it is current. The office manager preparing reports for top management should see that it is produced and distributed in time for its recipients to react and take action based upon that information. This necessitates careful scheduling on the part of the office manager. Again, the previously mentioned informal survey of senior managers found that many were of the opinion that 30% or more of the information they received arrived too late for them to take corrective action. What is meant by this comment is that when dealing with top management, the office manager must obtain a clear definition of the time frame required by top management to take effective action and influence the result reported to them, and he must schedule the production and distribution of reports accordingly.

Reports to top management may be prepared and issued either at regular intervals (for example, weekly, monthly, or annually), or whenever a particular situation or event occurs.

PERIODIC REPORTING

Periodic reports are the type most frequently used by office managers. The principal advantage of periodic reporting is that it ensures that senior management's attention will be drawn at regular intervals to the matters being reported on. On the negative side, however, periodic reports frequently become stereotyped and overloaded with detail. In addition, unless their relevance is regularly reviewed, periodic reports may continue to be prepared long after they are no longer needed. That is why many information managers advocate the use of the second report issue frequency—whenever a particular situation or event occurs.

EXCEPTION REPORTING

Many of the reports that the office manager submits to the top management may be classed as "operational" in nature, since they describe such things as the progress or status of a project. As operational reports, they will describe situations which indicate the operation is proceeding according to schedule, better than anticipated, or worse than anticipated.

Normal operations rarely require top management's decision or action. Consequently, there is no reason to issue a report informing them that normal operations are going on usual. However, if things are either better or worse than expected management must be advised so that they can take whatever action is necessitated.

The concept underlying exception reporting—alerting top management of only those things that require their decision—offers an excellent way for the office manager to reduce reporting work load and costs and to free senior management from having to devote valuable time and effort to reading about situations that do not require their intercession.

ALERT REPORTING

Alert reporting is a technique that, if used properly, makes top management aware of potential problems while there is still time to take preventive action or at least to minimize the impact of the problem upon the company.

Alert reporting requires that certain critical factors be indentified as indicators of possible problems. The critical factors are then carefully and continuously monitored. As soon as it becomes evident that these factors are undergoing change, senior executives are immediately notified. They then review the situation and decide upon an action to deal with the problem.

An example of alert reporting involves monitoring employee attendance and productivity levels during, for instance, a period of labor unrest—especially just before the negotiation of new bargaining agreements. Since a falling off in either of these critical factors would affect the organization's ability to meet its customers' orders and satisfy its contractual obligations, top management would make sure that attendance and productivity were carefully audited so that if it appeared that a work slowdown might be under way, they could immediately take action. For example, they could consider contracting with other manufacturers to fill orders; attempt to defer or extend delivery dates, or deplete inventories to fill orders.

ON-CALL REPORTING

On-call reporting involves the preparation and maintenance of operating data on a continuous basis, so that when top management requests specific, *current* information it can readily be obtained. Of all the techniques used by the office manager, on-call reporting is the most expensive to establish, since it typically involves collecting, coding, and storing information in a computer processable format (on magnetic tapes, disks, and diskettes).

The information compiled ordinarily relates to sales, costs, and production. By analyzing such information and putting it into a format that will satisfy management's needs, a variety of on-call reports can be prepared.

Presenting Data Effectively

Many office managers, in conveying information to their top management, fail to present it in a concise, easy-to-read, unambiguous manner. They tend to present lengthy, rambling narratives with uninterpreted or inadequately interpreted statistics. They often fail to emphasize the truly significant data that the senior officials should consider before arriving at a decision. Many of the reports that are submitted to top management are difficult to read and comprehend—factors that could conceivably lead to incorrect interpretation of the information and poor decisions.

The following techniques are essential to ensure that information is presented in the most effective way:

Select the reporting format that is best suited for the data or other information involved.

Condense and simplify all facts and figures.

Use comparisons to establish basic relationships and to clarify and highlight significant data and information.

Emphasize the data and other information that especially require top management's attention.

Reports normally have one of the following formats: (1) narrative, (2) statistical, or (3) graphic. The best form for the report depends upon the type of information to be conveyed and the recipient's familiarity with the information.

Narrative reports usually offer the most complete explanation of the matter at hand, since, in describing something that has happened within the organization they first ask questions about why and how certain events occurred and then provide the answers. On the other hand, narrative reports are the most time-consuming to read and the most susceptible to misinterpretation.

Statistical reports provide precise, detailed numerical data. The main disadvantage of statistical reports is that they do not present the situation at a glance. Senior managers themselves must often work at uncovering the *whys* and *hows* behind the reported statistics.

Graphics (charts, graphs, and the like) provide excellent comparisons of performance as well as a way of interpreting a given situation or relationship visually. A disadvantage of graphics as a reporting format is that they show rather than explain and that they frequently do not present precise information.

The office manager seeking the most useful, readily understood format will often find that combining all or some of the three formats will enable him or her to present the most precise and truest picture of the situation.

Assuring the Lowest Cost

According to surveys conducted periodically by the National Archives and Records Service (the organization responsible for developing programs to contain the government's paperwork work load and costs), reports submitted to top management are typically among the most expensive records created by an organization. After all, a report is usually a summary of information that is already contained in written form in other reports, correspondence, or forms. Such sources are often referred to as "feeder documents." They themselves may be summaries of other feeder documents, so that a report to senior management is frequently the apex of a costly paperwork pyramid for which much effort was spent in gathering, summarizing, reproducing, distributing, analyzing, and filing information.

It follows, therefore, that any reduction in either the quantity or frequency of reporting will have a geometric rather than an arithmetical effect upon costs, since by eliminating just one report we will probably eliminate several feeder documents. Similarly, were we to eliminate a single item from a report the net result might be to reduce many persons' efforts in accumulating and reporting such source data in various feeder reports. The office manager's objective, therefore, should be to minimize reporting costs by

Reducing the frequency with which the information is reported; changing from periodic reporting to situation or event reporting whenever possible.

Reducing the number of copies of the report being prepared and distributed. Restrict access to only those senior executives who can take action or make a decision on the basis of the information presented in the report. The office manager should be aware of and carefully resist the temptation to issue "courtesy" or "informational" copies of the report to top management personnel who do not require the information for either action or decision making purposes.

Redesigning the report for ease and economy of preparation. The common availability of word-processing equipment, office copiers that permit one to revise and update previously formulated data and produce copies equal in quality to the original, and similar equipment offers the potential for simplifying the preparation of reports. Rather than preparing reports from "scratch," the cost-conscious office manager can explore and select one of the alternate methods that permits him or her to use all or part of the previous report's captions and data in preparing the current issue.

PREPARING CORRESPONDENCE

There is a knack to writing in a convincing, persuasive manner, and, quite frankly, any office manager who hopes to win top management's support must acquire this knack. Correspondence specialists tell us that the secret to dealing with top management is no different than dealing with employees, customers, or even social acquaintances. One must

Gain the reader's attention immediately
Maintain the reader's interest in what you are describing
Present ideas convincingly
Suggest or imply a course of action

Office managers with a sales background will recognize that these are the same principles that are taught to salespersons—an apt comparison, since in many dealings with senior managers one will be "selling" a concept or a point of view or seeking approval for a recommended action.

Another common complaint of senior managers is that many employees write in a stilted, wordy style that is difficult to understand. Consequently, much of the impact of the message they wish to convey is lost, and both the writer's and the recipient's time is wasted.

The following guidelines can help one to develop a clear, effective style.

Plan the correspondence. To ensure that your message will be quickly and accurately conveyed, plan your correspondence carefully. First, keep in mind who the recipient is and make sure that all terminology, abbreviations, and jargon will be understood by him or her and that all situations reported will be of interest. If not, then more detailed background information must be furnished, or alternate words, abbreviations, etc., that are familiar to the recipient must be used.

Second, determine both the purpose and the objective of the correspondence. The purpose will be either to inform senior managers of something or else to request some action or decision. The objective should be defined as specifically as possible to ensure that all unnecessary and extraneous details will be eliminated. Again, defining both the purpose and objective is basic: if one cannot spell these out before beginning to write, it is doubtful that one's message will be properly conveyed.

Identify all main ideas. The next step is to simply list the main ideas one wishes to state. *Main ideas* may be defined as those that are critical to the recipient's understanding of the correspondence. *Supporting ideas,* on the other hand, are those that clarify and help the reader to better understand the main ideas but are not critical to the meaning of the correspondence.

Prepare an outline. The outline will serve as a guide for the actual writing. Aside from minimizing the possibility of omitting an important thought, an outline will also enable one to experiment with alternate sequences of ideas prior to the actual preparation of the correspondence.

Write from the outline. When the outline has been finished, it is used as the source from which a handwritten or dictated draft is prepared.

Select words with care. Specifically,

Use familiar words and phrases. Never attempt to impress the reader with the extent of your vocabulary by using uncommon, foreign, or technical terminology with which he or she may be unfamiliar.

Use action verbs rather than passive verbs (for example, say "Brown authorized the purchase" rather than "the purchase was authorized by Brown").

Be specific. For example, don't say "personnel" when you mean "stock clerks."

Include such personal words as "you," "I," "he," "she," "lawyer," and "accountant." Authorities such as Rudolph Flesch advise that if at least 15% of the sentences and 7% of the words contained in a text are personal, recipients will find the writing style interesting.

Avoid exaggeration. For example, don't refer to an "exhaustive search" when only one or two attempts were made.

Use sentences that are clear and easy to read. Specifically,

Restrict sentences to an average of seventeen to nineteen words in length.
Intersperse long sentences among shorter ones, for variety and change of pace.
Use a straightforward subject/action verb/object sentence structure.
Use punctuation properly. This will lead to increased clarity of meaning and greater comprehension and retention of ideas by the reader.

Facilitate the reading and comprehension of paragraphs.

Develop only one main idea in a single paragraph.
Restrict each paragraph to four to six sentences.
Introduce each paragraph with a sentence that tells the main idea that will follow. This helps to focus the reader's attention upon the main idea.
Continue the paragraph with a series of sentences that support the main idea with facts, figures, and details.
If the paragraph is complex, conclude with a sentence that summarizes the main idea that was just presented.

Apply the 4S writing formula. The 4S formula (whose principles are *shortness, simplicity, strength,* and *sincerity*) has, since its development nearly thirty years ago, proved useful in helping business writers prepare more readable and comprehensive correspondence. Here are the rules for applying the 4S formula:

For shortness
Do not repeat what was said in the request for the information you are supplying.
Avoid needless words and information.
Shorten prepositional phrases.
For simplicity
Know your subject so well that you can discuss it confidently and naturally.

Use short words, short sentences, and short paragraphs.

Tie your thoughts together so that the reader can follow you from one idea to the next without losing track of your reasoning.

For strength

Use concrete, specific words.

Make maximum use of active verbs.

Give the answer *first,* then the explanation if necessary.

Don't hedge.

For sincerity

Admit mistakes.

Don't try to overwhelm the reader by exaggerating, using complex vocabulary or grammar, or by being overly emphatic

Be neither servile nor arrogant when dealing, in writing, with top management.

CHAPTER 13

What an
Office Manager Does

Ask a group of college graduates planning to enter the business world what area of business they plan to enter or what type of job they would like to hold, and probably not one in a hundred will say "office management." Even after these graduates have attended a class reunion or two and the glamour of positions in sales or finance has evaporated, the idea of becoming office managers for their companies will still invite disdain and call up images of boredom.

In short, almost no one sets out to become an office manager. There is no maneuvering by eager young executives to push out someone presently holding the position; there is no file in the personnel department on prospective candidates for the job. And when was the last time office managers were invited to a career day at the local high school? However, dispite this apparent shortage of candidates, the business community has little or no trouble in finding people to fill the position.

"What an Office Manager Does" is the contribution of Keith J. Costello, Manager, Hardware and Technology Planning, at Hamilton Bank, Lancaster, Pennsylvania; formerly of Hershey Foods Corporation.

The assignment given the contributors to this book was to help the interested reader better understand what job standards are expected of him or her, to explain the scope of the job, and possibly to help that person perform more effectively in that job. And if ever a type of job needed a book that describes it more adequately, it is the job of office manager, especially that of the *new* office manager.

Please don't misunderstand me; this chapter is not the office management version of *The Joy of Sex*. Nor is it a complete how-to manual. However, given the lack of material to guide both potential and present office managers, it would seem that any pertinent information, suggestions, experiences, and examples would be helpful. What the reader *will* find in "What an Office Manager Does."

This chapter describes the duties that the office manager performs, the organizational structure within which the office operates, and the position of the office manager—that is, his or her role—within the organization.

HISTORICAL PERSPECTIVE

Although it's a cliché, the adage bears repeating: "To understand where you are, you must know where you have been." How has the position of office manager evolved as a separate function? Where did it originate? It seems likely that the function and position of office manager originated about the time that industries become large enough to require sizeable staffs, when industrial specialization began. As Western Europe became industrialized and markets grew, the need to keep track of increasingly complex and numerous industrial processes and markets also grew; more and more people were needed, and more and more paperwork was generated. Eventually, of course, someone was needed to manage the people and the paperwork—and that is when the position of office manager as an identifiable figure emerged.

As offices were broken into subareas (a process called *specialization*) and the size of office staffs grew, it became apparent to business managers that it would be more efficient to control business operations on a day-to-day basis. That meant someone would have to be continually on hand in the office, available to answer questions and make decisions. As an example, at one large company the responsibility for performing the myriad specialized jobs was subdivided and assigned to several departments that had little relationship to each other. Because the printshop began by producing price lists and promotional literature for the field salespeople, the sales department began to control the shop. Because the central file was originally designed for filing business documents generated by customer purchases, the credit manager supervised that file. Because communications between the home office and people in the field were sent over Western Union telex lines, the telex operator reported to the field warehouse manager. And because the switchboard was located in the personnel department, the switchboard operator reported to the personnel department.

There was no records procurement program. Office space was reallocated every other year. The purchasing department tried to standardize the purchase of office equipment and furniture, but because of the growth of the company buyers had to pay attention to other areas of the company. The annual office management budget of this firm, including the salaries of twenty-five people, was more than $1.25 million.

As other parts of the office, such as the printshop and the telex, began to need office support, it became clear that one central person was needed to manage and coordinate the services provided by the office. In addition, greater and more complex knowledge and expertise were required, and responsibilities had to be better defined. The new division of labor was this: salespeople were hired to sell a product, not to produce promotional literature.

This example illustrates how the position of office manager evolved in response to the need for maintaining better control over a growing number of support functions. At the same time managers of such areas as sales and credit were freed from responsibility for the support services and could devote themselves to the areas that they were hired to manage.

JOB RESPONSIBILITIES

An office manager's duties are many and varied. Often they are defined by the type and size of a particular organization. The function and duties of the office manager for an insurance firm, for example, will probably differ from those of the office manager for a manufacturer. The job scope for the office manager whose firm employs five hundred employees will be greater than that for a manager in a company employing fifty.

Depending on the industry, two office managers with similar responsibilities may assign different priorities to different tasks. Security and job safety, for instance, may be primary concerns to the office manager at a pharmaceutical company, whereas the office manager at a university will give these areas lower priority.

Numerous other factors must be taken into account in describing the position of office manager. Although an elaborate description could be developed that would allow comparison of the office management function in many varied industries, that is not the intention of this chapter. Here we are concerned with the practical side of managing an office, not with economic theory at the company level or with personnel management theory.

Records Management

In some large companies or in a company with extensive records the job classification of the person responsible for overseeing the records may be "records manager" rather than office manager. More often than not, however, it is the office manager who oversees the storage, retrieval, and disposal of company documents. These documents may be in one or more forms, such as hard copy (paper), microfilm, magnetic tape, or disks. Paper and microfilm receive the most attention; magnetic tape, punched cards, and disk storage are usually controlled by the electronic data processing (EDP) department. Any procedures that the office manager develops for storing paper and microfilm records should be compared with more sophisticated means of storage.

At some point information about office operations must be transferred to paper—for example, in the form of reports, memos, correspondence, customer orders, and manuals. This information can be handwritten, typed, or generated by a computer; after a document had been acted on, it is usually stored for subsequent retrieval. The storage of large quantities of information is one responsibility of the office manager.

In establishing procedures for storing information, the first question to be answered is, How long must the information be retained? If a records retention system has not been established, the task of storing records can get out of control and become a considerable expense to the firm.

Although instituting a records retention program is not complicated, it can be time-consuming. First, all company documents must be inventoried. This requires the cooperation of other department heads, since they are the people most familiar with the material. An "inventory card" is completed for each record in a given department's files, listing by title the purpose of the document, the age of the oldest set of that particular record, where the document is currently stored, and who normally uses the document. When the inventory is complete, a committee is formed to establish the maximum length of time the company must (or should) maintain each type of record. The committee should include a lawyer, to define the legal retention requirements; someone qualified to establish retention periods of records for tax purposes; and someone qualified to determine how long records must be kept for business and administrative purposes. In cases where the committee members cannot agree on how long a particular record should be retained, the longest applicable period should be adopted.

When a policy for retaining documents has been established, the office manager can turn to organizing the disposal of obsolete records—that is, records that are still held in storage but which are older than the retention period. In the disposal program consideration must be given to destroying records that the company considers confidential. Even otherwise obsolete records may contain sensitive information—for example, salary information on employees. In this case the office manager must make sure that the material is either destroyed or is exempted from the normal records retention period.

The office manager can now turn to the problem of storing the remaining documents. The first thing to be determined is what form the document should take. Must the hard (paper) copy be retained, or can the material safely be transferred to microfilm? In answering this question, one must remember that a significant trade off is involved. Microfilming is an expensive process, whether it is done in-house or through a microfilm service. In addition, microfilm reading machines or reader/printers will be required to retrieve the information once it is recorded on film.

Another question involves the length of time records must be retained. If the retention period is short, it makes little sense to commit the records to microfilm. According to one school of thought, microfilming any record that is to be held less than twenty years is not economically justifiable. Microfilm, however, remains an attractive storage medium because of the significant savings it affords in storage space and because the document can be made very secure. The latter advantage is often overlooked in evaluating hard-copy versus microfilm storage. With microfilm the need to see a complete file can be met by providing the user with a diazo copy while the original, or source, document remains under the control of the records center. When a file is kept in hard-copy form, a company risks losing a file that cannot be replaced.

If hard-copy storage is chosen, the manager must then choose an appropriate container. Storage boxes are available from several manufacturers. One should try to match the type of container with the storage facilities. For instance, how high will the boxes be stacked? What are the physical limitations of the employees who will have to move the boxes? How often must the boxes be gotten out?

Regardless of the storage medium chosen, strong consideration should be given to using centralized control. Setting up a central location for records provides several advantages:

Control over records that are entering storage
Orderly storage of records, which makes retrieval easier
Increased security
Greater assurance of adherence to the records retention program

Office Layout and Allocation of Offices

The office is at once a function, a collection of workers, and a facility. All of these elements must be taken into account when designing an office. The office manager is often the person in the organization best suited for gathering the information required in laying out an effective office.

In determining the most efficient layout, and before the layout is committed to paper, the planner must ask some basic questions:

What departments will occupy the area?
What is their function?
What is their current and projected size?

Projected additions to the staff should be estimated for a period equivalent to the period of normal planning forecasts for the firm. If, for example, the firm makes a five-year projection of sales, data should be available on the number of people needed to meet that forecast. This information will allow one to make a realistic estimate of the space needed, so that planners will not find themselves in a situation in which a plan has become obsolete because the firm has outgrown the allotted space even before it is occupied. In estimating space one must also take into account the special requirements of each department—the number of conference rooms; the space needed for the files in active use; and the space needed for special equipment such as word processors, copiers, and microfilm readers.

Next, the location of each department within the total facility is examined. The planner must look at the relationship of all the departments that will be housed in the facility. Which ones will be working closely together? What form will this interaction take? Will people in the various departments require frequent personal contact, or will communication be made by telephone or by memo? If it is the latter, what will be the volume of communication, how frequently will it occur, and how time sensitive is it likely to be? Note that the questions of frequency and time sensitivity must be answered—or at least estimated—for any mode of interdepartmental communication used, including the telephone and face-to-face meetings.

A good way to obtain this information is simply to interview people in each department and have them rank in the order of frequency the departments they need to communicate with daily. This will help the planner to locate the departments that interact with each other a great deal. To facilitate the flow of work, any two groups in which one group ranks the other first on its list should be located as near the other as possible.

Problems may be encountered, however. For instance, department A may feel that it should be located next to departments B and C, whereas department B may consider it more important to be adjacent to departments D and E; or a situation may develop in which a department sincerely believes that the company will fail if the department is not centrally located—that is, equidistant from every other department.

As soon as the placement of departments within a company has been resolved, job relationships should be worked out—in other words, who sits where. It is usually safe to assume that most of an employee's job functions are coordinated with those of some other employees in the same department. The workflow of a department can be greatly improved by properly positioning the people who work there. Something else that should be taken into consideration is the kind of supervision that the department head must exercise. Some department heads, for instance, feel that it is important to maintain visual contact with employees.

There is always a problem in defining just how much work space various employees need in order to perform efficiently. In attempting to answer this question, many companies have developed officewide standards. Unfortuantely these companies tend to base the size of the employee's office or work space on the individual's position or rank. A vice president may rate 250 square feet, a director 200, a manager 100, and so on. Although this system may be the easiest to administer, it is not necessarily the most efficient. A better standard is one based on job responsibilities, which provides the employee with just the amount of space he or she needs to do the work expected. For example, a buyer in a purchasing department may need shelving for catalogs and enough seating capacity to entertain visiting suppliers.

A key element in the overall planning process is to keep everyone who contributes to the planning informed and up to date on the proposed layout. This has the added advantage of making final approval easier and faster and of involving more people to ensure that nothing has been overlooked or incorrectly evaluated.

Planning for the occupancy of new quarters, although complex and time-consuming, is easy compared to finding additional office space in a building already occupied by the firm. The latter situation may exist when a firm finds that it is adding new personnel faster than anticipated and that it does not have enough office space to house the new employees. The office manager may find it necessary to put desks in conference rooms, ask people to share offices, shift entire departments from one location to another, or even to move a department out of a building altogether.

A company with inadequate office space can usually solve the problem by constructing new facilities or renting additional space. One alternative that is receiving attention is the *open office* concept. With this concept better use can be made of *vertical* space, thus making possible more work stations in an area that traditionally had a confined, closed-off office arrangement. However, the use of the open office concept is still controversial. The office manager must determine the value of this layout for his or her company by taking into account the company's mode and style of operation.

Equipment Selection

Selecting equipment and furniture for an office was once fairly simple. Supplies of pens, ink, and paper were maintained, and a desk and a chair were occasionally purchased when someone was hired. In the modern environment of rapidly increasing technologies, however, the decision process is much more complicated and time-consuming. Even if we disregard the technology factor, we can see that the number of manufacturers, suppliers, and vendors offering office equipment inevitably makes procurement more difficult, complex, and expensive.

Many organizations have assigned the responsibility for purchasing office equipment to one employee in the purchasing department who serves as a full-time buyer. However, even with this level of specialization the office manager is called upon to contribute to the selection of equipment, if not to the final purchase decision. Regardless of the type of item being purchased—whether it is pencils, typewriters, desks, or copiers—the evaluation process used to choose the best possible products for the firm is essentially the same. The office manager lists the product characteristics desired. Some suggested characteristics are

Reasonable price
High quality
Availability of good service from supplier or manufacturer
Ease of operation
Ease of expanding the equipment's capacity in order for the firm to meet new requirements

Before a selection is made each relevant factor is studied and assigned a priority. Proper preparation will make evaluation easier by allowing the office manager to specify the firm's needs to potential suppliers and will, in turn, give suppliers the information they need to better satisfy their customers.

One procedure used to simplify repeat purchases of office equipment items is to select one or two suppliers as the source of each product and deal only with those suppliers. This procedure

Yields benefits associated with quantity buying
Gives the firm added leverage in dealing with suppliers when problems arise
Offers greater standardization of equipment
Avoids overlap and duplication in evaluating purchase requisitions

Approximately every two or three years, the performance of suppliers is reviewed, and new bids are invited from other suppliers to make sure that the company is receiving the best price for the product or service purchased. For example, a firm may decide to examine its policy of using convenience copying equipment. The office manager first determines the features required. This can be done by getting the opinions of those who use the copiers most often. The manager also asks him- or herself:

How does quality compare with speed in various models?
What is the machine's collating ability?
How much of company funds should be spent for this purpose?

When these questions have been answered, the office manager is ready to invite bids from suppliers of copying equipment. Once bids are received the office manager evaluates the bids to make sure that in seeking economy the company is sacrificing as little quality as possible. One step the office manager can take to predict the future performance of the low bidder is to check with that bidder's present customers.

Office Services

The primary function of the office manager is to relieve the people who manage specialized operations such as credit or accounting of the need to coordinate the day-to-day operation of an office. Therefore it is logical to make the office manager responsible for managing the basic functions in an office. These functions include in-house printing, mail delivery and messenger service, telephone service, general maintenance, and arranging all aspects of business travel.

IN-HOUSE PRINTING

Placing the management of in-house printing under the office manager is easily justified. All one need do is compare the annual expenditure for material printed outside with the cost of the equipment and the personnel required to do the printing in-house. Another benefit of establishing an in-house shop is quicker turnaround time and reduced exposure of confidential material that needs to be duplicated to outsiders.

Starting an in-house printing service need not be expensive, nor should it require much expertise. The four basic stages involved in producing a printed image are

Typesetting
Plate making
Duplicating
Finishing

The first two are the most intensive in terms of time and hardware and thus are the most expensive. The duplicating and finishing stages are relatively easy, as well as being cheaper. Thus it is not unusual for an in-house printshop to perform only the duplicating and finishing operations and to rely on a commercial printer for typesetting and plate making.

All offices, regardless of size, require the production of printed material. Convenience office copiers can satisfy the need for up to 50 copies of an original; however, larger and more efficient equipment is needed to perform bigger printing jobs.

A job requiring as many as 250,000 impressions or involving the collation of a many-paged book or special paper cut to a specific size can best be handled by trained printers. Acquiring the equipment and skilled personnel needed to produce large print jobs in-house can offer management an attractive benefit–cost ratio when compared to using a commercial printer.

MAIL SERVICE

One of the most important departments of any firm is the mailroom. This department is also the least appreciated and the one most frequently taken for granted. The mailroom is responsible for disseminating written information throughout an organization. The percentage of written information that enters or leaves an organization by way of the mailroom almost certainly exceeds 90 percent.

The responsibility for handling such huge amounts of paper is made more complex by the increasing demand for faster processing and delivery. At the same time the cost of postage is rising, which means that the mailroom supervisor of even a small company must cope with an annual postal bill of a quarter of a million dollars.

Some advances have been made recently both in improving mailroom equipment and in understanding what kind of people are needed to staff the mailroom. The introduction of electronic technology has speeded the sorting and processing of mail. In addition there may be an economic advantage in using volume mailing when the volume is high enough for the mailroom supervisor to take advantage of the lower rates available for presorted, outgoing mail using zip codes.

The mailroom was once the entry-level position of an office. If a person showed potential, he or she advanced to a higher, better-paying job and left the mailroom. But this custom produced a high turnover rate and implied that any employee who stayed in the mailroom had, at best, merely adequate ability. With mailroom operations consuming more and more of companies' budgets due to the constantly rising costs of postage and equipment, companies have come to realize that they must examine more closely what is actually needed for the mailroom to function effectively.

TELEPHONE SERVICE

The telephone is probably the best-known piece of equipment in the office. Most people, however, take for granted its power to help us communicate. The cost of using this tool, however, cannot be taken for granted by management. Two costs are involved in telephone use in the office—an installation charge and a rental charge. Until recently an office manager had little control over either cost; now, however, equipment can be purchased outright, enabling users to eliminate monthly rental charges. Alternatives to telephone company long-distance dialing networks are also being developed.

The advantage of purchasing rather than renting telephone equipment monthly is now obvious. A firm's controller takes one look at the payback period and becomes enthusiastic about buying phones. Deciding to purchase is usually easy, but deciding which vendor to buy from is often difficult. This decision requires the same rigorous analysis as planning office space. Because of the technology involved in modern telephone communications systems, it is often advisable to seek the advice of a consultant in the appropriate field—for example, in communications, data processing, or management.

Some impressive advances have been made in communications technology, especially in developing the telephone as a business tool. In some ways the telephone is equal to the computer in its power to communicate. The capabilities of this tool should, however, be evaluated in light of a particular organization's operation. An office manager could, so to speak, buy a Cadillac when all the firm needs is a small Chevrolet stationwagon.

Technological advances in office equipment are likely to continue, with new features being introduced at a rapid pace. The office manager will therefore be cautious in deciding to purchase rather than rent, even when the potential payback is attractive. For example, a new telephone system that is up to date at the time of purchase can become obsolete within a year.

In the late 1970s the federal government significantly reduced restrictions on the sale of transmission services. Alternatives to direct long-distance dialing or to direct-distance dialing have long been available—for example, tie lines, foreign exchange, and leased lines. However, these services are expensive and require a high volume of traffic to be cost-effective. The WATS option is perhaps the most widely used alternative to direct-distance dialing. The problem with WATS, however, is the difficulty in controlling its use. People using it assume that a WATS line is a toll-free line. It is not. For either outgoing WATS service or incoming service, the cost is not inconsequential. Further, it is difficult to trace the party making a call, making it virtually impossible to assign charges appropriately.

A new competitor to WATS is the private carrier. Private carriers sell access to communications networks that are not a part of AT&T's Long Lines. The advantage of using a private carrier is lower charges; the disadvantages are the smaller networks and the often cumbersome access procedures.

Today's office workers have become accustomed to a safe, clean, comfortable work environment. This is due in part to state and federal laws enacted over the past forty years and in part to the realization by employers and management that providing such work environments benefits them as well. In return for investing in a better work environment, management gains a more productive office staff.

Every office must be kept reasonably clean. Thus janitorial service is a standard office expense. The office manager may wish to consider other expenditures in addition to the standard ones. For instance, is there a regular carpet maintenance program? How often are the offices painted? Is the furniture, in general and the chairs, in particular, cleaned regularly? These may seem to be mundane questions, but attention to detail should be as much a part of the maintenance program as of any other phase of office operations. No matter what equipment or furnishings are involved, the purpose of regular maintenance is to extend their useful life. The office manager who has a good maintenance program will help maximize both the efficiency and the effectiveness of the office.

Office Procedures

SECURITY

Whenever people gather to accomplish something, they find that they must first establish rules and procedures that will make the task of achieving a goal as safe and secure as possible. In an office the manager is responsible for establishing procedures for protecting not only individual workers but the business as a whole. Specific security rules, of course, vary according to the type of business, but some are needed in any business. Such rules often answer these questions:

Who may enter the office?
How are people with authorization to enter to be identified?
What provisions must be made for admitting visitors?
What are the responsibilities of those delegated to ensure office security?

When designing a security program, the office manager must first determine the level of security desired. It makes little sense to set up a program for tight office security if management feels that the risk is minimal.

Basic security is usually established through an identification program and the use of a security staff to enforce the program. Individuals may be issued badges or cards that identify them as employees of a firm and authorizing their admittance to the buildings and grounds of the firm. A security program may also be designed to restrict some employees to certain areas. The firm may wish to restrict employee access in terms of numbers, authorization, or both.

SAFETY

Workplace safety, on the other hand, is not a question of maximum or minimum levels. Building codes and insurance coverage dictate to a large extent the measures a firm must take to safeguard employees and physical property. The prudent office manager will, however, establish policies and procedures to ensure compliance with safety standards and will then make sure that employees are familiar with the policies and procedures. Some managers use a safety manual to help teach safety rules.

PREVENTING FISCAL ABUSE

The office manager is often given the responsibility for establishing procedures for protecting company assets from employee abuse. The asset that requires the most protection is money—the cash a business keeps on hand for daily operations. Access to company funds must be authorized and carefully controlled. Most large firms follow good business practices, practices any student of accounting could outline and follow. A surprisingly large number of small firms, however, make themselves vulnerable to abuse by not doing so.

The office manager must continually review company procedures to ensure that established policies are being followed and must adjust these procedures as necessary. A common problem is one that occurs when a firm with two hundred employees continues to follow policies in force when it had only twenty.

OFFICE ORGANIZATION

The task of managing an office can be divided into two areas—managing day-to-day operations, and developing new programs to meet future requirements. Without help, the office manager cannot expect to handle both areas efficiently. The work of the office makes it mandatory that the office manager entrust to others the responsibility for seeing that the office's services are provided. If the manager becomes overly involved in routine activities, little time will be left for other duties.

Thus far in this chapter we have been discussing the responsibilities of managers at a particular level of responsibility. The organization we are talking about is a manufacturing firm with sales of around $1 billion per year that is served by an office staff of about five hundred. The necessary level of service is high, and performance standards have been established to satisfy the company's needs. This particular business organization is divided into four areas of responsibility, or functions: printing, mail and messenger services, records management, and office services. The last function is not actually performed by a single functional team but by a group of unrelated service groups that must nevertheless be closely supervised. Some of the activities assigned to office services are travel arrangements, office supplies, and communications.

Individual areas under the office manager's control are assigned to area supervisors. An area supervisor is responsible for the daily operation of the area assigned to him or her, and management of the operation of that area is based on policies and procedures established by the office manager. The supervisor

Instructs employees in the performance of their duties and later reviews their performance
Interviews and selects new employees
Makes salary recommendations to the office manager
Dismisses employees for unsatisfactory work
In some cases controls the development and management of a budget

The area supervisor is also knowledgeable about the technical aspects of the job.

The office manager remains detached from the day-to-day operations but monitors the performance of area supervisors. It is a good idea to establish a reporting system that requires detailed, periodic reporting by the supervisor on the group's work. This report usually deals with performance as measured against standards set for the group. If the standards are not met, the area supervisor tries to determine why and then makes the necessary adjustments. It is the office manager's responsibility to foster good communications about how things are going within a department. The flow of communications should not be one-sided; information concerning the department should flow both from the top and from the bottom, as well as laterally. The manager will make sure that everyone with a need to know has access to pertinent information. A good way to develop this communication is through periodic staff meetings in which supervisors discuss the performance of their areas and the problems they have both encounterd and anticipate.

The other employees on the office services staff perform tasks assigned to them; these are usually clerical and are defined in job descriptions. Minimum standards of skill and performance must be maintained, or an employee should not continue in a particular position. The skills desired are those that are fundamental to clerical work. Many of these skills can be learned on the job under the supervision of the area supervisor. When an employee does not perform satisfactorily, it is usually because of lack of motivation or because the employee is not completely reliable. Even an employee with a high skill level is of little value to an organization if he or she is frequently absent from work.

A successful office management organization must be flexible. Management must be able to move staff members from function to function depending upon where the work load is heaviest. Backup support must be built into the organization for dealing with work load peaks or for covering personnel shortages caused by vacations and absenteeism. One way to deal with this problem is to use part-time or temporary workers. Another way is to make the regular staff more flexible by providing cross-training. Cross-training should go beyond merely knowing the job duties of another employee working in a related area; it should be expanded to give each employee a skill that will allow him or her to work effectively and efficiently in another departmental area or even in another division of the organization. For example, someone from the mailroom should be able to fill in in the printshop when the work load there is unusually heavy. Cross-training has advantages besides enabling managers to adjust for fluctuations in work loads:

It provides a reserve of trained replacement for filling a position that has been vacated.

It offers an employee job enrichment by providing diversified tasks and occasionally a change of work environment.

It increases the quantity and quality of an employee's skills, making the employee more valuable and thus more promotable.

The key to efficiency in the organization that uses cross-training extensively is the area supervisor. This person must accurately judge the volume of work to be done and determine how much additional help is needed. The area supervisor must also provide continuity—especially when employees are entering and leaving the group at frequent intervals—taking care that standards are maintained and that the quality of work does not decrease as volume increases.

The office organization that functions in these ways will be able to accomplish the routine tasks of the office. Beyond that, another area of responsibility that needs structuring is solving immediate problems and planning for the future needs of the office. Because an office is a dynamic organization, the office manager needs to continually be aware of changing requirements. The technology available for coping with these requirements is constantly changing as well. An effective office manager examines the most efficient ways to satisfy the demands on his or her office. At the same time suggestions will be offered from within the organization on how best to carry out projects or to perform particular jobs done by the office. The office manager will need assistance in evaluating the current operation of the office, the state of available technology, and the ramifications of adopting new procedures or installing new equipment. Although the manager can perform much of the analysis required, situations or problems may develop that demand the expertise and experience of employees from other areas of the company.

Some organizations use a "task team" approach to problem solving. When a problem affects the office, the manager is often called upon to head up the team. How it is constituted otherwise depends on the particular problem, but a representative from each department involved should be included.

SKILLS NEEDED BY THE OFFICE MANAGER

For every position within an organization a particular set of job skills is required if the job is to be performed well. The job description should be explicit in specifying the necessary skills, so that the organization will experience as little disruption as possible whenever the need to restaff arises. The job description is used to determine what abilities and skills are needed, if a person is to meet his or her responsibilities adequately. Although the job description may contain several necessary qualifications for the successful performance of a position, one requirement is usually given extra weight: the ability to work effectively with people. This is especially true for the office manager, who must organize a number of people into an efficient, well-motivated team.

The office manager does not operate in a vacuum. He or she needs the work and cooperation of numerous other individuals. This is true whether the manager is working with area supervisors, task team members, or office employees in general. The office manager can demand cooperation, but unless the cooperation is given willingly, it is likely to decline, and quickly. The most successful office managers are those who can gain their employees' respect, liking, and willing cooperation.

Every organization has characteristics that distinguish it from other companies in its field, since every organization is made up of a different group of people. In viewing the office as a dynamic suborganization of a larger dynamic whole, the office manager must continually be aware of the special "personality" of his or her company, which tends to reflect the personality of the senior managers. The distinguishing characteristic might be that numerous—or very few—approvals are required before a change of policy is initiated, or it might be that new technology is adopted quickly or very slowly. Does the firm consistently choose the top of the line in equipment or services when presented with a clear choice of options, or is it more likely to select a less expensive option? Such characteristics are manifestations of the values and attitudes of the company's senior managers. Unless the office manager recognizes this, the chance of getting senior managers to adopt new policies or programs or to authorize the installation of new technology is greatly reduced.

Other necessary skills, besides the ability to work well with people, are those usually acquired through higher education. Although a degree in business is not a prerequisite for success, someone with college or university training generally has an advantage. More that a casual familiarity with business practices and with financial decision making techniques is advised. Although it is not essential that the office manager be able to perform regression analysis or to set up a balance sheet properly, a knowledge of business theory, plus the ability to ask relevant questions, is important. The ability to speak the language of the business community is the essential element.

Other areas in which the office manager needs to have a basic knowledge are personnel management and general management theory. Once again, it is not necessary for the good office manager to develop expertise in the field of personnel management, but he or she should be familiar with the views of experts in the field and be prepared to put these views into practice where applicable.

The office manager needs to be acquainted with just about every aspect of the business in which his or her firm is engaged, since sooner or later he or she must deal with problems that involve all the various facets of office operation. In developing a solution to a particular problem, one must take into account the effect of the recommended solution on the business as a whole, not just the effect on the departments directly involved. The ability to anticipate the effects of a course of action is a valuable one. It should be kept in mind that systems analysis looks not only at the short-term effects of an action but at the long-term effects as well.

In summary, the office manager must be a good general manager and a good administrative manager. The skills required can be gained through formal education, through professional affiliations, or through on-the-job experience. The chance of success in office management increases with the individual's level of preparation. Once a person has started working as an office manager, there are many avenues open to either develop new skills or to refurbish techniques that have become rusty through disuse. One of the best ways to achieve either objective is to join a professional managers' organization, such as the Administrative Management Society (AMS). The purpose of AMS is to improve managers' performance by sponsoring seminars, publishing material that discusses management techniques, and gathering managers in formal and informal meetings and conferences where they can share problems and solutions.

Another good source of information for the office manager is the many periodicals and magazines dealing with the office and with office management. Some valuable ones are *Administrative Management, The Office,* and *Modern Office Procedures.* Published monthly, each journal helps the office manager keep abreast of information about the profession.

The office manager's position is a highly visible one. The responsibilities of the position are varied, testing the skills and talent of anyone who is ambitious and who enjoys facing the challenge of new and sometimes difficult problems and managing a vital part of a business operation.

CHAPTER 14

The Successful Office Manager

To be effective the office manager must, above all, manage people successfully. Because an office, by definition, consists of people, the level of success achieved depends largely on the manager's direction and leadership. It makes little difference whether the office is staffed by chemical engineers or by inventory clerks; managerial ability is the single most important characteristic of the successful office manager.

It might at first seem that this ability is innate, but that is hardly the case. The ability to manage must be learned. Essentially this ability consists of using a knowledge of human nature to develop a technique for motivating people to reach agreed-upon goals. The successful—or, to be more precise, the effective—manager is one who gets to know his or her subordinates and who uses this insight to motivate them to work well and diligently. This is true no matter what business a company is involved in. Many people consider management to be a difficult task, when in fact it merely involves using common sense. What makes the

"The Successful Office Manager" is the contribution of Joel R. Culmone, Director, Compensation and Benefits, Yale New Haven Hospital, formerly of Emery Air Freight Corporation.

task of management appear difficult is the time and effort it seems to take; a manager must continually think about his or her managerial responsibilities. The moment one's thoughts wander, problems are certain to arise.

Because managing people is by far the most important ability in an office manager's repertoire, this chapter concentrates on areas of office management that are directly related to each other: communicating with employees, hiring, motivating, appraising employee performance, taking disciplinary action, and the legal aspects of office management. In dealing with subordinates the office manager should always be careful to treat them with respect, be honest with them, give them a reason to grow in their jobs as well as provide room in which to grow, explain rather than dictate, and be sensitive to their backgrounds, feelings, and needs.

COMMUNICATING WITH EMPLOYEES

Communication is fundamental to the operation of an office. It is the single most important factor in successful management. Communications works both ways, however—information must flow *to* as well as *from* management. A predominately one-way flow can short-circuit communication and result in inefficiency and lowered production.

Let's consider the two types of communication—upward and downward. What techniques are available to the office manager for improving communication within an office? Putting out good news is one effective method. Suppose that a company increases its paid holidays from nine to ten. Such news, properly communicated, can engender a positive attitude among employees. In other words, good news can be an effective morale booster. Another effective way to improve employee–manager relations and thus raise morale, is for the office manager to hold brief meetings at which such items of company news are explained to employees.

Sometimes, however, news must be announced that will not meet with universal approval. Let's say that a company has just introduced a new performance appraisal program that establishes standards intended to make employees more accountable. A group meeting would be held to announce the program and explain it more fully. If an office manager has developed a rapport with his or her subordinates, the meeting should go well, and questions should come easily. Here, too, there must be give-and-take: ample time must be allowed for questions and discussion, especially when a major policy change such as an appraisal program is announced. A single, brief meeting is not enough. Employees tend to view with skepticism announcements concerning complex new programs, procedures, and policies, especially if these can be easily distorted by misinformation or rumor. They are likely to become uneasy and to worry about the impact of such a change on their jobs. If they are still worried after a meeting is held to clarify an issue or a policy change, they are likely to become disgruntled, which could lead eventually to lowered productivity. One effective procedure is to follow up a general meeting with individual sessions in which you and the employees discuss, say, a performance appraisal program and how it could affect them both personally and as a group.

Good communication between manager and employee about important matters is best accomplished face to face. Routine information can be transmitted more formally through bulletin board notices, memos, or newsletters. One error that managers often make in communicating with their subordinates is to formalize important information in writing—with few or no private discussions. The written communication that anticipates every possible question has yet to be written. A written memo also tends to put employees at a disadvantage, erecting an artificial barrier between them and managers that becomes more and more difficult to overcome as time goes along. Many employees feel that it is improper for them to question a written memo. They may believe that a memo or an announcement is an edict that cannot be questioned effectively, or that should not be questioned closely if they want to keep their jobs. The best way to allay such feelings is to meet them head-on. In such meetings as those discussed above (especially in the case of the performance appraisal announcement) a good follow-up to the group meeting is to post on the bulletin board the details of the changes discussed.

Consider another situation: You have recently hired a clerk, and it is now the clerk's first day at work. What should you, as the office manager, do to familiarize the employee with the job and make him or her effective as quickly as possible? First, you should analyze the job for the new person, discussing what it consists of, how it should be performed, and the level of performance expected. Having done so, you might perhaps feel that the new employee is now adequately prepared to assume the responsibilities of the position.

A period of time passes (say, four months), during which you have simply allowed the new employee to perform the work—without, however, having discussed his or her performance or progress with the employee. At this point, when you finally decide to assess his or her work you discover that the performance has been merely average. However, because you have not kept abreast of his or her progress during the past four months, you find yourself in a difficult position to either criticize or commend the employee. As a result, you decide on an easier alternative, which is to allow the clerk's performance to continue as it has for the last four months. The harder alternative of confronting the performance issue under these circumstances is unquestionably difficult.

Many office managers allow such situations to develop, but they are wrong to do so. Although that initial discussion with the new clerk is valuable, it must be followed up frequently, regardless of how well or poorly a person performs.

In the case of average performers, how can the office manager know what a person is capable of? How does the manager find out whether the clerk is capable of being a superior performer, and, if so, what will motivate him or her to try? In the present example, the manager does *not* know—because two ingredients of good communication are missing: feedback and counseling.

It is unreasonable to expect an employee's performance level to increase if the employee has been given an orientation but no indication of the performance expected at periodic intervals. In the case of the average employee mentioned above, no discussions were held about areas in which performance could be improved, and no suggestions were given for reaching the desired levels. Neither, as we have noted, is it reasonable to discipline the employee. Even in merely considering disciplinary action, the manager should keep in mind that any such actions must be applied equally to everyone who fails to meet performance standards. No matter what action is taken, it must be applied to all employees who warrant it, or the manager will be accused, rightly, of playing favorites. Fairness should be the guiding principle. Employees must be counseled, and job performance must be evaluated continuously—not in generalities but in specifics that are clearly stated. The office manager is entitled to expect above-average performance from each employee—if realistic standards are established and constant evaluation and suggestions are made to help improve performance. Communication should be an ongoing activity, whether a policy change is to be announced or a new employee has just joined the department. The communication process should also occasionally include chitchat that is not directly job-related. The outside interests of employees are ideal subjects. For example, you can talk about tennis with a secretary who is an excellent player or have a chat with a clerk about woodworking who does it for a hobby. Once you can talk freely to employees about non-work subjects, you should find it easier to discuss work-related matters.

The office manager should try to talk to employees often—if possible, every day—regardless of what the conversations are about. The manager needs to be sensitive to employees' moods; they can signal attitudes that might need to be discussed. For example, the manager of an office with twenty-five employees took pride in how well she knew her subordinates and spoke to each of them every day. Thus, she noticed that the mail clerk was beginning to withdraw from the rest of the employees. Once the life of the party, he had become aloof. Because the mail clerk's performance of his duties was virtually unchanged, the manager thought that it might be a good idea to leave well enough alone. When after several days, his mood had not changed, however, the manager, who felt that she had developed a rapport with him, decided to find out why. It turned out that the clerk was becoming increasingly dissatisfied with himself; he envisioned himself remaining a mail clerk for his entire career, although he considered himself capable of assuming more responsibility, greater challenges, and more diversified work. But he would never be able to prove his ability, or so he thought. The manager began talking to the mail clerk more often, asking about his work, his interests, and his ambitions. Eventually she was able to counsel him and to suggest what he could do to prepare himself for advancement. The clerk's outlook brightened. He became, if anything, more productive and finally developed into an employee with a future at the company.

Although no one meeting or series of meetings can take the place of rapport between the office manager and a subordinate, meetings are a useful tool in achieving effective communication. Meetings have as many purposes as there are policies, problems, and announcements. An office manager might, for example, wish to discuss the company's medical insurance policy with employees or explain or discuss a particularly bad or good business quarter. Each meeting is an opportunity not only to inform and to clarify but also to hear from employees and learn what is on their minds, what questions are uppermost, what their mood is. It goes almost without saying that the office manager should keep an open mind. He or she should also be alert to trends. If several similar questions are asked, that may signal strong employee interest in the topic. The manager should make a note (mental or written) and investigate such interest at the first opportunity. At the same time the manager should not allow meetings to become gripe sessions. Complaints, yes; gripes, no. Nor should a meeting ever be dominated by one employee. Finally, questions should be answered directly, succinctly, and honestly. If you, as the office manager, are conducting the meeting and do not know the answer to a question, say so, adding that you will find out as soon as you can. Then do so.

The key is openness. Do not be so formal that employees will be afraid to approach you. Check the following list to determine whether you are communicating effectively:

Employees usually come to me with their problems.
Employees know at any given time how I feel about their problems.
Performance appraisals do not catch employees by surprise.
Rumors about work, working conditions, or company policy are few, and those that do occur are short-lived.
I am familiar with the career goals of my subordinates and am generally aware of their personal interests.
I frequently have private talks with each employee.
When I tell an employee something, I explain it and give the reason or reasons.
Questions are always raised at employee meetings that I conduct.
Employees are kept informed about company policies and procedures, as well as about how the company is doing.

Remember, treat employees with respect; do not condescend or patronize; be responsive. Remember, too, that communication within the company must flow both upward and downward.

HIRING

Hiring is one of the most important responsibilities of any manager. The office manager who can find and hire efficient, productive employees ensures his or her future with the company; conversely, the manager who hires incompetent people regularly is headed for a downfall. All too often, however, office managers view the hiring aspect of their work as onerous. Certain steps must be learned. The first step is to review the job to be filled. Although most office managers are sufficiently familiar with the jobs in their departments to feel that they do not need to spend time reviewing them, they would do well to review the job descriptions and work procedures. Such a review should include

> The credentials required for the job—for example, education, skills, experience (including length)
> A detailed breakdown of the requirements into the items *necessary* for success in the job advertised and those that will virtually guarantee success
> A list of the job's responsibilities
> The levels of performance expected at predetermined intervals— for example, initial (or probationary); at six months; at one year, etc.

While it may seem logical to use published job descriptions if your company has them, it is better not to. Many jobs can change both rapidly and significantly; thus a formalized description of a job may be merely a "snapshot" of the job as it existed at a certain time, and a job description may be seriously out of date by the time an opening occurs. In view of the rapidly changing technology, a computer job, for example, is likely to change dramatically over just a year or two. This is especially true in fast-growing companies, in which jobs and job duties often evolve rapidly.

Once you have thoroughly reviewed and updated a job description, you are in a better position to discuss the job precisely with applicants. Next you should decide on the procedure to be followed in filling the position. The first step often is to post the opening for the company's employees, some of whom may be interested because the opening represents an opportunity for advancement. The employees are also in the best position to know of someone outside the company who might be interested. Successful applicants from either source would undoubtedly save the company time and money that would otherwise be spent in recruiting. Another clear benefit of posting openings is that it avoids alienating employees who might view turning to an outside source as evidence of a lack of confidence in them.

The announcement should be short and clear: job title, brief description, salary range, and starting salary (if known). It should include a statement such as: "Interested employees who feel they are qualified should speak to [name] by [date]." When you receive applications, interview the applicants privately and rate them. Then tell those who are unqualified why they cannot be promoted.

If the position cannot be filled by the company's employees, prepare for the next step. In recruiting from outside, use some or all of the following sources: business schools, high schools, junior and senior colleges, community colleges, employment agencies, minority placement services, classified advertising, private associations, and rehabilitation agencies. The personnel department can also be helpful in filling positions, especially when the company is large, spread out, or highly structured.

Let us assume that you have advertised for applicants and have solicited applications from other sources. You will soon be getting responses—by letter, telephone, and even people who just walk in off the street. The first step in handling these applicants is to screen them. Screening usually consists of asking questions that can be used to determine as quickly as possible whether an applicant meets the requirements. An applicant who does not have the necessary qualifications should be dropped from consideration unless he or she has compensating skills. Applicants who meet all the requirements should be formally interviewed. Telephone and letter applicants are fairly easily screened. Because of the office manager's schedule, it may not be possible to screen every applicant who comes in. However, walk-in applicants should be given the opportunity to fill out an application, and an appointment for an interview should be set up.

In reviewing résumés and written applications, watch for the following danger signals:

Job hopping: the applicant who holds a job for one year, then another for one year, another for ten months, and so on

Employment gaps: the applicant who has been out of work for significant lengths of time

Inconsistent experience: the applicant who appears to have changed careers with each job change

Inconsistent or sluggish salary growth: the applicant who moves from one job to another with a good salary increase but who takes a pay cut in a later job move or one who shows evidence of consistently meager salary increases

Keeping these signals in mind, screen each application or résumé and arrange interviews in the near future for those who appear to be qualified on the basis of the initial screening.

The purpose of the job interview is to learn enough about the applicant to get an idea of how well he or she will perform in the job being offered. One type of interview that is counterproductive is the one that is designed to intimidate the applicant into raising his or her defenses, so as to reveal how the applicant reacts to stress. Even when such a tactic works, what is revealed about the applicant is virtually useless. A more effective tactic, and one that is fairer to the applicant, is to be casual yet businesslike in the interview. An applicant who feels truly comfortable with the interviewer will reveal all that the hirer needs to know about the potential employee and his or her qualifications.

Proper preparation is a great aid in conducting an effective interview. For example, you should

Select a private room

Make company materials available

Be prepared with a detailed list of questions and a format for the discussion

Allow no interruptions whatsoever

Schedule so that sufficient time is allowed for each interview

Follow a predetermined pattern in each interview:

First, try to put the applicant at ease. For example, ask about the weather or about whether the individual was able to follow the directions to the office without difficulty.

Next, outline the interview procedure by telling the applicant what you hope to accomplish. By doing this, you can remove some of the mystery—about the interview itself, about the job offered, and about the company.

Then probe for information about

    Experience: is the applicant's experience closely related to the position offered? How successful (that is, effective) was the applicant?

    Education: What is the applicant's educational background, and what were his or her objectives?

    Ability and personality: What are the applicant's strengths? Liabilities?

    Outside activities: What are they? What bearing do they have on the position under discussion? What do they indicate about how the applicant will perform in the job?

    General: Why is the applicant applying for this position (aside from needing the money)?

Provide information about the job and the company. Encourage the applicant to feel positive about the company while at the same time acquainting him or her with the details of the job.

Give the applicant a chance to ask questions.

Tell the applicant what the next step is and when it should occur.

As soon as the applicant leaves, record the results of the interview. By doing so at this time, you are more likely to remember all the details of the interview.

In the interview, it is generally more useful to ask open-ended questions than questions that can be answered only with a yes or no. To repeat, only two people should be in the room—you and the applicant. If the applicant answers a question in a way that indicates that there is more to be said, wait for it; do not say anything for a moment. Silence can be surprisingly effective in encouraging the applicant to be more forthcoming with information.

The next step is to review what you have learned from the applicant. A thorough evaluation of the individual's academic background, employment history, career orientation, and, critically important, the ability to deal with people is essential. The ability to deal with people is something that can be evaluated only after a series of in-depth questions during the interview that probe how he or she has dealt with peers, superiors, and subordinates, and how stressful interactions were handled at each level. An excellent line of questioning would be to have the candidate describe the personality type whose interactions he or she finds most difficult to deal with and how such interaction has been handled when it was necessary. Rate each applicant according to these criteria, as well as against all other potential candidates and rank them—first choice, second choice, and so on.

Use caution. Certain traps await managers who do hiring:

Do not allow yourself to be overimpressed by a single outstanding trait that you have noted in an applicant. Such a trait can overshadow all others, some of which might turn out to be very detrimental. For example, do not be misled by the applicant who, on paper, has had extensive experience or impressive job titles. Look for the facts; let the impressions form later.

Avoid setting overly restrictive standards. Qualifications that are unusually high or unusually narrow could shut out many worthy applicants.

Studies have shown that interviewers tend to rely on initial impressions—those formed during the first few minutes of an interview. Do not look for evidence supporting a preconceived notion about an applicant. An effective interview is an objective interview.

The final step in the evaluation process is to check references. If you can, speak directly to immediate supervisors; they are probably more familiar with an applicant's work and tend to be more candid than managers and personnel representatives in their evaluations. Questions should be objective and should concern only job-related matters. A word of caution: do not run reference checks unless the applicant has given authorization to do so by signing a consent statement on either the application or a separate form.

What comes next? The job offer! Phone the applicant or invite him or her to come in. Explain the company's desire to have the applicant fill the job. Restate the job title and salary and briefly describe the duties. Then ask whether the applicant is still interested. If the applicant accepts, follow the acceptance with a letter confirming that he or she has been hired and stating the pertinent conditions of the job. If the answer is no, write the applicant, thanking him or her for expressing interest in the job and the company and wishing him or her success. Because a physical examination is rarely a condition of hiring, it can—and should—be scheduled after the job offer has been made. Both the offer and the letter of confirmation should state whether the offer is contingent upon the applicant's passing a physical.

MOTIVATING

An important attribute of sound management is the ability to stimulate, or motivate, employees to achieve both departmental and company goals. Ideas abound about the best motivational tactics, many of which fall into either the authoritarian category ("Get a move on or you'll be out the door!") or the lenient category ("Don't worry about meeting only a third of your quota; I know you're trying.").

The vice-president for manufacturing of a moderate-sized corporation once told his colleagues and the company's senior vice-president that in his opinion the most effective way to manage was to inspire fear in one's employees. It is interesting to note what went on in this vice-president's division under such a regime. Managers reported only good news to the vice-president, never bad news. When problems arose, it was difficult to determine responsibility because every subordinate was pointing a finger at another subordinate. All kinds of scheming went on behind the vice-president's back. Primarily because his leadership style was counterproductive, he did not remain long in that position.

Another example provides a look at the difficulties encountered in the lenient style of leadership. An office manager with responsibility for eight office workers tried to be a friend to each worker. Because he disliked discipline, he hardly ever used any. However, his group was not the carefree "happy family" that might have been expected. Some of the group performed well, and some did not. The manager gave out merit raises that varied little for the good, average, and poor performer. It soon became clear to the productive workers that they were doing more work for virtually the same pay and recognition. They concluded that good attendance, punctuality, and performance meant nothing, since everyone was treated the same. The result was that over a period of time the group's performance declined sharply—enough so that the need for managerial training for this particular manager became obvious.

In past times, management exercised almost dictatorial power. It was virtually unheard of for employees to question company policies, and discipline was administered at the whim of supervisors. Subordinates dared not protest directives for fear that to do so would get them, at the least, reprimanded and at the worst fired. Today, however, management on the whole treats employees with respect; employees' opinions and suggestions are frequently sought. This change in attitudes reflects the social changes that have occurred in our society. People now question and challenge far more than they did twenty years ago; they are less prone to accept traditions and values they do not understand or agree with, and challenges to individuals and institutions representing authority are no longer odd occurrences. The decline of "blind acceptance" has affected business as much as it has government. However difficult it is to manage in times in which people recognize their rights and seek greater self-fulfillment, the situation does provide a golden opportunity. Harnessing this greater awareness into managerial participation can yield far greater productivity than its exclusion. Companies now use their workers as the first line in the fight against inefficient production. Quality circles, as a process in which small groups of employees meet to discuss improvements in the work situation, have become an excellent vehicle for encouraging worker input into managing the business. Originally an idea which developed in this country, it has become characteristic of the progressive and effective Japanese management style. Above all else, allowing worker involvement provides a motivational boost that few other techniques can match.

The following are some basic ways to motivate subordinates:

When you tell an employee to do something, don't make the request sound like a command. Explain what it is you want done, why it must be done (if you can't explain why, perhaps the task shouldn't be performed), and when it should be completed.

After you have explained what you want done, ask the employee whether he or she has any questions. If there are questions, discuss them thoroughly. Ask the employee whether he or she foresees any difficulties in doing the task in the time allotted. If difficulties are foreseen, ask for reasons.

Periodically, ask how the work is going—whether it is on schedule and what problems, if any, have been encountered.

If the task is going well and proceeding on schedule, compliment the subordinate. If it is not, constructive criticism may be in order: restate the deadline or the special instructions and ask to be kept informed of anything that could affect the subordinate's ability to meet the deadline.

When the task has been completed, offer honest praise for good work. Remember the rule: it's a good practice to praise publicly and to criticize privately. Even with those whose performance you find unsatisfactory, temper negative criticism with positive comments; if a lackluster worker has performed well in some respects, point out the good things. But do not get into the position of praising an employee when there is only a weak or a nonexistent reason to do so—for the simple reason that it will be clear to everyone involved that you are not being sincere.

To a large extent, providing motivation depends on knowing your subordinates. What kind of work do they like to do? What are they particularly good at? What will motivate them? One way to answer these questions is to give your subordinates challenging assignments. Such assignments are also a valuable method of providing additional training. Take the following example. A clerk has been advancing steadily until he has reached the level of senior clerk III. The next level is one that is exempt for professionals. At his present level, the clerk begins to have doubts about his abilities and where he is going. Is he in over his head? His manager senses this and, bit by bit, begins to redirect the clerk, using assignments that challenge him but which the manager knows the employee can handle. It soon becomes evident that the clerk has not only mastered the duties of the senior clerk III position but that he has gone beyond that level. This was accomplished step by step; after the first assignment was completed successfully, more difficult tasks were assigned. At each step the clerk was given the direction and recognition he needed and deserved.

Keep your subordinates informed about their performance, which should be assessed at regular intervals. As an example, a medium-sized company introduced a form for appraising employees' work. The form had several categories in which the employee was to be rated. The idea was that the subordinate and the manager, after filling out the form separately, would get together and compare notes. After the form had been introduced and tried for the first time, a manager complained that it was unworkable because subordinates consistently overrated themselves. Apparently this manager felt that his rating and that of his subordinates were incompatible. They may have been, but that did not mean that the system was unworkable. The fault may have lain with the manager—with his perception of his employees' performance. It may have been the manager who was out of touch; in fact, communication both upward and downward was suspect. The manager should have taken the discrepancy between ratings in the appraisal form as a danger signal, an indication that his subordinates were operating without knowing the proper standards of performance. If that was so, why *wouldn't* they consider their work to be excellent? As it turned out, this indeed was the problem.

PERFORMANCE APPRAISAL

Nearly every company reviews employee performance regularly, usually at intervals of six months or one year, and usually to provide a basis for salary increases. The review procedure can also be used to provide feedback to employees about their performance. As both the office manager and the review officer, you are now in a position to affect how much an employee earns. Thus, you should make certain that your appraisals are objective, consistent, and fair. Most inexperienced managers approach the employee review as a one-time, painful exercise which, once it is done, can be forgotten about until the next review time. Such an attitude could not be more wrong. A proper appraisal for the next review begins the moment the current review ends. If the review has been conducted properly, it becomes a routine procedure with predictable results. Throughout the period between reviews, the manager should be making notes on the positive as well as the negative aspects of each employee's performance. A good way to do this is to put two sheets in each employee's personnel folder, one for good performance and the other for poor. When an employee goofs, insert a note in the folder to that effect. However, first discuss the performance or incident with the employee. Do not put in writing anything that has not already been discussed. Document everything, whether good or bad, and include the date of occurrence and the date on which you discussed the matter with the employee. If this is done properly, your subordinates will be aware of what is in their personnel files, both favorable and unfavorable. Be careful about what is rated. If it is not related directly to the job performance, omit it.

For example, many companies include the category "leadership" in their reviews, even when the appraisal is being made of a file clerk or secretary—two positions for which little leadership is required. Another category often found in rating forms is "attitude." What do you, as office manager, do about the inventory clerk who never makes a mistake, who does every report on time, and who devises new ways to save time and money, but who is not very friendly in the office and relates poorly to people? At the other extreme, what about the good-natured, fun-loving employee who, while only an average performer, has a great work attitude? The job is what counts. Unless the position is one that involves wide exposure to people, the importance of "attitude" as a factor to be rated is minimal. Because both are highly subjective, neither attitude nor leadership stand up under scrutiny as qualities to be rated. Although different office managers define leadership differently, they should remember that one of the most difficult tasks they face in their position is justifying a particular rating, one that everyone knows is subjective.

Although many factors must be rated, performance in all nonexempt office jobs can be rated in terms of the following qualities:

Quantity of work
Quality of work
Cooperation with other workers
Time at work

Each criterion can be related to job performance, and that should be the office manager's only concern. Give examples of performance to document why you reached a particular rating. Because managers commonly use "check-off" rating forms, the very ease with which the process can be done tends to lull them into producing ratings that are indefensible and that do not stand up to scrutiny. Make sure that there is a reason for each item checked off.

In every performance appraisal program there is one underlying assumption—that an employee is fully aware of the performance expected in the job. The new employee presents a marvelous opportunity to review a position and to tell the employee what is expected of him or her. By the same token, it is necessary to review periodically the duties and responsibilities of long-time employees, since jobs can change so much over the course of time. Bear in mind that if an employee does not know what is expected of him or her in a job, that employee cannot—and should not—be taken to task for not measuring up. Such a situation occurs with considerable regularity in business offices when appraisals are arbitrary. I have known numerous employees who resented their bosses because they had unjustly penalized them for allegedly failing to meet commitments which only the managers know about.

Employees must be given advance notice about the performance appraisal; a week is usually sufficient time. It is also a good idea to ask the employee to give some thought to his or her performance in the meantime and to identify both positive and negative aspects. In preparing for a review, you, the office manager, should also be ready to review the employee's performance and to highlight areas in which you think improvement is necessary. This appraisal should be conducted in two steps: analysis and outline. The *analysis* should be of past performance, and the *outline* should be of the course you believe the employee should follow in the future. This type of appraisal should not be a hasty one; take the time to analyze and discuss the employee's work thoroughly. Schedule the appraisal at least two days in advance, allowing time for adequate discussion. Before the appraisal, prepare a list of the topics to be covered. When the discussion begins, take up the positive aspects of the employee's performance first, and then discuss them in detail. Next go into the negative aspects—always, however, accompanying the criticism by pointing out potential areas of improvement. As these areas are noted, discuss the part you expect to play in helping the employee improve specific skills. The appraisal should end with a general discussion of the subordinate's performance. If the appraisal is good, conclude with comments to that effect, possibly adding that there are no major problems, just a few areas where certain practices and skills could be improved.

Throughout the appraisal interview, remember not to conduct a one-sided discussion. Allow time for the subordinate to react to your comments about the various topics that arise. When each topic has been discussed, ask the employee what he or she thinks the appraisal should be, and why. This will provide an opportunity for exchanging points of view. Ask yourself, for example, what the employee is actually saying in giving a particular appraisal. Does it vary much from the appraisal you had in mind? If so, what are the reasons? For instance, have you properly communicated with the employee between reviews? In other words, listen to what the employee is saying. When something new comes up, do not be afraid to tell the employee that you will review your own appraisal to find out whether your appraisal and the employee's can be brought into line with each other. It is important to remember that the performance appraisal is, or should be, an updating of the ongoing appraisal process—a process whereby an employee's work is continually assessed and the assessment is kept both objective and job-related.

A word of advice: keep dress and personal behavior codes in perspective; do not let personal appearance or innocuous office behavior unduly influence an appraisal. If you have standards of dress and behavior at work, correct violations through disciplinary action, not through negative appraisal. In other words, the appraisal process should never be used as a substitute for discipline. The only true objective of a performance appraisal is to measure the performance of an individual against the objective standards established for a specific job.

DISCIPLINING

It would be nice if workers never needed to be disciplined and if an office manager could just conveniently dismiss the few troublemakers who inevitably show up. Although the first condition is obviously utopian— human nature just does not work that way—you, as office manager, can take steps toward that goal. You can, for instance, set up standards designed to standardize performance in the office. You can also establish rules of conduct guiding the behavior of your subordinates. At a time when businesses and business practices are coming under greater legal and regulatory scrutiny by the courts and by state and federal agencies, it is more important than ever that companies, when they must take disciplinary action, do so in a manner that will avoid legal difficulties as much as possible.

In one company, a part-time employee was dismissed after being absent twice and late seven times over a period of seven months. The office standard was two days' leave for personal reasons per year and three instances of tardiness. The employee's tardiness ranged from a few minutes to an hour and a half. During this time the employee had received three warning letters. However, an examination of the office's records revealed that another employee in the office who had taken three personal days off was still employed and that a group of employees in another department of the company were operating under more liberal rules. Was the termination justified? It wouldn't seem so. Virtually anyone, I think, would agree that a limit of two days off for personal reasons and three instances of tardiness per year is unrealistically strict. Furthermore, the fact that two departments of the same company were using different standards adds up to an inconsistent overall policy. Assuming that the employee was a typical employee of this company, going from three written warnings directly to termination indicates that the employee was not treated fairly, that "due process," as it is called in law, was not followed. In this example we have seen the lack of three fundamental criteria of a sound disciplinary system: *consistency, fairness,* and *due process*. Discipline usually involves two areas of behavior: general conduct and job performance. The legitimate enforcement of discipline requires that standards be set in both.

Conduct

Most people understand what is meant by "good conduct." Too many managers, however, try to enforce a narrow personal code for conduct at work. How many of us, for example, have noticed relatively petty rules being enforced—for example, rules forbidding the wearing of specific articles of dress or forbidding employees to leave their desks except at narrowly prescribed times? A proper—that is, workable—rule is one that establishes standards of conduct that are directly related to productivity in the office. Clearly, if a rule is unenforceable, it is not worth having. Standards of conduct must be maintained, of course, but they must also be realistic standards that contribute to the proper functioning of an office. Rules governing insubordination, theft, vandalism, gambling on company premises, drinking on the job, and taking drugs at work—all are related to productivity and the general well-being of a company.

Rules, because they govern such a wide variety of human conduct, must of necessity be ranked in order of importance. Gambling, for instance, is usually not considered as serious as stealing; the first is, within certain bounds, a minor offense, whereas the other is usually viewed as major. Once work rules have been categorized as major or minor, the appropriate disciplinary action for each can be established.

Rules for disciplinary action should not be so broadly phrased that no room is left to take special circumstances into account, nor should they be phrased in terms of ultimatums. They should, wherever possible, be flexible and avoid such statements as "Insubordination will result in termination."

In one example, a supervisor had a fight with her husband and came to work angry and visibly upset. She proceeded to vent her anger on her subordinates. She told one of them to run an errand even though she knew the employee was already working against a deadline that did not allow him to take time to run an errand. He became upset as he tried to tell her the problem, but she interpreted his explanation as insubordination and immediately set out to discipline him. According to the rule, which stated that "Insubordination will result in termination," the employee should have been fired. Here was an employee doing his job who was confronted by an emotionally upset supervisor making dubious demands. Was the rule too broad? It it was, it would have been better to define it more clearly. The rule, better stated, might read: "Insubordination is a serious offense that, depending upon the particular incident, may result in disciplinary action up to and including discharge."

It is also an error to try to anticipate every situation that might arise. Often the result of such an attempt is a lengthy code of ethics that resembles the Ten Commandments. In publishing such a catalog you might be ignoring the fact that the sole purpose of establishing rules is to make the workplace productive, safe, harmonious, and reflective of the company's goals.

Once work rules have been established, what about enforcement? Let's take an example and carry it through all the stages.

It's lunch break on Monday. Mike, a supervisor, goes into the lunchroom, were he finds, Jim, one of his subordinates, gambling for money with two men from another department. Mike goes back to his office and sends for Jim. They discuss the departmental rule that prohibits gambling for money on company premises. Mike tells Jim that their discussion in a warning, and that Mike will also report the incident to the supervisors of the other two who were gambling. This is step one.

Ten days later, Jim is again found gambling, this time with three other employees. Again, Mike calls Jim into his office and tells him that this is the second time Jim has violated the rule against gambling. He reminds Jim of the first warning and informs him that the second disciplinary step has to be taken. Later that day Mike sends Jim a letter warning him about the offense and spelling out the details—the date of the first offense and the discussion they had at that time. Mike says the purpose of the disciplinary action is a corrective one, not a punitive one. This is step two.

Three weeks later, Jim repeats the gambling. Mike responds with a warning letter labeled "Final Written Warning." They discuss the matter once again, and Jim is reminded of the previous two offenses. Mike repeats that the objective of the disciplinary action is to get Jim to change his behavior, not to punish him. In this final letter, Jim is informed that the next offense could result in a three-day suspension. This is step three.

A month passes, and Jim does it again. Mike calls Jim in to hear his explanation, but Jim has no satisfactory explanation, none that would excuse his repeated violation of the rule forbidding gambling. Mike gives Jim another written notice and recounts Jim's earlier offenses. In a letter, he suspends Jim for three days, stating that the next offense could result in termination. This is step four.

Most people would probably agree that if Jim continues to gamble during working hours he should be dismissed. He has flagrantly violated a reasonable rule, one that employees should make an effort to observe. If Jim had stopped gambling on company property, the disciplinary rule would have served its purpose. When it is necessary to dismiss an employee, however, it becomes clear that a company's disciplinary procedures have failed, at least in the sense that they have not been effective—either because of the employee, the disciplinary procedure, or both.

The steps outlined above illustrate the due process procedure that is essential to maintaining discipline, regardless of the circumstance. What procedure is established and what measures are taken to enforce the rules is another question. It is important, though, that the process be fairly lengthy and that an employee be given several chances to straighten out. Of course, if an employee is caught stealing a typewriter, there should be no multistep procedure; the employee should be fired immediately. Whatever rules have been adopted, however, employees should not be disciplined for committing violations of rules that have never been formally discussed with them. Ideally, a handbook should be given to each employee, outlining the company rules and policies. These rules and policies should also be posted prominently—for example, on all available bulletin boards. Make sure that there is little or no chance of an employee's not knowing about a rule or policy. As long as this possibility exists, discipline is threatened. Any disciplinary program that is not intended as a corrective program is an ineffective program, hardly worth the paper it is printed on. "Due process" exists so that employees will have the opportunity to correct their mistakes; It is important to communicate the objectives of disciplinary procedures to employees both before and after administering them.

Performance

Discipline is also properly used when an employee performs unsatisfactorily, although here it is handled somewhat differently. The steps taken resemble those taken to correct violations of rules of conduct. In a real sense discipline for inadequate or poor performance involves counseling more than it does specific disciplinary steps. As we have seen, an employee's first day is the time to review the duties and responsibilities of the job. As time goes on, if the employee's performance is unsatisfactory a discussion with the employee is indicated.

Again, let's take an example, step by step. Sid is the printer for an office. He handles all of the office's printing in addition to operating a special photocopier. The office nearly always has a heavy work load. One Friday Sid's manager tells him that fifty-five books, each thirty-two pages long, must be printed and ready for distribution by the following Thursday. Sid and his manager estimate that the job will take two days. The manager tells Sid that this job has first priority, that all other jobs must wait. On Tuesday afternoon the manager checks on the status of the print job and discovers that Sid has not even started it. For some reason Sid is working on a printing job for the sales department, a job with lower priority. The manager calls Sid into his office and expresses his dismay at the situation. When he asks whether Sid can make the Thursday deadline, Sid says he may not be able to. When Sid is asked why he did not start earlier, he explains that he had already begun the job for the sales department when the manager gave him the book printing job and that he did not want to drop that job midway. The manager reminds Sid that he had been given a clear priority and had been told that he must drop everything and finish the book job by Thursday. It is now clear that overtime work will be necessary; Sid works six hours that night and finishes the job early Thursday, on time. That morning the manager calls Sid in again. The manager wants to know why Sid did not follow the priority they had discussed, why he had made it difficult to meet the agreed-upon deadline. The manager points out that the company must spend money for overtime for a job that should and could have been done during normal work hours. They go over Sid's explanation again. The manager comes to the conclusion that Sid simply ignored the instructions and tells him that his performance is not satisfactory and that he should consider this a formal notice of poor job performance. The manager writes a memo about the discussion and puts it in Sid's personnel file.

Three weeks later Sid prints one hundred and fifty copies of a twenty-page sales catalog. The catalog is almost illegible. There are smudges where the ink was not allowed to dry properly, and the type is uneven. The manager calls Sid in again and asks for an explanation. All Sid can say is that he did not realize that the job was being done poorly at the time he was doing it. When asked why he had not spotted the problem and tried to avoid it, Sid tells the manager that if certain parts of the press had been cleaned and proper inking had been done the printing would have been of much better quality. It is now clear to the manager that Sid in fact did know about the problem and that he knew how to correct it. The manager points out to Sid that such shoddy work will be readily apparent when the catalog is sent to the company's field locations, that it will reflect poorly on the company, and that time and money will now have to be spent to redo the job. Sid is reminded that this is the second time he has turned in a poor job. He is given written notice of this and the earlier instance.

A week later the manager of another department comes to Sid with special large prints that must be reduced. Sid tells the manager that the photocopier is not in working order. When the manager asks Sid whether the machine will be ready by Friday, Sid says it will. On Friday the manager returns only to find that the machine is still not working. The manager asks Sid when the company repairman was notified about the problem. "Yesterday," says Sid. "It just kept slipping my mind because of all the other work I have to do." Sid and the manager discuss the matter, and Sid is put on notice for the second time. The manager tells him, "If there is any way I can help you, let me know. This carelessness of yours is costing the company money, and it's becoming increasingly serious for you."

Less than two weeks later Sid lets the paper supply run out before reordering. Twelve days after that he leaves the photocopier on with a jammed feed, causing the unit to overheat and be damaged. Each instance is followed by a written notice stressing the increasingly serious nature of Sid's offenses. After this many violations, it is clear that Sid is both careless and somewhat uninterested in doing better work. The only course now is termination. Depending upon the extent of the performance problem, suspension is sometimes used between the written notices and termination. In the example just cited, however, it appears that suspension would have been futile.

A final point: administering discipline is often unpleasant, but it is far worse *not* to administer discipline it when it is necessary. The manager who does not enforce standards as a way to increase the productivity of subordinates jeopardizes his or her future and potentially harms that of the company.

LEGAL CONSIDERATIONS

The increasing role and influence of the government in the affairs of individuals and business has produced a growing number of regulations that the informed manager should know about. Prominent among them are the regulations that govern employment practices. Some of the major acts passed by Congress include the Civil Rights Act of 1964, the Age Discrimination in Employment Act, the Equal Pay Act, the Rehabilitation Act, the Vietnam Veterans Act, and the Fair Labor Standards Act.

The Civil Rights Act states that there shall be no discrimination in employment on the basis of race, color, religion, sex, or national origin.

Originally interpreted as applying only to hiring practices, the act now applies virtually to all business activities. Promotion, discipline and training are some activities affected.

The Equal Pay Act states that equal pay shall be given for equal work. The act also prohibits pay discrimination on the basis of sex.

The Rehabilitation Act prohibits discrimination on the basis of physical or mental handicap. If an applicant for a job is confined to a wheelchair but is fully capable of and experienced in the job that is open, according to the law the individual must be hired, even though that might mean that a company would have to make certain changes in its office layout to accommodate the person. Unless financially devastating changes would be necessary, the employer has no choice. The regulations provide a wide definition of handicap. Alcoholism, for example, could be considered a handicap. Generally, any condition that poses an obstacle to securing employment would be judged to be a handicap.

The Vietnam Veterans Act prohibits discrimination against a disabled veteran of the Vietnam War who was a 30% or greater disability.

The Fair Labor Standards Act requires an employer to pay employees the base rate of one and one-half times their wage for all hours over forty worked in one week. The law also requires that employees covered under the act be paid at least the minimum wage. (Those categories include virtually all office employees.) The Fair Labor Standards Act also establishes categories of "exempt" and "nonexempt" employees. Those defined as exempt are just that: excluded from the overtime provisions of the law. Professional employees are exempt; other employees are nonexempt. The law specifically states the qualifications for exempt status.

Much has been written about these and other laws and how they work, but an overview will help the reader appreciate their emphases. Individual states have added their own laws to supplement the federal laws, and in some cases state laws go beyond the federal laws. In many states privacy legislation restricts the information that may and may not be withheld from employees. In general, employees have the right to know what is in their personnel files and to review the material. (This is another reason why all the material in a file should be objective and job-related.)

In setting up a personnel file it is a good idea to establish both a medical file (for records of preemployment physical examinations and medical claims) and a primary personnel file for each employee. The latter should contain only job-related information such as attendance records, performance reviews, discipline received, and salary history. Employees should be allowed to examine these records if they choose.

What if someone calls you for a reference check on a former employee or you call a company to check on a potential employee? What should you ask, and what should you say? The critical element is objectivity; anything an office manager may ask for or give must be objective. A statement representing a judgment or interpretation could mean trouble. If it is a statement that can be interpreted three different ways by three different people, how can it properly be used as an ingredient in deciding whether or not to hire?

If a reference for a former employee is requested by another organization without any evidence of authorization by the employee, the only information relating to the employee that should be revealed is the job title and the dates of employment. There is no room for judgment or interpretation in those facts. You may, however, receive a reference request through the mail with the signature of the former employee authorizing the release of the information requested. With or without that authorization, the guideline remains: objective facts only! If it is authorized, you can release additional information such as last salary and salary history, promotional history, and number of days absent. Again, each of those are facts not subject to interpretation. Stating that an individual was "an average worker, couldn't get along with his supervisor, or did poor work" could put you in a very difficult position.

If you call for a reference, the same guidelines apply. Do not ask a former employer to make judgments. In practical terms, their judgments about a person may be far different from your own: one company's poison may be another one's delight. The specific written authorization of the prospective employee is necessary before any reference check. With that, you can question another company about the dates and amounts of salary increases and the average merit increase and time sequence. This will give an indication of whether the individual was treated as an average, below-average, or above-average worker in terms of compensation. It is also wise to ask the former employer the reason the employee left. Does that reason coincide with the reason given by the applicant?

Giving or using judgment information may seriously jeopardize the applicant's ability to secure a job. In an increasingly competitive job market, challenges by applicants against former employers are likely to increase. The defense against such charges is objectivity. Any information you may give or use which is not objective and provable may place your organization in a very messy situation from which a costly and embarrassing solution may result.

There is an on-going evolution of laws and regulations regarding the workplace and serious discussion today about modifying the regulations that govern the administration of affirmative action programs by the Equal Employment Opportunity Commission and the Office of Federal Contract Compliance Programs. Perhaps the most crucial issue to come will be the debate over "comparable worth." The issue, simply stated, is whether two jobs that are the same in terms of level of contribution and difficulty should receive the same compensation regardless of the pressures of the market. If, for example, a technical sales representative had the same basic qualifications and job difficulty as a programmer, the expectation is that both jobs would have the same salary grade. While the comparable worth issue is far from settled, it may have a dramatic impact on organizations in the future. It is a wise practice to subscribe to a service that keeps you informed about all pending and enacted legislation so as to anticipate their impact.

Once again, the principal criteria in the relationship between the office manager and the employee are objectivity and job-relatedness. The manager should not react toward employees on the basis of subjective judgments or unsupported personal opinions, and all of his or her actions toward employees should be taken with the objective needs of the office operation in mind. Although in managing an office properly it is important to give attention to work safety, office layout, delegation of work assignments, and training, the proper interaction of people is the office manager's most crucial concern. The office manager who respects his or her subordinates, as well as those higher in the company, and lets this respect guide his or her actions, will be well on the way to becoming a successful office manager.

CHAPTER 15

Establishing the Regional Office

This chapter describes the procedures involved in acquiring and setting up small regional offices that hold approximately ten to thirty staff members. The guidelines presented here should be helpful to employees charged with this task, although the reader must of course adapt these suggestions to his or her company's particular requirements. Moreover, the rapidly changing nature of office technology requires users to become knowledgeable about current advances in the field. (This knowledge can be acquired either through direct experience or the currently available literature. The periodicals *Facilities Design and Management, The Office, Interiors,* and *Administration Management* are useful sources.) In addition, a strict adherence to the practical rules for selecting, acquiring, designing, and opening a new regional office will not in itself ensure success; a more intangible, subjective, yet crucial ingredi-

"Establishing the Regional Office" is the contribution of Margo Corson, Director, Facilities Management, Mathematica, Inc.

ent must be recognized—human behavior. The process involves both personal and professional interaction with a number of actors (such as company management, realtors, architects, landlords and their representatives, general contractors, construction crews, telephone company equipment vendors, and movers). To achieve a time- and cost-efficient process of selection and acquisition, the person responsible for establishing the office must have a knowledge of these other fields and be able to balance his or her own company's needs and interests against those of these other actors.

I have gained my experience in this field of office management as Director of Facilities Management for Mathematica, Inc., an economics research and computer software development company headquartered in Princeton, New Jersey. Over the past few years I have established nine offices in both the United States and Europe for Mathematica's software subsidiary Mathematica Products Group (MPG). These offices have provided space for MPG's regional sales and technical assistance staff, and each office has also contained a classroom used by MPG for training customers to use the company's software products.

This chapter is divided into eight additional sections. The first seven of these described the major steps in the office acquisition and set-up process. These steps are (1) initial discussions with management about facilities requirements, (2) interaction with the realtor and office selection, (3) office design, (4) lease negotiations, (5) construction, (6) telephone installation, and (7) moving procedures. A concluding section highlights some important overriding factors.

INITIAL DISCUSSIONS WITH MANAGEMENT

Before MPG management decides to open a full-scale operation in a particular city, region, or foreign country, it sends its sales force to the area to generate business. Periodically management reviews sales performance in the new area through revenue and growth projections to determine the feasibility of expansion. During this initial phase, which could range from six months to two years, the sales forces are housed in temporary offices under a full-service lease. Services are provided not by the parent company but by administrative and office services personnel contracted for through the building's owner.

The services included in the lease provide for Furniture (in each
   office)
     One desk
     One bookcase
     One credenza
     One filing cabinet
     One desk chair
     Two or more visitors' chairs
Electricity
Heat/air conditioning
Directory listing
Telephone equipment and answering service
Secretarial service (the lease states the number of hours included in
   the base rent and the rate per hour used over this number)
Other general administrative services
Conference room
Copier services
Security services
Mail services
Telecopy services
Word processing services
Air Express
Courier services
Coffee services

These temporary offices are primarily taking off places for sales personnel, since the salespeople spend most of their time visiting with prospective clients to generate further business. However, when revenues and
growth necessitate, MPG decides to expand not only its existing work
force in the new region but also its office space.

Then begins the task of acquiring and setting up the new office. The
person responsible for the task (called here, for the sake of convenience, the *facilities manager*) meets with management to discuss the
following questions:

How many and what types of employees must the new office accommodate at the outset?
What is the projected growth of this office?

What (on the basis of past experience) is the highest amount that the company will pay for rent.

Will the office need a classroom? More than one?

How many conference rooms?

Does the company prefer a specific geographical spot for the office location?

Where does the work force live?

Where are most of the clients?

Does the company want proximity to an airport?

When does the company want to move into the new office?

Who is the key person in the regional office with whom the facilities manager will interact?

This discussion will yield company estimates about the number of present and projected personnel and thus will provide a foundation for estimating the approximate level of services, amount of furniture, and the space that must be available to accommodate them within the limits of the budget. The costs of acquisition, interior reconstruction, furnishings, telephones, and moving must also be estimated at this time. These estimates are quite rough, and they are generally based on prior experience, although in some cases vendors will provide rough cost estimates for their services, and the realtor will provide approximate rental and construction costs for the city. These estimates will provide a space and cost framework for managerial review and approval.

THE REALTOR AND THE SELECTION PROCESS

The realtor is one of the most important actors in the process of acquiring a regional office. Thus one of the most crucial decisions in the entire process is to choose the most appropriate realtor, especially since the rental obligation frequently entails hundreds of thousands of dollars and it would be unwise to entrust this responsibility to haphazard choice. The realtor can greatly simplify the entire process with his or her knowledge of the city's physical layout (knowing who's who and where they are located), the general mode of operation (determining whether things move fast or slow), important statutes and codes, and reputations of prospective landlords, managers, and owners, and with his or her experience in the negotiating process.

I select most of the company's regional offices with the help of a national brokerage firm. Relying on an exclusive broker ensures that both his or her interests and the interests of the office manager will be bound together in mutual dealings and that the company is represented exclusively by one person, which helps to ensure the best possible deal. The realtor's commitment to a company and his or her knowledge of the company's particular requirements (developed through rapport and a long working relationship) will ensure that the firm obtains what it needs to remain a viable operation within that city. It also frees the facilities manager of much tedious groundwork, which enables the manager to use his or her time more productively. Selecting an exclusive broker also helps to ensure that the company gets the best office space available to it. For example, until you have signed a lease, you are still in the market; if a really "hot" piece of space were to become available on the day you were scheduled to sign a lease, only an exclusive broker would bring it to your attention. For the most part, brokers are not committed to *you;* they are committed to the deal.

However, there are times when it is necessary to deviate from the "exclusive broker" theory—in particular, when a company's exclusive broker either does not have an office or has an insufficiently solid sales force in the region in which the company must establish its office. In such cases a facilities manager should use a broker who has a solid, well-established reputation in the area. The method of selecting such a broker depends largely on the size of the deal to be negotiated. If office rentals are high in the city in which the company is setting up the regional office, the exclusive broker should help the facilities manager choose an appropriate alternative broker, and the two brokers share responsibility for selecting the office site and split the commission. However, if the deal entails a smaller amount of money (that is, when splitting the commission between the two brokers creates no clear financial incentive of either to engage in aggressive negotiations), then the facilities manager can simply resort to telephone calls to his or her business contacts in the area to determine what realtors they know and how other businesses' needs have been met. In some cases the company's regional sales personnel prove to be good sources of contacts.

Once the realtor has been selected, the next step is to call the realtor to provide him or her with the specifications:

The number of rentable square feet required
Where the space should be located
The approximate dollar amount
The approximate deadline

The number of square feet can be estimated by using the following process (following the open office design concept). Generally speaking, 150 square feet of office space are allocated per person; this usually allows enough space for sales staff, technical staff, educators, and managerial staff. Added to this amount are the square feet necessary for small (200-square-foot) or large (300-square-foot) conference rooms; one or more classrooms of approximately 850 square feet each; work, copier, and kitchen space (200 square feet); and reception areas (200 square feet). The number of square feet will vary slightly according to the shape of the space. Rectangles are the most efficient, since a building's "loss factor" is smallest for rectangles. The loss factor is the ratio of common areas (lobbies, halls, elevators, restrooms, and utility service areas) to the total number of square feet of the building. To figure the loss factor of a building, subtract the usable space (U) from the rentable space (R) and divide that answer by the rentable space:

$$\text{Loss Factor} = \frac{R - U}{R}$$

Except for buildings that have an excessive or under-excessive loss factor, this square-foot formula can be applied to most locations.

Using this basic information, the realtor conducts a "space survey" of the suitable buildings in the area and sends the office manager a report that generally includes the following information:

Map of building
Building address
Owner/architect
Age
Rentable area
Number of floors
Floor size
Annual lease rate
Available area
Parking ratio

Along with the survey the realtor will send his or her recommendations about which spaces are suitable to a company's needs. The space survey will help the facilities manager review the office spaces available and narrow down the number of choices according to the following criteria:

Availability date
Cost
Location and accessibility
Proximity to transportation and to potential clients
Aesthetics

Of the five criteria, availability date, cost, and location are the most important factors. The availability date should coincide with the company's ability to vacate the existing temporary office or, if possible, to terminate the present lease. The rental costs must be within the budget; the office building must be easy to reach; and the traffic flow to and from the airport by public transportation facilities must be quick and smooth. Proximity to these facilities will greatly reduce travel time and inconvenience and, thus, save the psychological and energy resources of the staff. In MPG's case it is also most important that the office be located as close to the company's clients as possible so as to make it easy for them to participate in the education program. The choice of neighborhood is also a factor—especially with respect to neighboring buildings, restaurants, and other amenities.

In the process of using these characteristics to narrow down choices, the exchange of ideas and interaction between the facilities manager and the realtor is critical; the facilities manager solicits suggestions from the realtor and the realtor from the facilities manager. It is crucial that ideas be generated and analyzed concerning such things as the various codes and statutes relevant to the city and the problems that might be encountered with them, and, in particular, the rent escalators used to determine future base rents, operating expenses, and taxes. In most cities the rent escalator clause is based on the Consumer Price Index (CPI), while operating expenses and taxes escalate with actual costs. These escalator clauses can, over time, contribute substantially to the cost of the space; in comparing leases, the facilities manager must project and compare influences on costs both currently and over the life of the lease.

At this stage the facilities manager should call the regional sales representatives and arrange to meet with them when he or she visits the region. This gives the facilities manager a chance to acquaint him- or herself with the representatives, to show them color photographs of the type of office that will be set up for them, to see the things that will have to be moved, and to solicit any ideas the representatives have about their space needs. Their ideas about suitable locations can be particularly useful.

The next step is to visit the city and the selected office sites with the realtor. Unless upon entering the building the facilities manager makes a quick "no" decision, the checklist shown in Figure 15-1 should be used for each space visited. The facilities manager should write notes of the details, since after seeing several office buildings the details of each might easily be forgotten or confused. The checklist covers primarily physical characteristics, so the facilities manager must also keep in mind the "psychological" and aesthetic factors for both the prospective employees and the company. With respect to the latter, the facilities manager should be concerned about how the building will represent the company's image to visitors. It is important to match the image with the surroundings. (For example, MPG has a solid, well-established reputation. I therefore reject lobbies that are flamboyant or flashy, and I reject office suites that cannot be adapted to a more conservative yet not overly staid image. I also consider the personalities of the people who operate the elevators and information centers.)

If the space appears potentially suitable, the facilities manager might find it advantageous to meet informally with the landlord or his or her representative while visiting the building to discuss initial concerns or to ask questions about the space. In turn, the facilities manager will answer the landlord's questions about what the company represents and its type of business.

After visiting the potential sites, the facilities manager meets with the realtor to narrow the choices down to two or three, even if the second and third are not nearly as desirable as the first. (The second and third choices can be used as alternatives should the first site not be negotiated successfully, and they can also enhance the bargaining position. In negotiating the lease and the work letter with the landlord, the facilities manager must be willing to switch to these other choices at any point if the negotiations are unsuccessful.) At this point the realtor also pro-

Figure 15-1. Space Checklist

Date_____

City_____

Location

In what part of the city is the space located?
What is the address?
Are there any special details about this location?
How far away is the airport?
Does the building have a special name?
Is there public transportation to the building?
What is the name or number of the major access roadway to the building?

Lease

Is this a straight lease or sublease?
What is the term of the lease (number of years)?
Can it be sublet if the company outgrows the space before the end of the
    term?
What are the number of square feet:
        Rentable?_____
        Usable?_____
What is the price of the space?
        Gross_____
        Net_____
If the quoted price is gross, does it include or exclude electricity?
If electricity is excluded, what is the average going rate per square foot?
If the quoted price is net, what is included? What is excluded?

        Cost of heating and air conditioning?
        Electricity?
        Janitorial?
What are the going rates per square foot for each?
What additional charges should I expect to pay in the future?
        Increase on base rent
        Operating expenses
        Tax increases
Will a security deposit be required?

Parking

Is there parking for tenants?
Is the garage covered or exposed?

Figure 15-1. (*continued*)

How many spaces are allocated per square foot?
How does the garage operate?
Is there an attendant?
What are the attendant's hours?
What parking problems might our students encounter?

General building characteristics

What is the percentage of our space relative to the entire building?
What does the lobby look like?
    Composition of floors?_____Color?_____
    Composition of walls?_____Color?_____
    Lighting?
    Are there plants?
    Is it an inviting, friendly lobby?
Are there lobby attendants?
Is there a security guard or system? How does it work?
What are the building hours?
Is there a directory in the building?
Is there a freight elevator? If so, what are its hours of operation?
Where is the cafeteria located? Is the cafeteria located in the building?
What floor is the space on?
Are there floor directories upon exiting the elevator?
What type of corridors lead to the space?
    Colors
    Carpeting
    Lighting
Can we put up a directory sign for the students at the elevator exit?
How far is the space from the elevator?
What does the inside of the elevator look like?
How far is the space from the restrooms?
What do the restrooms look like?
Do you need a key to enter?

The space

What does the entry door look like?
What is the configuration of the space?
How does the space fit in with the rest of the floor? What is it next to?
   (Ask for a floor layout.)

Figure 15-1. *(continued)*

Is the space next to a heating, ventilating, and air conditioning (HVAC) air
   shaft?
Is the space next to anything else that could create noise?
What is the view?
   North
   South
   East
   West
What are the windows like?
Are the window coverings included in the work letter? If so, what are
   they?
Will the window coverings block out light or allow light to filter through?
What is the building's standard carpet color?
Is the carpet a loop? Is the carpet a pile?
Is the carpet glued down or installed over padding?
What is the building's standard paint color?
Is there a music system? Can the music system be controlled by each
   tenant?
What does the standard ceiling look like (2 × 2, 2 × 4, exposed or con-
   cealed spline)? What is its acoustical rating?
What does the lighting look like?
What is the ceiling height?
Is the space near plumbing or water (for the kitchen)?
What do the internal office doors look like? Wood or paintable?
What do the closet doors look like?

vides the facilities manager with a blank copy of the lease and a copy of
the work letter (see Figure 15-2). The work letter describes the alterations or construction that will be made at the landlord's expense and
provides the date for the submission of the tenant's plans and specifications to the landlord, the cost of any above-standard items, specifications of (HVAC) heat, ventilation, and air conditioning systems and of
available electrical facilities, and other details pertaining to the tenant's
installation.

   The facilities manager then meets again with the key personnel at the
regional office to inform them about the prospective space and to invite
them, if their schedule permits, to visit and inspect the space.

Figure 15-2. The Building Standard Workletter or Agreement

1. **Partioning**
   Thickness and quality of gypsum wallboard
   Partioning between suites to be slab to slab
   Sound ratings
   Allowance per square foot (sometimes this is unlimited)

2. **Suite entry door**
   Size
   Number per square feet of space
   Composition
   Description of lockset

3. **Paint**
   Colors available
   Number of coats
   Finish on door frames

4. **Floor covering**
   Carpet name
   Type of installation
   Type and color of vinyl base
   Allowance per square foot if alternate carpet is used

5. **Interior doors**
   Size
   Composition
   Stain or paint finish
   Closet or lockset details
   Number of doors per square foot

6. **Ceiling**
   Manner of installation (hung-exposed or concealed spline)
   Size of panels
   Acoustical rating

7. **Suite entry door lettering**
   Will describe building standard

8. **Window covering**
   Type and name of manufacturer

9. **Electric and telephone outlets**
   Number of outlets per square foot of rentable area
   Electric loading capacity

Figure 15-2. *(continued)*

10. **Lighting**
    Number of lights allowable per square foot of rentable area
    Fixtures: size, manufacturer, number of tubes, lamps supplied and installed
    Are fixtures also source of return air?

11. **Floor loading**
    Number of pounds per square foot of live load ·

12. **Closets**
    Number per square foot of rentable office space
    Door description
    Shelves
    Rods

13. **Heating and ventilation**
    A general description of how the system works, and type
    Energy management
    Zones per square foot of rentable space
    Diffuser size
    Hours of operation

14. **Plumbing**
    Number of wet stacks–drink fountains

15. Details and schedules of how to submit tenant drawings.

16. Statement of whether landlord supplies and pays for architectural drawings or whether the tenant is responsible.

17. Schedule of response time between tenant submission of drawings, estimate from landlord for above building standard allowances, and tenant response time for such costs.

DESIGNING THE OFFICE

Having chosen the most suitable of the office spaces, the facilities manager then makes appointments with the building's space planners, designers, or architects—the next actors in the process. Together they will discuss preliminary layouts to determine whether the space can accommodate the company. A rough sketch is then made by using the guidelines from the facilities manager's previous discussions with management and the list of space requirements for each function. Figure 15-3 lists the criteria. If the sketch is suitable, the designer or architect will produce more detailed working drawings. This process is interactive, usually requiring between five to six "cuts" before reaching a final decision on the design. This interaction takes place after the facilities manager returns to his or her company's headquarters. It might be useful to ask the company architect to review the plans to ensure that the furniture will fit in properly and to determine whether another better layout is possible. At this point the furniture dealer begins to develop a list of items that the facilities manager must order for the office. During this process the facilities manager also circulates the plans to key members of the regional staff and company management.

Figure 15-3. Instructions to the Architect

Number of staff
    Present_____
    Future_____

Location and specifications of the following:
    Reception area
    Employee work stations
    Classrooms
    Conference rooms
    Storage closets
    Supplies closets
    Coat closets
    Kitchen/coffee area
    Copy room
    Telephone room

Millwork requirements (kitchen, cabinets, built-in credenzas)

HVAC requirements

Lighting (any special)

Electricity and any excess capacity

Telephone

Plumbing

Open landscape office designs are increasingly being used today. Three primary reasons for this choice are that

Open office designs require less space than standard partitioned offices, and, with the rapidly escalating cost of office space, savings can be realized. Savings are often so great that the extra costs associated with purchasing partitions and other fittings needed for the open design are usually offset by the rental savings at the end of the second year or early in the third year of the lease.

With most companies it is difficult to project exact growth in a particular city. Consequently if an office must be expanded quickly, the office landscape panels can be taken apart and switched and a new office added without noisy construction disrupting the entire staff.

The outside window areas are available to all the staff.

At the time that staff are moved from private offices to an open landscape, some common complaints do arise—most notably, that there is less privacy and more noise. However, these complaints can be offset by using acoustical and curved panels, as well as wooden writing surfaces and panel caps, to absorb sound; careful coordination of colors, as well as task lighting, and more comfortable *ergonomic* chairs than used in standard offices to make the space attractive and comfortable; and office designs that ensure the necessary privacy.

To standardize the furniture and thus avoid morale problems, the facilities manager should choose one furniture manufacturer (I use Herman Miller office furniture for MPG). The following elements should be considered in choosing the manufacturer:

Cost: the cost of furnishing the space should be in a reasonable ratio to the cost of renting space

Variety and design

Maintenance: parts that can easily be cleaned, fabrics that can be replaced

Adjustability: substitution, ability to move around

Longevity and durability

Human factors: rounded corners, soft edges, light weight

Acoustical rating

Concealed energy distribution

Manufacturer's reputation and availability of the products throughout the company's operating area

With respect to choosing the appropriate panel heights, noise levels and aesthetics are important considerations. Because managers need privacy for sensitive discussion, they require high partitions, normally 80 inches, and their offices are located directly near windows or are separated in some other way from professional staff. The technical and professional staff usually require medium-height partitions, because they do not generate an inordinate amount of noise and they may frequently be away on trips for the company. The reception area requires low partitions because they permit greater visibility; conversely, support staff (typists and work processors) need medium-height partitions because of the noise they generate.

The final step in the design process entails a review of the architect's drawings. The facilities manager should go over each area very carefully; details are extremely important. All aspects of the drawing should be measured and checked. For example, a wall that is off by only a couple of inches can cost hundreds of dollars to convert during construction. If the facilities manager decides to change the design after the landlord's pricing is complete, the lease might require the company to pay for the architect's time. Thus the following should be examined carefully:

Wall placement
Hall widths
Traffic flow
Door openings
Precision of millwork drawing
Lighting
Placement of electrical and telephone outlets and switches
HVAC air flow and special air
Ceiling gridwork layout
Are all columns marked on plan?
Closets (show shelves or coat rods)

Once the drawings are complete, the facilities manager is ready to submit them to the landlord for pricing (except when the landloard has agreed to pay for the extras). The landlord replies with an estimate of the cost of construction. The estimate will detail what work the landlord pays for and what work the tenant pays for. After review, the facilities manager might be able to have the landlord pay for all or some of the above-standard costs; he or she might also want to ask to have construction costs added to the rent. Since rent escalators could also be tacked onto this price, depending upon the economy, the facilities manager must be careful to avoid unnecessary escalations of costs. Construction begins as soon as the lease is executed.

NEGOTIATING THE LEASE

An office lease represents a large financial commitment for a company and it is in negotiating the lease that the most expensive errors can occur. In addition, because of inflation, the manner in which leases are written has changed drastically in the last ten to fifteen years. Before the sixties, short-term leases with no escalator clauses were common. Beginning in the early sixties, longer leases were written, and escalator clauses were added to cover potential cost changes. As mentioned before, these escalations can contribute substantially to costs and are a major negotiating point. The base-rent escalator usually equals the increase in the Consumer Price Index or a percentage of that rate for each year following the tenant's negotiated base year. Another escalator involves operating expenses. Landlords commonly require a tenant to pay operating expense increases in either of two ways: (1) on the basis of increases actual cost or (2) on the basis of a formula created by using porter's wage and fringe package costs. Operating expense increases vary greatly from city to city, from lease to lease, and from landlord to landlord. If a wage formula is used, the facilities manager and the realtor determine whether the formula is a fair representation of current operating costs. Increases in taxes are also billed and added separately in leases; however, they have not climbed as rapidly as the base rent .escalators and the operating expenses. It is importnat that the tax escalator clause state whether the current tax rate and building assessment will be used for the first year of the lease. Otherwise an increase could occur even before the building is occupied.

In addition to escalator clauses, the following are the negotiable business aspects of a lease:

Rental price: The rental price will be determined by the extent of the services provided by the landlord and possibly by the scope of alterations that the landlord will be required to make.

Ratio of rentable to usable space: In addition to the actual space occupied, the *rentable* area includes certain public areas, mechanical facilities, and common areas, such as lobbies, restrooms, and corridors. The *usable* area is an area defined as the area actually occupied physically by the tenant (including columns). It is important to determine the efficiency of the building by analyzing the ratio of usable space to rentable space.

Space and floor design: The efficiency of the floor space is determined by the configuration of the floor in relation to the core area, and the maximum number of windowed walls in relation to the usable area on the floor.

Electricity: Is it metered or included in the rent? The rate may vary according to the rate classification of the building. In addition, the rate can be subject to a survey of the actual electrical consumption. Facilities managers generally have the right to conduct a survey should they dispute the landlord's rent inclusion charge.

Work letter: This outlines the extent of the alterations or construction that will be made at the landlord's expense. While most landlords will provide a standard work letter, it is advisable for the tenant to have its designer or architect prepare a work letter that outlines the specific requirements of the tenant.

Expansion provisions or lease back: According to the size of the space, a landlord may consider leasing back a portion of the space initially leased in order to provide for projected expansion during the lease term. This eliminates the necessity of having to sublet a portion of the premises that is not immediately required by the company. (With the present slowing down of the economy I do not find landlords amenable to this.)

Right of first refusal: The landlord is required to notify the tenant of space becoming available on a designated floor at the end of a specified period. At this time the tenant has an opportunity to determine his or her requirements for expansion and can negotiate for the vacated space.

Cleaning specifications: If the rental is to include cleaning, a detailed schedule of the landlord's janitorial cleaning specifications should be included as part of the lease. The extra costs of floor waxing and carpet cleaning, which are generally at the tenant's expense, should be considered.

Repainting: Is the lease term long enough to provide for repainting at landlord's expense?

Right to sublet: Will the landlord agree not to withhold consent to any subleasing (within reason), and does the owner have the right to recapture the space? (When lease costs were soaring, I found that landlords would grant the right to return the space to the landlord only should a subtenant be found. Now that the economy is slowing down, they are much freer to grant the right to sublease.)

HVAC: What is the cost for overtime heat or air conditioning? What are the legal holidays on which the building is closed?

Substantial completions or alterations: Facilities managers should ensure that they negotiate ample time for notifying the landlord that the alterations have been completed. What is the latest date at which the tenant will require occupancy or delivery of the premises? (No company wants to have to move into a building on a week's notice.)

Alterations (during occupancy): Is the facilities manager required to use only the landlord's contractor?

Rental concessions: depending upon the proposal, a landlord might consider abating some rental payments to cover some of the incidental construction and relocation expenses of the tenant.

Amortization of tenant's costs: A landlord might consider amortizing above-standard leasehold improvements of the tenant over the term of the lease, thereby minimizing the tenant's initial cost outlay. This is usually applied to the lease, adding an appropriate interest factor. (Again, one must be careful not to have the percentage of CPI added to this amount.)

Security deposit: This usually equals one month's rent. It is sent to the landlord upon executing the lease, along with the first month's rent. (Because of MPG's national recognition and business reputation, I am not generally required to give a deposit.)

Condition of building: Has the building been adequately maintained? Does it require any physical improvements or mechanical improvements that the facilities manager wants the landlord to pay for to meet his or her needs?

If the lease being negotiated is a long-term commitment that heavily favors the landlord or owner or is coupled with the possibility of committing hundreds of thousands of dollars in company revenues, company attorneys should review or negotiate the legal terms of the lease. On the other hand, if the term is short, the financial commitment small, and the lease is fair or recommended lease amendments are accepted, attorneys might not be necessary. In this case the facilities manager should ask the realtor and his or her boss to review and provide input into any clauses with which he or she is uncomfortable. However, due to the progressive increases in the costs of leasing, attorneys are more frequently necessary than in the past. The lease is executed (that is, signed by landlord and tenant) when all the lease terms are agreed upon. If at this point the drawings are complete and construction estimates are agreed upon, the reconstruction will begin.

CONSTRUCTION

If the facilities manager is located near the office being worked on during construction, he or she should check on the progress weekly; however, this is not always possible. Therefore it is important to have the drawings sent to key regional personnel and to discuss the details of construction with them so that they can oversee this part. Generally speaking, this stage proceeds quite smoothly. This is where it pays to have reviewed the plans carefully ahead of time. Occasionally the facilities manager will request changes because a wall will be put in the wrong position, or he or she might find that something that looked fine on paper does not look well in reality. Fortunately this happens very infrequently. When construction is complete and the furniture is due to be installed, the facilities manager should visit the site to check all construction, using the "punch list" shown in Figure 15-4 as a guide to remember certain items. The facilities manager should make a detailed list (made most easily with a tape recorder) of what must be done and where, and who is responsible for completing each task. Because the company will move into the office before every detail is completed, the

Figure 15-4. Construction Punch List

Is company name on the directory?
Count electric outlets.
Count phone outlets.
Count lights. Do they all work?
Count switches. Do they all work? Are they missing covers?
Check lights. Do they all work?
Check any rheostats.
Window coverings:
   Are they properly adjusted?
   Does all hardware operate?
Count doors.
Check paint for necessary touch-up.
Check carpet and vinyl base.
Are closets complete?
Check kitchen plumbing.
Are windows clean?
Check door hardware.
Check directory signs.
Check music system.
Test door keys.
Check HVAC system.
Check security system.
Check parking permits.
Are janitorial staff aware you are about to move in?
Is construction cleanup complete?
Examine millwork.

facilities manager should appoint a person from the regional office to monitor the completion of all items.

TELEPHONE INSTALLATION

When revisions on the working drawing are nearing their completion, the facilities manager should begin to evaluate what phone system will be used. Again, the first consideration is present and future staff size; the second considerations are system and station features, price, and service.

Three to four private systems, including Bell Systems, should generally be reviewed. When reviewing private systems, the facilities manager, by using his or her numerous business contacts, should search out the private companies that are used widely in the vicinity of the new office. Quality of service is very important; thus, he or she should ask numerous questions about the repair and dispatch location, response time, and number of users in the near vicinity.

In general, MPG uses a "Request for Proposal" (RFP) for telephone service that outlines our specific objectives and goals. The RFP shown in Figure 15-5 was developed from materials received through our participation in an MCI telemanagement course on "How To Buy a PBX." The proposals that are received are reviewed, analyzed, and rated by the following criteria:

Does the vendor's equipment meet the company's basic list of requirements?
How do the system features compare?
How do the station features compare?
What do other users say?
Is training provided?
Is the maintenance record satisfactory?
Is the financial analysis favorable?

During the review process the facilities manager should remain in contact with the key regional staff person to ensure that he or she is fully aware of the systems being reviewed, the pros and cons of each

---

Figure 15-5. Request for Proposal for Telephone System

Purpose and Overview of Requirements
This solicitation requests a proposal for a telephone system to be utilized by Mathematica Products Group (MPG), a New Jersey–based software sales firm, for its_____ regional office being constructed in_____. We are searching for a vendor to provide excellent, timely service. Therefore, attached you will find a map pinpointing our exact location. We have_____square feet on the_____ floor of [*give full address*]. A floor plan of the suite layout showing the tentative location of instruments and the location of the telephone equipment room is attached. We will have_____sales and technical staff move into the space on_____and anticipate growing to_____by_____.

Figure 15-5. (*continued*)

We request a system that will do the following

Present a professional image to the public.
Serve us and have us available to our customers.
Provide a system that is dependable.
Provide a system able to stabilize, reduce, and monitor costs.
Provide a system that will change to meet future needs.
Provide access to WATS or another least-cost calling facility.
Allow ease of internal communications.
Be expandable to accommodate future growth.

All responses concerning this RFP should be submitted to MPG and must meet the requirements and specifications stated herein.

All vendors intending to bid must have their bids submitted to [name of person to whom bid should be sent].

Any questions pertaining to preparing the bid can be made to [*contact person*], Monday through Friday, between the hours of 9 A.M. and 5 P.M. at [*telephone number*].

Proposals received by MPG will be treated as confidential and will not be released to any other outside party.

The bidder must include all costs to be incurred by MPG in installing the specified system.

Any extra cost not specifically detailed in the proposal shall not be incurred unless specifically agreed upon in written form by_____of MPG, Inc.

The successful bidder must certify that

All work will be performed by appropriately trained personnel.
All equipment is new and unused unless otherwise stated.
Vendor personnel will leave MPG premises in acceptable condition upon completion of work, removing all rubbish and refuse created by their work and/or repairing or replacing damaged walls, floors, ceiling, and furniture.
A complete system test will be made to ensure satisfactory performance of all switches, cables, consoles, and instruments.
This proposal will include a detailed description of the system elements needed to successfully implement the package, labor, materials, equipment, and services offered.

All vendors must be able to produce a customer list of users with the system operating at their location.

Bidders will be notified of acceptance or rejection of their proposals by phone or letter no later than_____.

Figure 15-5. *(continued)*

Technical Specifications

The supplier must provide a complete technical specification and detailed description of the following:

A. Overall system size
   1. Maximum number of lines
   2. Minimum economical number of lines
   3. Number and size of cabinets, if any
   4. Traffic loading
   5. Traffic capacity
B. Trunks
   1. Type and quantity of central office trunk
C. Console
   1. Describe face layout
   2. Cover size
   3. Lamp indicators
   4. Extension status
   5. Call displays
   6. Special functions
D. Telephone instruments
   1. Describe operation of
      a. Conventional single line
      b. Conventional keysets
      c. Special sets/electronic instruments
E. Station wiring
   1. Number of pairs for single set
   2. Number of pairs for key instruments
   3. Number of pairs for electronic instruments
   4. Special requirements (fire-rated wiring/nonrated wiring)
F. Expansion
   1. Capacity of system or cabinet
   2. Increments of expansion
G. Features
   1. Specify the features operations of your system in the following way:
      a. Provided in basic software package: (1) system features; (2) station features
      b. Optional features available: (1) system features; (2) station features
H. Physical requirements
   1. Equipment area, based on 25% annual growth rate
   2. Electrical requirements

Figure 15-5. (*continued*)

3. HVAC requirements
4. Conduit requirements
I. Installation
   1. An outline of the installation plan, including time frame
   2. Requirements for equipment room access, storage, building access, or any other special requirements
   3. A complete training plan for console operator and station users
J. Guarantee and acceptance
   1. Details on manufacturer's and vendor's guarantee and terms of coverage
K. Maintenance
   1. Location and actual number of local maintenance personnel who are qualified to service the system
   2. List of all site spare parts
   3. Number and location of nearby users of system now installed and being serviced
   4. In the case of a distributor, a written guarantee by the manufacturer that services will be provided for a period of not less than five years
   5. Time frame for responses for major problems
   6. Time frame for responses for minor problems
   7. Copy of the maintenance agreement
   8. Training on restart procedures in the event of a power failure
   9. Statement of warranty and list of items covered
L. Vendor qualifications
   1. History
   2. Credit information
   3. Names and telephone numbers of five customers in this area who are presently using the same system
M. Financial requirements
   1. Payment options
      a. Outright purchase
      b. Lease/purchase (provide three and five year options)
      c. Straight rental
      d. Available alternate pricing
   2. Installation and other one-time charges
   3. Sales taxes
   4. Amount of investment tax credit (in the case of lease purchase, this is kept by the lessor or lessee)
   5. Itemization of maintenance plans with all associated costs
   6. Sales/lease contracts and service contracts

one, and the direction the company is pursuing and why. This important interaction should never be overlooked; the eventual user's input cannot be undervalued.

When the process is complete, a report that includes the RFP, proposals, and analyses is written and presented to management. The system is then ordered. The next step is to coordinate dates with the vendor. After that time the facilities manager should remain in contact with the vendor to determine the targeted cutover (systems startup) and when the vendor expects to start the work.

At the time of installation, the facilities manager or his or her representative will visit the regional office; the representative should know what was ordered and where it is to be placed, should be able to answer the installer's questions, and should be "tough" when necessary.

Installers can be notorious for not giving the "straight scoop," and they sometimes disappear. (I once had an installer tell me he was going to the basement of the building to check cabling—he never returned!) The facilities manager must keep a record of the names and phone numbers of the responsible persons in the company with whom he or she is dealing, since it might be necessary to call to follow up if someone is not performing his or her job correctly.

After the system is running and while the installers are still on the premises, the operation of the console and the station user sets should be checked. After any problems have been taken care of, the system is complete and ready for the staff to use.

MOVING

On the facilities manager's first visit to the regional office that is to be moved, he or she asks a staff person to make an inventory of furniture and estimate the number of boxes to be moved to the new office. If the staff is housed in fully serviced offices, the move generally involves only boxes. An adequate estimate is ten to fifteen boxes per office (for secretaries, twenty to thirty boxes). This will give the facilities manager some idea of what to tell the moving companies. Three reputable companies are called; they should be given the estimated moving date and the name of the staff contact person at the regional office and then asked to set up times to visit the office and to give an estimate of the cost of the move. If there is an appreciable difference in moving prices, the facilities manager chooses the agent whose estimate is lowest. (However, because of our long association with the one particular agent of a national moving company, I prefer to book the move through this agent if there is no appreciable difference in price. This established relationship allows me to recover quickly in the event of an unexpected problem or if there is any damage or loss during the move.) One to two weeks before the move, the facilities manager sends the regional staff a list of moving instructions and a memo informing the staff when, where, and how they will be moved. It is also a good idea to encourage a major office cleaning at this time. The instructions sent are shown in Figure 15-6.

Figure 15-6. Moving Instructions: An Employee Checklist

Desks

Desk drawers must be emptied.

You should remove and personally take to your new office personal effects such as money, fountain pens, clocks, pictures, plants, etc.

Index cards should be secured by elastic band. Other files shall have the follow-up brace pushed tightly against contents.

Calendar pads, letter trays, ashtrays, paper weights, and small items must be placed in cartons.

Bookcases

Bookcases must be emptied and contents packed into cartons. If shelves are removable, *all* shelves as well as the bookcase should be labeled with the destination room number.

It is suggested that any small hardware used for holding shelves be placed in a carton in order to be available when the bookcase is ready to be put together again.

Standard files

All files are moved upright, with contents intact.

Follow-up braces in drawers shall be drawn forward tightly against contents.

Lateral files and storage units

Storage units located above lateral files will be moved separately from the file; therefore, *do not lock* file or storage units. Label *both* storage unit and file with the destination room number and name.

Storage units shall be emptied and contents packed in cartons.

Files must be emptied.

Figure 15-6. *(continued)*

Special files
    Contents of tub files shall be moved in normal position. Empty and pack
        in cartons all two-door storage cabinets.
Typewriters and large-sized calculators
    Typewriters, adding machines, and other small business machines shall be
        labeled to correspond with companion desk. If small enough to fit in a
        box, definitely do so.
Miscellaneous items
    Glass tops, desk blotters, waste baskets, and chair pads shall be labeled
        with room number and name.
Chalkboards
    Label: movers will remove from wall.
Procedure to assemble moving boxes properly
    Fold small flaps down first. Then large flaps are folded on top of small
        ones. Tape the middle seam with two pieces of masking tape. Do not
        crisscross the bottom flaps. Do not use Scotch tape.
Moving don'ts
    Don't pack cartons full to overflowing. Use an extra carton instead.
    Don't forget to tag everything with a label showing room number and
        name. If a piece comes apart, tag each part or section.
    Don't fail to remove from desks such personal things as money, lighters,
        fountain pens, etc. Take care of them personally.
    Don't place boxes or waste baskets on desks. They might scratch or scar
        the surface.
    Don't leave clothing, rainwear, etc., in coat closet of office.
    Don't be reticent about asking questions about the move.
    Don't lock lateral file or storage units.
    Don't throw cartons away; break them down and they will be reused.

At the time of the move the facilities manager or a designee goes to
the regional office to coordinate the move. On this trip the facilities
manager should be sure to bring very comfortable shoes, since one will
be on one's feet most of the time. An hour or so before the move the
facilities manager visits the old office to check whether all items to be
moved have been properly packed and marked for their destination. The
boxes are counted. When the movers arrive, the manager stays with
them until the loading is completed. Before the movers leave for the

new office, the halls and loading area are checked for any items that might have been forgotten. The facilities manager meets the movers at the new office to oversee delivery, making sure that everything has safely arrived. Details are very important. One missing box can create disaster and ruin all the previous hard work.

The day after the move accessories, plants, and signs are put in place, and the facilities manager and regional staff persons make decisions about additional items needed to make the office more comfortable. These items are purchased or requisitioned, and the office is completed.

CONCLUSION

While the practical steps described above will help ensure success in setting up an office, several overriding, less tangible factors also need to be kept in mind. First, from the initial managerial meetings to the day of the move, it is crucial to ask questions and pay careful attention to all the details. A small item overlooked at the beginning can become a major annoyance in the future.

Second, experience has shown that you need to be prepared at all times for something unexpected to crop up. At any moment labor strikes, bankrupt landlords, missed dates, and a host of other critical factors could require a quick change of plan.

Third, in negotiation it is also critically important to be forthright and honest, but tough. This often feels like balancing on the edge of a sword. You are in a position of representing and creating an image of your company with each interaction. In the middle of a tough negotiation, do not lose sight of your end goal.

Fourth, with your company's future in mind, operate and make decisions as if you owned the company or were the president.

Questions
and Answers

---

1. *Is one specific skill more important than others in ensuring the office manager's success? Can an office manager be deficient in one skill (such as written communication) and still hope to function effectively?*

Communication skills are the most important skills for a successful manager. An office manager must be able to express his or her thoughts accurately and unambiguously, in both written and verbal form, if he or she is to be able to interact with superiors, peers, and subordinates. Without this ability all other attributes will suffer. For example, the office manager who is unable to express him- or herself clearly will be unable to train or motivate subordinates as effectively as one who can do so. An office manager who is deficient in any skill other than written or verbal communication can still perform admirably in the job provided that he or she recognizes the deficiencies and takes some action to correct them (such as by hiring subordinates who are proficient in areas in which the office manager is deficient. (Chapter 1))

2. *Is there a specific ground-level position that is considered to be an ideal starting point for advancement to the position of office manager? What prior experience would be useful?*

The office managers who were asked this question at the 11 March 1982 meeting of the New York City chapter of the Administrative Management Society suggested that the would-be office manager seek employment in either the personnel management or records management fields. Each of these professional-level functions typically affords an individual the opportunity to work as a member of the office management team while acquiring interpersonal and managerial experience and skills that will serve him or her well in the future. In addition, entry-level positions in these two areas generally provide a career path leading to the position of office manager.

Prior experience in a service job or one which has involved public contact is beneficial. Only through such experience can the prospective office manager determine whether he or she has the temperament and attributes essential for success as an office manager. (Chapter 1)

3. *How difficult is the transition from serving as an office manager in a small company to serving as an office manager in a large company? What problems are likely to be encountered?*

The difficulty is more a matter of adjustment than of actual operating difficulty. The small-company office manager is primarily a jack-of-all trades who will frequently have the opportunity to become involved actively in the day-to-day problems of his or her function. In a large company the office manager is more likely to be a subject specialist (such as a wage and salary analyst or a records manager) who has been promoted to the top office management job and who must rely heavily upon his or her supervisors to provide supplemental technical knowledge. The small-company office manager frequently has the opportunity to become involved in actual operations; the large-company counterpart generally must function more in an executive or managerial capacity. (Chapter 2)

4. *To what extent should the prospective office manager specialize in the specific functional responsibilities of office management?*

This depends upon the office manager's staff. If the staff includes supervisors who are technically competent in their areas of specialization and who keep abreast of the state of the art, the office manager will have little need to specialize in their areas as well. However, if high-caliber supervisors are not available the office manager must acquire such specialized knowledge as quickly as possible. (Chapters 1 and 2)

5. *To what extent should an office manager have a working knowledge of the various equipment, machinery, and systems within his or her area of responsiblity?*

Again, assuming that he or she has knowledgeable supervisors responsible for such functions the office manager need have little more than simply a general understanding of such equipment. If such persons are not present, however, the office manager's knowledge must be more extensive. (Chapters 1 and 2)

6. *Given the multitude of tasks and procedures in office management functions, to what extent should the role of the office manager consist of oversight rather than hands-on involvement?*

Again, if competent subordinates are present the office manager's job might be more oversight than hands-on, allowing him or her to function as a true manager. However, if no such individuals are on staff the office manager's job must necessarily entail a hands-on approach. (Chapters 1 and 2)

7. *After having established new or revised procedures to create the most efficient office management function, does the office manager risk processing him- or herself out of a job?*

I don't think so. Office management is a dynamic, constantly changing profession. When one problem is solved, another appears on the horizon. There are constant challenges facing every office manager; it is extremely unlikely that the office manager will ever achieve that enviable position when he or she, like Alexander the Great, has no more worlds to conquer and is no longer needed. (Chapters 1 and 2)

8. *Is the position of office manager a vehicle for career growth and advancement?*

The office manager's position is unique in that he or she continually interacts with everyone—from the president to the newest mail clerk. Accordingly the office manager has a wonderful opportunity to showcase his or her abilities and talents and to lay the groundwork for advancement within his or her own organization. In fact, many administrative vice-presidents are former office managers. (Chapters 1 and 2)

9. *Could you provide a fuller explanation of the* administrative specialist *concept?*

The administrative specialist concept involves the centralization of the various administrative and clerical support activities under the responsibility of an office manager. As a result the various operating executives are freed of the responsibility of planning for and managing activities. (Chapter 2)

10. *Could you provide a fuller explanation of the term "work-measurement analysis?"*

Work-measurement analysis involves a quantification of the various work produced by a given individual (e.g., pages typed or pieces of mail delivered), and the use of those quantities to establish a "standard" (or average) level of performance that may be used for work scheduling, staffing requirements, and employee performance evaluation. (Chapter 4)

11. *Although a chargeback approach to providing support services seems to be cost-effective, will the approach have a negative impact on attitudes by placing additional stress on the individual who is responsible, in addition to his or her other duties, for monitoring his or her department's use of these services?*

Not really, since the cost-effective utilization of available resources is a primary responsibility of every manager. Monitoring chargebacks to preclude misuse and unauthorized use is merely one technique whereby the manager may discharge this responsibility. Thus it should cause minimal negativism. (Chapter 1)

12. *Under the "decreasing-bonus-as-performance-increases" incentive plan, aren't there still some advantages to being productive (such as gaining a better reputation or increasing the likelihood of advancement)?*

Yes, but in the author's experience most people will limit their productivity if their earnings begin to decline once they have attained a specific output level. In addition, peer pressure sets in when the decreasing bonus arrangement is employed. The attitude is, Why kill yourself for a few pennies? The intangible benefits, while they exist, are decidedly of secondary importance. (Chapter 10)

13. *Isn't a group- or team-participation incentive plan more company-oriented than worker-oriented?*

Yes. The group or team approach is designed to achieve a higher level of *overall* output than would be possible using other incentive plans. With this approach the individual worker is secondary to the group, the idea being to bring peer pressure to bear upon those persons whose output is impeding the group's incentive earnings power. The "star worker" is not as recognizable with the group or team approach; therefore one might conclude that it is more company-oriented than worker-oriented. (Chapter 10)

14. *Isn't the use of television monitors and telephone systems in reception areas more expensive than using receptionists (given the costs of acquisition and continual maintenance)?*

No, not when the *total* costs of using receptionists is measured. In addition to salary and fringe benefits, one must also provide a backup receptionist to substitute during vacations, sicknesses, lunch, and rest periods. Obviously a cost analysis would have to be conducted to ascertain the exact break-even point, but organizations such as J.C. Penney Co. (which have substituted closed-circuit television monitors for receptionists), and American Airlines and Continental Can Co. (which use telephones) have found that cost savings begin in the very first year and continue thereafter. (Chapter 6)

15. *Are mail-delivery robots cost-effective (given acquisition and maintenance costs)?*

Studies conducted by the author at a major life insurance company and a Connecticut-based conglomerate indicate that a mail robot's purchase price (approximately $15,000) was equal to the cost of a typical mail clerk's annual salary and fringe benefits. By amortizing this purchase across the IRS-authorized amortization period of five years, the cost of the robot, even including maintenance costs, will typically be returned within one year. (Chapter 6)

16. *With respect to copying services, how can the office manager ensure that authorized employees can have access to copy services after hours and on weekends if the various copy equipment is to be locked?*

The use of "operating keys" (meterlike devices that are inserted into receptacles built into the copying machine in order to complete the electrical circuitry and allow the machine to function) provide an excellent way to restrict after-hours copying and still allow authorized employees to gain round-the-clock access. Such devices would be issued to each department head, who would control their use by issuing them to those persons who normally work after hours. It must be realized, however, that no organization can eliminate unauthorized copying; the best it can hope to do is minimize it. The use of an "operating key" will help hold down unauthorized use, particularly if the department head is judicious in charging it out for after-hours use. (Chapter 6)

17. *Doesn't background music contribute to noise in the office and thus increase the possibility of noise distraction?*

No, the type of music provided by Musak and others who offer background music is very unobtrusive. The instruments that play such music are light in tone (strings rather than brass), and the volume at which the music is played is quite low. As a result, one is aware of the music but not usually distracted by it—that is, one hears it but does not listen to it attentively. (Chapter 7)

18. *What are the adverse effects of stockpiling?*

The main problems are (1) the possibility of waste (spoilage) from over-estimating future requirements; (2) the risk that prices will not increase to a point at which the carrying costs of inventory are offset; (3) the need to provide space for such stockpiles in warehouses; (4) the additional record keeping involved in accounting for such inventories; and (5) the reduction of profits during the period in which such stockpiles are purchased. (Chapter 11)

19. *Can an office manager enter into a "business" by selling unused, overstocked items to other organizations?*

Yes, and many do. By placing ads in local trade papers, sending mail to local businesses, and otherwise letting it be known that one has unused and overstocked items for sale, the office manager can generally find a ready market and return additional "sales" dollars to the employer's till. (Chapter 11)

20. *Would you recommend that an office manager form a local group of "office managers" to exchange relevant information?*

Very definitely, if there is not a local chapter of the Administrative Management Society in the vicinity. (Chapter 2)

21. *Is restricting access to supply rooms (although it reduces waste and pilferage) a possible time-consuming practice, since some employees would otherwise have quicker access than would be possible if they had to go through the procedure of telephoning or filling out requests?*

Yes, but organizations that have adopted such practices, such as American Airlines and Turner Construction, feel that the dollar savings from overordering, pilferage, and waste are significant enough to justify any inconvenience that may be caused by restricting access. (Chapter 11)

22. *How should a centralized storage medium be set up and managed?*

A centralized storage medium, or business records storage center, can be compared to a library. Material housed in the center should be indexed, catalogued, and inventoried. Signout procedures should be enforced, as should the proper authorization to review records to ensure document integrity and security. (Chapter 11)

23. *Why do experts consider the microfilming of any record less than twenty years old economically unjustifiable?*

The twenty year rule applies only if a firm is initiating a microfilming program. The start-up cost of equipment and personnel in a microfilm operation are often greater than the cost of storing material in original form. However, if material is to be stored in original form for longer than twenty years it becomes more economical to convert the material to microfilm. Of course the quantity or volume of material must also be considered. (Chapter 6)

24. *With respect to office allocation, what other individuals either within or outside the company can the office manager depend on to help in such allocation?*

The office manager might wish to employ the services of an outside consultant or office design firm to perform the allocation study. The techniques used to develop an efficient space allocation system are time-consuming. An outside firm will have the manpower available to perform a detailed analysis of office interactions. (Chapter 3)

25. *What are some of the advantages and disadvantages of the open office concept that should be taken into account when the office manager is planning office layouts?*

The advantages of the open office concept include the more efficient use of floor space, greater flexibility in rearranging office layouts, and reduced cost of removing accoustical and visual distractions. The principal disadvantage is the inability of a work-group supervisor to maintain visual contact with employees in an office layout where partitions are used. (Chapter 7)

26. *What are some ways to control the abuse of WATS lines?*

WATS lines should be "turned off" after 5:00 P.M., since direct dial rates are cheaper at the end of the business day. Calls placed over the

WATS lines can be traced back to the individual initiating the call by using specialized telecommunications equipment. (Chapter 6)

27. *What are some procedures for setting up a "task team"?*

There are no set rules or formulas for selecting task-team members. A firm's operating style will dictate how a task team is formed. The objective of the team, however, usually defines the skills required as well as the number of people needed to realize that objective within the time constraints defined by management.

It is wise to include on the task team a representative of any department or work group that might be affected by the recommendations of the team. This will ensure that all elements of the problem are covered. Implementation of any recommendation will be easier if those effected have input in formulating that recommendation. (Chapter 4)

28. *What type of jobs would* not *be covered under the regulations of the* Griggs *v*. Duke Power Company *decision?*

Generally, those jobs that require specialized knowledge or skills that can be determined only by setting minimal standards and testing all applicants to ensure that they meet those standards (lab technicians, computer programmers, typists, stenographers, etc.). (Chapter 5)

29. *Whom should an office manager consult to obtain more information on the concept of self-insurance?*

The organization's insurance broker, or the American Management Association at 135 W. 50th St., New York, NY. (Chapter 3)

30. *To what extent should an office manager encourage his or her subordinates to seek additional and more challenging responsibilities both within the company and with other organizations?*

Theoretically the office manager should encourage his subordinates to reach their full potential, even if it means that they might leave the organization. However, in actuality the office manager should strive for longevity among his staff by providing career paths and job challenges that will motivate superior employees to refuse any opportunities outside the company. (Chapter 14)

31. *What methods should an office manager use to neutralize criticism on the part of one or a few well-liked, influential employees when a new system or set of procedures is implemented?*

An effective way is to invite such employees to air their opinions at an open meeting of all persons who will be involved in the new system, and to respond truthfully and unequivocally to any criticisms they make.

Another is to include such influential critics among the group that is planning the new system, either as members of the working team or as members of the advisory (or steering) committee. In this way unfounded negativism is confronted and effectively rebutted. (Chapter 14)

32. *To what extent can an office manager allow "democracy" within his or her group of subordinates without risking the loss of authority?*

As long as there are prescribed goals and the subordinates neither violate company policy nor exceed budgetary limits it is advisable to allow them freedom to run their own functions. As far as disagreement is concerned, once a decision has been made to adopt a particular plan or course of action complete cooperation and support of all are essential. Everyone must adopt the decision as his or her own and proceed with it, unless a new previously undiscussed approach surfaces as more effective. (Chapter 14)

33. *What type of tradeoffs have to be made between ensuring the welfare of subordinates and adhering to the profitmaking policies of the company?*

Fortunately, evidence continues to mount which indicates that employee welfare versus profit of the company is not an either/or situation. That which meets the most basic welfare need of the employee—development of a feeling of worth, involvement, and a degree of control over one's job—is the most critical and once met will do more to engender high productivity, and hence profit, than any other single factor.

34. *How does the office manager balance the interests and rights of his or her subordinates with the interests and policies of top management and the company?*

The office manager must first realize that he or she is a member of management and is part of a team that directs the operation of the organization. In exercising his or her duties, concern for the desires of employees should always be present, and every effort should be made to accommodate those desires. The efforts to do so, however, must end when they begin to impinge upon the effectiveness of the organization or run counter to its objectives. Any organization that tailors its actions solely to the desires of its employees is not a viable one and cannot survive. More simply stated, go as far as you can in meeting the needs of your employees, but stop when those actions oppose the needs of the organization. (Chapter 14)

35. *What methods can be used to ensure that subordinates keep abreast of and well-informed about policy changes that are announced through notices on bulletin boards or through memos?*

The effort to ensure that employees are kept informed can be limited to only those policy changes considered major, such as a change in discipline or attendance policy. Where there are major changes, it is always wise to have group meetings to continue discussion and, if necessary, conduct one-on-one discussions. Where a particular policy change might have a selective effect on some individuals, one-on-one meetings are advisable. In addition, an office manager should follow up with more memos and update bulletin board postings to reinforce the change. (Chapter 14)

36. *Ideally, can disciplinary actions be applied equally to subordinates (given the different job functions and stresses of various employees)?*

Discipline *must* be uniformly applied. Anything less creates a system that is unfair, indefensible, and simply not worth having. Different jobs do entail different levels of responsibility and stresses; however, those differences should be accommodated by differences in pay grade, salary, and perhaps benefits. Let's say you pay an individual to perform a job, and you pay another individual more to perform a higher-level job.

If each of them performs at 50% of the expected level for their respective jobs, you should treat them as equally as you would treat either one if he or she violated the same safety rule. (Chapter 14)

37. *How does an office manager balance authority with the attempt to provide open communication and empathy for his or her subordinates?*

A good communicator will not usually have to fall back on the authority of his or her position. When employees feel comfortable talking to their supervisor and when they feel that he or she understands their situations, assigned tasks, rules, and policies are, in most cases, accepted after discussion. If that is not sufficient to induce the desired performance, the next alternative is to use the leverage of authority. When that happens and proper communication has existed, it is unlikely to damage the rapport that has been established. Mutual understanding opens many doors, and effective communication is the key; constant exercise of authority will ultimately erode that communication. To explain and justify takes an extra effort; however, do so, because you'll sell your approach rather than mandate it, and it will become more effective with your subordinates. (Chapter 14)

38. *Likewise, can overcommunication or openness have an adverse effect upon an office manager's objective stance toward his or her position?*

The idea behind proper communication in management is that where there is understanding there is compliance. As long as communication from the manager down is objective, relevant, and accurate, there will be no adverse effect on his or her position. The only danger of overcommunication is when a point that is already understood and accepted by subordinates is repeated constantly. That type of overemphasis is demeaning and would probably be perceived as an insult by those to whom it is being communicated. (Chapter 14)

39. *How can personal meetings realistically be conducted every day with subordinates without interfering with the myriad other duties of the office manager?*

Personal meetings need not be conducted every day. What should occur every day is some type of conversation, a good deal of it casual. This can be anything from idle morning chatter about weather difficulties to a particular hobby in which the subordinate has an interest. The advantage of these ongoing dialogues is the better understanding the manager gains about the employees. If you know your employees well, you can easily detect changes in attitude, find out the reasons why, and usually prevent them from affecting performance. It takes time away from other duties, but not a great deal; after all, effective management itself takes time. (Chapter 14)

40. *To what extent is a company or an office manager responsible for providing help to, say, an alcoholic, so as not to jeopardize that employee's future or career growth?*

It is morally and legally proper for the manager to offer help to an alcoholic. If the manager were to take action against the alcoholic without ever having tried to direct the employee to those who could provide help the decision to fire could run afoul of the law. A suit could be filed claiming alcoholism as a handicap which the company made no reasonable attempt to accommodate. If you offer help and the employee refuses, you can properly proceed with action. The motivation to do so is as practical as it is legal: turnover is expensive. If you can salvage an employee, you have not only saved that cost but perhaps gained a greater degree of company loyalty as well. (Chapter 14)

41. *If there are conflicting demands by different departments for the location of their work areas, to what extent should the office manager defer to departmental wishes, and on what basis?*

Techniques exist that allow the office manager to determine the interrelationships among various departments. These techniques use quantitative methods and should be used to produce the arrangement that affords the most efficient layout possible. (Chapter 14)

42. *Are there specific company characteristics (size, location, production modes, etc.) to which each of the three office management organizational structures (centralized, decentralized, and centralized-decentralized) is most appropriate?*

Yes. The centralized function is best suited to small-to-medium–sized organizations operating in a compact, single location. The decentralized function is most suitable for large organizations that occupy numerous floors in the same building or that are so spread out that centralization becomes a logistical problem. The centralized-decentralized approach is generally best for large, dispersed, multilocation organizations. (Chapter 2)

43. *In large companies, to what extent should the office manager be held accountable for the actions of those to whom he or she had delegated responsibility for supervising various functions?*

In any organization, regardless of size, the office manager (or any manager, for that matter) must be held accountable for his or her subordinates' actions. The adage that "one delegates authority, never responsibility" holds true. The office manager must be held accountable for his or her subordinates' success or failure. (Chapter 14)

44. *To what extent is top management responsible for expressing their information needs to office managers (as opposed to vice versa)?*

Ideally, determining information needs is a two-way street. The recipient of information should give his or her preferences about format, type of data, and so forth to the originator, who should try to satisfy those needs. Continual feedback thereafter is necessary to ensure that the report continues to satisfy the recipient's requirements and that all reported data are still required for either decision making or control purposes. (Chapter 12)

45. *Given the wide range of skills and attributes necessary to ensure the success of any office manager, are there minimal educational levels that should be prerequisites?*

I posed this question to ten office managers attending the 11 March 1982 meeting of the Administrative Management Society's New York City chapter. The consensus was that while no formal educational background is essential to the success of an office manager, the broad-based college-level course of studies leading to the B.A. degree (including courses in expository writing, speech, psychology, and business organization) provides a background that will help the prospective office manager during his or her business career. Such courses help to develop communicative and business skills—factors essential for success in office management. (Chapters 1 and 2)

46. *If an office manager finds it productive to enroll in any educational course relevant to his or her job, is the company responsible for tuition reimbursement?*

Typically, based upon my experience in conducting after-hours courses at New York University, the American Management Association, American University, and George Washington University, companies will reimburse office managers for job-related course fees. As a rule such reimbursement extends to tuition, books, fees, and even travel costs. Such attendance is valuable, since it not only exposes the office manager to state-of-the-art office management techniques but also provides contacts with other office managers that can prove beneficial in the future. (Chapters 1 and 2)

47. *What type of educational courses are recommended for the office manager, especially given the wide range of skills and attributes necessary for the position (motivational skills, verbal and written communication skills)?*

A number of universities offer courses on managing people. These can vary from full-credit courses to one-to-three–day seminars. This is an excellent initial preparation for the office manager, since most such courses deal with communication, motivation, discipline, and delegation. Beyond such an overview course, others that would provide useful information would be those dealing specifically with personnel administration, motivational techniques, and behavioral methods. Seminars on legal restrictions in the workplace can provide excellent knowledge to prevent costly errors (i.e., information about EEO, the Fair Labor Standards Act, OSHA, and the National Labor Relations Act). A number of excellent books are also available that address each of these areas. (Chapters 1 and 2)

48. *To what extent should the office manager have a knowledge of corporate tax structures in deciding whether to lease or purchase various equipment for the company?*

The discussion to lease or purchase should be made individually for each type of equipment on the basis of *current* tax laws and taking into account the current tax advantages and disadvantages of leasing or purchasing. It would be wrong for the office manager to attempt to make such a decision alone or to attempt to acquire the knowledge about his or her organization's tax structure needed before one can make such decisions. It would be far more practical to rely upon a specialist (the organization's CPA, for example) for advice about whether leasing or purchasing would be more desirable from a tax standpoint. (Chapters 3, 6, 15)

49. *To what extent is the office manager responsible for knowing the various federal and state regulations and statutes that apply to work standards and hiring and termination practices?*

The office manager who has responsibility for subordinates is expected to know all relevant legal statutes. In most cases violations cause action against the company rather than the individual manager. While the manager does not usually face any individual charges, one may ponder what position he or she would be in vis-à-vis the organization if his or her actions have exposed the company to expensive and perhaps publicly embarrassing charges. A primer in all relevant laws is strongly recommended for every office manager. (Chapter 14).

50. *What publications giving federal laws and regulations can the office manager obtain to ensure that workplace standards are adhered to?*

The office manager should become familiar with the building code standards enforced by the state and local governments. Also, the firm's insurance carrier can be of assistance in identifying safety hazards. (Chapter 7)

51. *In an interveiw, what techniques can be used to allay the applicant's anxiety toward the interview once the substantive portion of the interview has begun?*

Depending on the nervousness of the applicant, more time may be spent in the very beginning discussing non–job-related subjects: the trip there, the weather, the town the applicant comes from—anything to which the applicant may respond without much fear or without much thought. Another technique is to begin with questions that are less stressful and easier, and then work up to those that are the more thought provoking and perhaps stressful. It should not be viewed as a failure if the applicant is still nervous. Some people create their own stress, and this should be learned from the interview as well. (Chapter 14)

52. *In judging the applicant during the interview, what criterion is most important? For example, is experience more important than behavior or appearance?*

The relative importance of the criteria is dictated by the individual job. For instance, for a customer service clerk who greets customers and makes clerical entries, good appearance and the ability to talk with people may be the most important criteria. The person hired to run the printing equipment might have experience that far outweighs the importance of education or appearance. The accountant, on the other hand, might have a legitimate need for education and experience. No one criterion can apply to all jobs; each one must be considered independently. (Chapter 14)

53. *How qualified is an office manager without a graduate degree to interview a candidate for a position that requires a graduate degree?*

This would depend upon the depth to which the office manager would delve. If the office manager is not qualified to evaluate the applicant's overall competency, he or she can conduct the interview in the presence of an employee or a consultant who is able to evaluate the applicant's capabilities. The general rule is that when in doubt the office manager should include a person who is capable of judging the applicant's abilities. (Chapter 14)

54. *Should a reference check on an applicant who is currently employed be conducted? Wouldn't this be a betrayal of confidence if the applicant lost his or her job as a result?*

As a rule a reference check need not jeopardize a person's current position. The office manager may check with prior employers, police departments, and credit bureaus if the employee is unwilling to have his or her current employer contacted. To avoid problems, many organizations include the question "May we contact your present employer?" on the employment application. (Chapter 14)

55. What role does the office manager play in the office union?

Ideally the office manager should represent his or her management in all dealings with the union—contract negotiation, adjudication of grievances to supervisors and working cooperatively with the union and the company in matters relating to health and safety, work rules, wages, and benefits. The astute office manager wishes to be seen as a flexible person who, while serving the organization's interests, is willing to right a wrong protested by the union, for the betterment of all. (Chapter 9)

56. If there is an office union, to what extent can an office manager provide input into choosing or implementing an incentive program?

There is nothing about an office union that precludes the office manager from presenting ideas for an incentive program. The office manager's ideas, together with those of the union, will form the basis for the plan that is ultimately adopted. The actual implementation of the program, however, will probably be the office manager's (or his or her designee's) responsibility. (Chapter 9)

57. What are some of the advantages, concisely speaking, of organizing an office union rather than not having one?

I assume that you mean from the employee's point of view, since I am unaware of any ways in which an employer benefits from his office workers organizing. Employees gain from the enactment of labor agreements that tie their wages to the cost-of-living index and by removing to a great extent such subjective criteria as their supervisor's personal feelings toward them from the assignment of duties or selection for advancement. (Chapter 9)

58. Could you explain "decertification" in relation to an employee's decision to quit a union?

Decertification does not apply to individual workers leaving the union. Rather, it is a vote of "no confidence" by the employees and amounts to an assertion that they do not wish to be represented any longer by this union (or perhaps by any other). (Chapter 9)

59. *Could you provide a more concise distinction between a "craft-based" and an "industrial-based" union?*

A *craft-based union* is one in which all members hold the same job classification (e.g., machinists, meat packers, morticians). However, members of craft unions need not be employed in the same industry (e.g., some members of the International Association of Machinists work in the automobile industry, others for aerospace companies, and still others for railroads). Members of *industrial unions,* however, do work in the same industry (e.g., the health care industry) but do not hold the same job classification (e.g., some are nurse's aides, others are orderlies, and still others are laboratory technicians). (Chapter 9)

60. *Could you explain more fully the use of "authorization cards"?*

An authorization card is a written expression of interest by an employee of a given company in having a specified union or employee association represent his or her interest in dealings with his or her employee. The union organizer is required to produce these signed authorization cards to justify the union's request for certification. (Chapter 9)

61. *What is the office manager's role in relation to the shop steward?*

Usually the office manager, as management's representative, will deal directly with the shop steward in matters relating to interpreting the current labor contract, employee grievances, and work rules. Typically these two individuals will interact almost daily; therefore mutual consideration and respect are essential. (Chapter 9)

62. *What is the office manager's role in any office's attempt to organize into an office union—that is, whose side should he or she be on?*

The office manager has no choice if he or she is to remain in his or her position. As a key member of management, the office manager must support the organization's opposition to the formation of an office union. (Chapter 9)

63. *What are the criteria used to select an "exclusive broker"?*

Generally speaking, the selection procedure is long (six months to two years) because you will have to try different firms to see which is best. You will want a national brokerage firm with affiliates or subsidiaries in the cities where you are likely to do business. This information can be found in major city newspapers or gained from discussion with business associates who know of firms or agents with good reputations. Begin by working with one or two firms on a deal-by-deal basis. Observe the agents' interactions how precise their explanations are, and their attention to detail; professionalism, excellent knowledge of real estate, experience, assertiveness, promptness, effectiveness with landlords, and their ability and initiative in representing and understanding your company are important points. Ask each for a proposal outlining their "exclusive agent services" and a client list so that references can be checked. You should choose the realtor that meets these criteria and with whom you feel most comfortable in a professional relationship. (Chapter 15)

64. *If the projected number of employees for a regional office is to double in, say, the next six months, should an office manager negotiate a larger space than necessary at present or come back at a later time to negotiate an alternative site?*

The answer depends largely on the location, price, size, and market conditions during the time of your office search. If the market is "soft" (i.e., much empty office space available, not too many clients, declining prices, and a slow economy), you can expect to come up with a deal that will satisfy you. Let's say you want a total of 4,000 square feet of contiguous space—2,000 at the start and 2,000 six months later. Give the realtor the information, and determine whether there is a landlord with acceptable space. You might find one who will agree to hold the balance of the space or will agree to your taking the 4,000 square feet on the lease commencement date and be willing to abate rent to offset the cost of the extra space for the first six months. If the market is "tight" (i.e., space is moving fast, there are many clients, and prices and the economy are rising), you might not be so fortunate. You might also have to simply take all the space to ensure having contiguous space. A careful cost study should be done. You will need to see how much it will cost to carry the extra 2,000 square feet for six months as opposed to taking temporary space and relocating everyone in six months. (Chapter 15)

65. *Do rent escalators vary from office to office and from landlord to landlord, or are they standarized in each particular city?*

Usually, in the course of time landlords have jointly created the city standards, but most are willing to vary their deal slightly. (Chapter 15)

66. *Are rents due annually or at the discretion of the landlord?*

In the United States rents are due monthly; in Europe they tend to be paid quarterly. (Chapter 15)

67. *Who is responsible for paying for above-standard building costs?*

The tenant, except in the case of a negotiated agreement whereby the landlord has agreed to pay for all or a portion of the leasehold improvements. (Chapter 15)

68. *Who is responsible for contracting for the construction of the office space—the landlord or the tenant?*

Generally the landlord. Usually if the landlord has contractors with whom he has already done business and/or the city code requires that union workers be used, the landlord will require you use the contractors he or she has chosen. If one is familiar with the city and the job is small, one might consider doing the general contracting. However, general contracting (which I use in the home office) is very time-consuming, and any savings generated by performing the general contracting work yourself could easily be used up by paying for your time. Therefore construction contracting should be left up to the landlord. (Chapter 15)

69. *Is it desirable to tear down an existing office designed in the traditional compartmentalized way in order to construct an open office design?*

If the space meets all your criteria and the landlord is willing to assume the costs of this—yes. Otherwise a construction estimate for the work would have to be made to determine whether this would be economically desirable. (Chapter 15)

70. *What are the criteria used to select a furniture manufacturer?*

Price

Features of Furniture: Design; Color, Acoustical ratings; Standardized panel sizes; Flexible and responsive components; Durability; Repairability; No planned obsolescence

Supply Factors: Delivery time; Easy availability of stock; Established manufacturer, responsible to user problems; Established distributor with good reputation

Manufacturer responsive to solving user problems

Reputation of distributor

(Chapter 15)

71. *With respect to rent increases to meet rising operating expenses, would you explain in more detail the formula created by using the "porter's wage and fringe package cost"?*

A penny (or more) is added to the operating expenses for each penny negotiated in the porter's hourly wage, including the fringe benefits package. Your realtor should be able to provide you with some "city" history, so that you can calculate approximately what you will pay. (Chapter 15)

72. *Would you discuss in more detail the concept of "amortizing the tenant's costs"?*

The landlord actually acts as your banker. He will agree to pay the upfront "over building standards costs" and recover that amount by increasing the price per square foot cost figured in the lease.

For example, you negotiate the following deal:

3,500 square feet at $15 per square foot for 5 years, total cost $262,500.

Let's say the over building standards costs are $30,000. The landlord tacks on interest to the $30,000 (let's say $20,000), so now we have added $50,000 to the lease cost of $262,500. The lease will cost us $312,500 for 5 years, or $62,500 per year divided by 3,500 square feet. This changes the price per square foot from $15.00 to $17.86. This is when you need to be careful! The landlord can now make more profit on your lease when he or she adds on the operating expenses because your base rent has increased. (Chapter 15)

73. *Does an office manager ever enter into a competitive bidding process for a piece of office space, and, if so what does it entail?*

Yes—however, not often and not in the true sense of a "competitive bid." If there is another client interested in the same space you are, your realtor will probably know and give you a status report—such as that leases are being reviewed or are in the process of negotiation. According to the information you have, you can choose to wait and see whether the negotiation succeeds or fails. I would not be willing to pay an "over the market" price for any piece of space. If you escalate the base rent, you will unnecessarily escalate the cost of occupancy over the term because the percentage of increase is calculated on your base rent. (Chapter 15)

74. *With respect to telephone system selection and installation, who is responsible for these tasks—the facilities manager or the company's communications coordinator?*

The vendor selection is handled by the facilities manager, with information supplied from an analysis conducted by the communications coordinator. (Chapter 15)

75. *What does a company do if after having prepared for the move construction is unexpectedly delayed?*

Communicate with all relevant parties revising dates, postpone furniture shipments, phone installation, etc. Be ready, it happens—keep going! (Chapter 15)

76. *After the new regional office is operational, what role does the facilities manager continue to play at the office site?*

The facilities manager will be consulted on major problems that the regional office manager cannot resolve with the landlord, phone company, or construction company. If more furniture is required, the facilities manager will assist with that acquisition. (Chapter 15)

77. Do the same relocation formulas apply to a small company as to a large company with several smaller regional offices? What are the similarities or differences?

In most respects the formulas are similar. A small firm would not need to conduct a search for an exclusive broker. The chief executive officer of a small company will probably play a major role in the decision process and negotiation stages. A less experienced person may implement the plan and oversee that all tasks are completed on time. (Chapter 15)

Glossary

Accountable Income. Income generated by the profitmaking organizational elements of the company

Adjacency Requirements. Intra- and inter-departmental requirements for locating certain individuals or organizational elements in proximity to each other for ease of communication and efficient workflow

Allocation Approach. A method whereby the company finances the office function simply by allocating expenditures and budgetary funds without demanding accountability

Ambient Lighting. The lighting arrangement used throughout the entire office setting

Authorization Cards. Cards that indicate the identity of persons who have been given authority for particular actions (e.g., authorizing purchases)

Bargaining Committee. The group of persons selected to participate in the collective bargaining arrangement as representatives of employees who wish to form a union

Bedaux Plan. An incentive plan under which a group or team pools incentive payments and distributes them equally among all members

Buying Cooperative. A group of companies in one area that band together to make bulk purchases of supplies to reduce overall costs

Call Screening. A computer-based technique that limits telephones to calling only specified area codes

Carrying Costs. Costs incurred in stocking items prior to their use, as well as the costs incurred through subsequent waste, pilferage, and obsolescence

Carterfone Decision. An FCC ruling in 1969 that allows a company legally to connect any telephone manufacturer's equipment to local telephone lines

Chargeback Approach. A method whereby the company bills user departments for the costs incurred in providing various services and supplies to them

Check-Writer Machine. A machine that embosses or perforates the check amount to guard against forgery

Collective Bargaining. A concept used in union negotiations, whereby management and workers are represented by bargaining units that negotiate employment conditions and arrangements within the workplace

Convenience Copies. Reproductive copies made only for individual copying requirements

Copying Service Network. An office's copying service arrangement that provides reproduction services to fulfill individual and company requirements

Cost Efficiency. The wisest, most economical use of funds after analyzing the tradeoffs among expenses for machinery, personnel, and processes

Diazo Copy. A reproduction prepared by the interaction of a strong light and ammonia vapors

Distributive Copies. Reproduction copies made for bulk copying requirements

Due Process. The concept used to determine whether an employee should be fired or reprimanded for violating company rules, whereby employees are to be treated fairly and equitably according to standards governing the entire workforce

Economic Order Quantity (EOQ). An equation used to determine the optimal amount of units to be purchased to ensure that the quantity of a given item is bought at the lowest overall cost

Election Observers. The persons responsible for overseeing the vote balloting for or against union organizing activities

Electronic Mail. A system that reduces textual and graphic material to digital format for transmission over telephone lines

Empire Building. A common practice of office managers of indiscriminately adding to their department's staff, equipment, and services without first ensuring that the additional costs will be offset by demonstrable tangible and intangible benefits

Flow Chart. Diagram or tabular material that depicts workflow or procedures flow for given organizational elements

4-S Formula. A report writing method to ensure accurate, informative, and concise reports, keeping in mind the principles of (1) shortness, (2) simplicity, (3) strength, and (4) sincerity

Fringe Benefits. Compensation paid to employees (e.g., health benefits, vacation pay, and sick leave) over and above their wage rate

Functional Analysis. An evaluation of system components by using representative samples of those components to standardize the system

Golden Handcuffs Approach. Providing employee benefits attuned to their predicted needs

Grievance Procedure. A process whereby a complaint is lodged by an employee about an alleged violation of work rules

HVAC System. A heating, ventilation, and air conditioning system

Individual Improvement Plan. A program designed to identify skill areas in which an employee is deficient and to formulate a specific plan to correct those areas

Industrial Engineering. The discipline involving the cost-efficient use of manpower, machinery, and work methods to achieve operational efficiency

Open Office Concept. An office arrangement that uses portable dividers to section off an entire office complex into individual offices or carrels

Operational Efficiency. The concept used to design an efficient procedure for a given work function

Organizational Elements. The various components within the company structure that provide specific functions (administration, accounting, reproduction, etc.)

Pareto's Principle (80/20 Law). A workflow principle that states that 80% of the total operational and cost benefits that can be attributed to any systems analysis can be achieved by 20% effort. To attempt to attain greater than 80% benefits would generally be uneconomical, inefficient, and unrealistic.

Percentage of Efficiency. Individual productivity divided by the standard level of performance according to time quotas for various work processes and functions

Performance Criteria. Standards used to assess an individual's work performance

Position Incumbent Specifications. Work and educational background and experience that a person should possess to fill a specific job

Price Volatility. Inflationary uncertainty about the costs of an item over time

Procurement Costs. Expenses incurred in order to obtain the required supply of a given item (e.g., filling out forms, delivery services)

Records Management. A program of systematically transferring records from office files to inactive storage or destruction, based on declining legal, regulatory, and internal reference requirements

Records Series Concept. A method whereby all related records are filed, accessed, and destroyed as a unit

Reflectance Value. The level of light reflection given off by furniture, walls, and ceilings

Reflective ("Veiling") Glare. Glare created by light bouncing off an object, such as furniture, walls, and ceilings

Residual Mail. Mail that cannot be sorted by three-or five-digit zip codes due to insufficient volume so as to receive presorting discounts

Scientific Management. The concept of sound managerial philosophy applied empirically

Short List. A list of final applicants for a posted position

Sound-Masking System. A system that produces a moderate, unobtrusive sound to increase the noise level to offset the sounds emanating from employees, equipment, and movement within an area

Source Glare. Glare that shines directly into a person's eyes

Span of Control. The number of individuals that an office manager can directly but efficiently supervise

Squeaky Wheel Principle. Concentrating efforts on those who complain the loudest rather than on those who need those efforts the most

Standard Level of Performance. Under an incentive system, a method whereby individual productivity is tied to the type of work performed and the standards for completing the work

Stockless Procurement. A method whereby a vendor is under contract to keep supplies on hand to be purchased when needed, so as not to tie up an organization's existing space

Stockpiling. A method whereby items are bought in large volumes at prevailing low prices to reduce anticipated cost increases

Supply Obsolescence. Overbuying supplies that will not be used and will become obsolete

Systems Analysis. An evaluation of the relationship among workers, equipment, and procedures that comprise a system's function

Task Lighting. Lighting fixtures that are used in particular office settings

Therbligs. Four basic symbols—flow-charting used to indicate workflow and work procedures

Time Study. A method used to establish a standard level of performance for a specific job

Turnaround Time. The time taken to complete a given work project or task

User Departments. The specific departments within an organization that request and receive support services

Value Analysis. A cost reduction technique whereby every component of a product is evaluated to assess whether any component is unnecessary or uneconomical

Wage and Salary Administration. A program designed to ensure that salaries for certain positions are competitive with those of other companies

White Mail. First-class mail

White Noise. A low-volume, almost inaudible sound-masking system used in an office or sales area to cover up (or mask) various distracting noises made by machines, personnel, and movement

Workplace Standards. Standards that govern the quantity and type of space provided to various positions and the type of furniture and office necessities provided

Index

AMR International, 13
Appraisal, in record retention policy
  development, 107, 110–115
Architects and office design, 41, 305, 306
Architect's drawings, review of, 308
Architectural controls of noise levels,
  155
Area supervisor, 260, 261
  and cross training, 262
Area Wage Surveys, 78
Association for Systems Management,
  12, 78
Association of Records Managers and
  Administrators, 12
Atomic Energy Commission, and records
  retention, 114
Attendance reporting
  and computer payroll system, 176
  employees, 169–170
  management personnel, 170
Attitude, as part of employee evaluation,
  281
Audits
  and record retention, 111–112
  telephone bills, 134
Authority, 22, 333
Authorization card, 191, 193, 340
Automation, and office workforce, 60–61

Background music, 159–160, 327
Bank, and cash payroll, 171
"Bargain" supplies, 226–227
Base salary, relation to incentives, 204
Bedaux plan, 205
Better Business Bureau, and organized
  scams, 226–227
Bids, for office equipment, 254
Blanket purchase order, 221–224
Bottlenecks, 46
Brand names vs. private brands, 224–225
Budget for incentive plans, 203
Building codes, 259, 337
Building condition, office lease negotia-
  tion, 311
Building costs, 342
Bulk mailings, 96–97
Bulletin board notices, 268, 332
Business Equipment Manufacturers
  Association, 13

Business knowledge, 11
Buying cooperative, alternative to contractual buying, 224
Byrnes Anti-Strikebreaking Act of 1938,
  184

Call screening, 135
Career paths, 19
Carrying costs, office supplies, 218
Carterfone decision (1969), 130, 131
Cash bonuses, 76
Cash flow, impact on incentive plan
  payments, 203
Cash payments, of employee wages, 171
Centralization
  record storage, 250, 328
  supply room, 228
Centralized office management structure,
  17
  advantages/disadvantages, 19
  case history, 24–26
Certification of union, 191–193
Certified mail, 96
Chargeback costs, 4, 5, 325–326
  case history, 26
  copiers, 129
  office supplies, 230–231
  postage, 98
  telephone expenses, 135
Checks, as employee wages, 171
Circulation space, 141, 145
Civil Aeronautics Board, and records
  retention, 114
Civil Rights Act of 1964, 289–290
Cleaning specifications, 310–311
Clock card, 169, 176
Closed plan, office space, 145, 146
Code of Federal Regulations, 113
Collective bargaining, 183
  agreement, 193
  inclusion in unit, 191
College placement offices, 68
College scholarships, 83, 189
Color, impact on employees, 160
Commercial computer services, 177–178
Commercial service bureaus, 27, 85
Communication, 11, 267–271, 322
  and decentralized office management
    structure, 20

Private offices, 146
Processing times, and manpower resources evaluation, 73
Procedures, rearrangement of steps, 56
Procurement costs, office supplies, 218
Product discounts, 80, 84
Production standards, 49
Productivity, 2
  and background music, 160
  and color, 162
  and environment, 140, 157
  and financial incentives, 197
  impact of measurement and incentives, 199
  and incentive plans, 198, 210
  and lenient leadership, 277
  and lighting, 149
  and reception services, 88
  and staff size, 64
  and standards of conduct, 284–285
Professional associations, 68, 74
Professional meetings, 75
Profile for office supplies, 222
Profit accountability, and decentralized organizational structure, 20
Profit sharing, 84
Profitability, and productivity, 199
Project definition in systems analysis, 46–49
Promotion from within, 66
Public contact, as prior experience for office manager, 323
Public transportation, and new office site, 37
Purchase costs, and lack of office supply standardization, 214
Purchasing, office space, 39–40
  task force members' roles, 41

Qualified managers, and centralized organizational structure, 19
Quality circles, 278
Questions, appropriate for job interview, 71

Random storage system, inactive records, 123
Rate classification of U.S. Postal Service, 90–97

Ratio of rentable to usable space, 310
Real estate broker
  criteria for selecting exclusive, 341
  and new office selection, 33, 296–299
Real estate consultant, 40, 41
Reception services, 87–89, 326
Records
  evaluation of need for, 56
  and information gathering in systems analysis, 51–52
  long-term reference value, 111
  preparation for inactive storage, 124
  timing of transfer to storage, 110
Records inventory form, 109
Records management, 104–125, 323, 248–250
Records retention program, 106–119, 249
Records retention schedules, 105
  form, 117
  imposed by federal government agencies, 114
  job applications, 69
  and office relocation, 42
  review of, 116
  and space needs, 144
Records retrieval, from storage, 125
Records series concept, 108
Records storage center, 328
Recruitment of personnel, 61–72, 273
Recycled office products, 225
Reference value of records, internal, 110–111
References of job applicants, 71–72, 276, 291–292, 338–339
Regional offices, 293–321, 341, 344
Registered mail, 96
Rehabilitation Act, 290
Relocation formulas, and company size, 345
Rent, 310, 311
  escalator clause, 299, 342
  increases, 343
  payment schedule, 342
Repainting, and office lease negotiation, 311
Report preparation for top management, 234–240
Representation election, 191, 192

Turnaround times, and manpower resources evaluation, 73

Unattended reception areas, 88
United Auto Workers, 188
United States . . . *See* specific departments and agencies (e.g., Defense Department; Federal Trade Commission; Internal Revenue Service; etc.)
U.S. Postal Service, 90
record retention requirements, 113

Value analysis of office products, 216–217
Vendor selection, blanket purchase order, 223–224
Vendor storage, 229
Ventilation. *See* HVAC systems.
Vice-president for administration, 15–16
Vietnam Veterans Act, 290
Volume discounts, and purchasing, 213
Voluntary deductions from wages, 171

Wage and Hour Law, 169
Wage and salary administration, 76–77
Wages
computerized report preparation, 177
federal reporting requirements, 173–174
method of payment, 171
Wagner Act of 1935, 183
Water sprinkler systems, in record storage areas, 120
WATS lines, 136, 257, 329–330
Weight restrictions, postal service, 92–95
Welfare and Pension Funds Disclosure Act of 1958, 184
White noise, 157
Withholding statements, 174
Woman, as job applicant and interview, 70–71
Word processing, 136–139
equipment and static electricity, 147
illumination recommendations, 150

Work areas locations and departmental conflicts, 334
Work backlog, 46
Work division
and office organizational structure, 22–23
payroll preparation and distribution, 172
Work experience, as job qualification, 65, 66
Work letter, 303, 304–305, 310
Work measurement analysis, 64, 325
Work methods, 73
and need for additional workers, 64
Work rules, 181, 284–285
enforcement, 285–286
Work sampling, as information gathering in systems analysis, 52
Work standards, legal statutes, 337
Work tables, 122
Workflow
and office space configuration, 35
and staff placement, 252
Workforce
quality and educational fringe benefits, 80
supplementing, 85–86
Workload
and manpower resources evaluation, 73
staffing for average, 85
Workmen's compensation, 85
Workplace safety, 259
Workplace standards, 163–164, 337
for space, 34
Writing style, in correspondence, 241, 242–244
Written communication, limits to, 268
Written reports, as communication with top management, 233

Zip codes, nine-digit, and presorting, 97

DATE DUE

GAYLORD			PRINTED IN U.S.A.